We Are Israel

A Mystery Wrapped in an Enigma

Damian P Myler

Copyright © 2024
E-Book ISBN: 979-8-9918571-0-9
Paperback ISBN: 979-8-9918571-1-6
Paperback ISBN: 979-8-9918571-2-3
Hardback ISBN: 979-8-9918571-5-4

Dedication

I want to dedicate this to my mother, who is in Heaven right now. Mum Megan Hughes was her maiden name before marrying my dad and becoming a Myler. As a child, she had scarlet fever and almost died. After that, she had many health problems. She fought life with a tenacity and strength that was truly admirable.

Often, she would have little energy, and the doctor couldn't figure it out. She would, at times, cough up blood, at which point the doctor sent her to get her chest examined. It wasn't till she was pregnant with her third child that the stand-in physician made a startling statement.

He said that the doctor he was filling in for should be struck off the registry for malpractice because he had misdiagnosed her for tens of years. He informed her that she did not have a lung problem but a heart problem. She had a major heart operation with experts from around the country assisting in Manchester Royal Infirmary.

My mum was a real hero. She had two major heart operations, with two of her valves being replaced and one repaired. Out of 4 heart valves, she had one intact; she recovered from cancer curvature of the spine, and a broken hip. Towards the end, she developed dementia, but could still remember me, even just before she passed.

What an inspiring woman of faith and tenacity. She was almost 80 when she passed away, I love you, Mum, forever!

About the Author   Damian Myler

Damian Philip Myler is a dedicated scholar and devout Christian who has passionately studied the Bible for over 40 years. Since becoming a Christian in 1976, Damian has read the Bible cover to cover more than seven times, delving deep into eschatology and biblical hermeneutics. His commitment to understanding the Scriptures has been a driving force in his life, leading him to uncover profound connections between ancient texts and modern languages.

Damian's educational background includes a Diploma in Management Studies from Brunel University, where he gained expertise in Financial Management, macroeconomics, Information Technology, and Strategic Management, among other fields. He also holds a Level 5 technical qualification in Electrical and Electronic Engineering from Wigan College of Technology, equivalent to a BSEE in the USA.

His professional journey has been marked by a rich and varied career in telecommunications and project management. Damian has served as a consultant and project manager on high-profile projects across the globe, including work for the Seoul Broadcasting System, the Elihu Harris State Office Building, and Merrithew Memorial Hospital, among others. His technical expertise spans voice and data network design, fiber optic transmission, and specialized signaling, making him a sought-after expert in his field.

Damian's passion for uncovering the truth led him to embark on a 30-year odyssey, beginning in 1987, with the study of a book and belief system that would shape his life's work. This journey culminated in his books "English is Hebrew" and "We Are Israel," where he presents groundbreaking research on the connections between the ancient Hebrews and the modern English-speaking world.

Damian's writing is fueled by a deep spiritual conviction and a desire to share the earth-shattering revelations that have been poured into his soul. His work invites readers to discover the divine heritage woven into the fabric of our history and to explore the hidden truths that connect us to the promises made to the patriarchs of old. With meticulous research and a profound understanding of biblical prophecy, Damian's books offer a unique and compelling perspective on the extraordinary connection between the Bible, Israel, and the English-speaking peoples.

Table of **Contents**

Dedication 2

About the Author   Damian Myler 3

Contents.. 5

Introduction 11

   Where Are We on the Biblical Calendar 13

CHAPTER 1 -The British are coming-Covenant 17

   Covenant, known as Brit.. 17

   Abraham The First Brit with Skin in the Game! 17

   The Bible's Amazing Promises 19

   Abraham and Sarah's HEY day.. 20

   Isaac's pending birth is marred by conflict. 20

   Abrahamic covenant promises, summarized. 21

   Isaac 22

CHAPTER 2 - Jacob's Story and His Birthright. 25

   Jacob 25

   The White House 26

   Jacob winning streak.. 27

   Jack got Hip & butt tap... 29

   Wrestling with God.. 30

   Jacob showing his true colors. 30

   The Lady Di Problem 31

   Coat of Many Colors, and dream 31

   Joseph in Egypt.. 32

   Joseph keeps faith through thick and thin. 32

   The silver lining.. 34

   Living the dream... 35

   Corrie Ten Boom 38

   Story of Tamar.. 38

   The Red Hand of Zerah (Gen 38) 39

CHAPTER 3 Egypt, Joseph, and Moses. 41

   Archeological & Historic Evidence for Joseph - Egypt.............. 41

   Imhotep — Joseph 41

   Joseph Promoted to Lord of Egypt 43

   The Joseph's Hay Day 44

   Let My People Go Pharaoh 13 Times.................................... 45

CHAPTER 4 — The Exodus.. 46

   El Arish — Sukkot Etymology 47

   Four Proofs for the Location of Tharu — El Arish...................... 48

Archaeologist Claims: Tharu, Sinai (Biblical Succoth?) 50
Military Fort, Naval Base & Prison, Succoth-El Arish-Tharu. 51
Rhinoculura — Tharu — Cut Nose Off. 53
New Chronology of Egypt 54
CHAPTER 5 - The Exodus -New Route. 56
From Pillar to Post 56
Here today, gone tomorrow 58
Exodus Ron Wyatt's Route, Sukkot, El Arish — 59
Israel on the March — The Cross 60
CHAPTER 6 - The Tribes & Their Emblems. 62
Symbols, Blessings, and Promises. 62
Rueben 62
Judah 63
Joseph — Ephraim — Manasseh 63
Joe, a fruitful vine 64
Dan is known as a judge (policeman) and lawgiver. 66
The Cross of Jesus (Yeshua) in Ancient Israel 66
CHAPTER 7 - Priest to Kingship 70
Israel Asks for a King 70
Kings of Israel 70
Kings of the Northern Kingdom of Israel 71
2 Kin14.23,26-heavy suffering in Israel 71
Kings of Judah After Solomon 970-930 72
Warnings to Judah Before Final Captivity 72
CHAPTER 8 - Judah's Fall – Jeremiah. 75
Jeremiah's Commission 75
Israel Driven from God's Sights 76
Where Did Jeremiah Take the Remnant? 77
Astonishing Promises of God Reiterated 79
Waymarks pillars, high heeps 79
What did the Israelites look like? 80
Prophetic fulfillments are Key to Finding Israel. 81
CHAPTER 9 – Egyptian trade & migrations. 82
Gold Mining in Ancient Egypt 83
Israel set out early to treasure hunt or escape. 83
The Ruling Class 88
Jonah-Aran-Nineveh, 761-760 BC. 89
The People of Tyre 89
Dan's continued serpents trail 89
Kittim-Chittam 91
A People Prophesied to Invade Israel from Islands 91
CHAPTER 10 – British-Hebrew links. 93
Ancient Jews Spoke Gaelic 93
Th'Ar(s)hish — Irish Connection 93
Pillars of Hercules – Embellishment of Samson 94
Solomon Tin – Cornwall England connection. 94

Phoenician — Israel..96
Metallurgic evidence linking Solomon to Britain.......................96
CHAPTER 11 Birthright not to Jews. 98
Birthright and lost ten tribes 98
Assyria..100
Sins of Jeroboam-main reason for Israel's demise. 101
Babylon Neo Babylonia Chaldean Empire – 625-538 BC.........103
Babylon Nabonidus and Belshazzar, Co-regent's 555-538 BC. 104
Medes and Persians 538-332 BC Darius and Cyrus. 105
Scythia 107
Literary Evidence...108
CHAPTER 12 - Greece 110
Greek Alphabet...111
Athens — Cecrops — Calcol — Darda..............................112
Miletus 113
    Thales of Miletus 113
    Theater Seats in Miletus 114
Lacedaemonians of Greece..114
Greek-Ireland connection 115
CHAPTER 13 – Ireland-Irish-Hebrews 118
Ireland..118
Did the Irish come from Magog?....................................119
    Map – Table of Nations 120
    The Ethnographic division into races 121
Irish – Russian 122
Abraham – Go west, young man! 122
Tuatha De Danan's – 123
    Dan ability to work in Gold, Silver and Fabrics 130
    Snakes in Ireland?..131
    The Number Three..132
    Cross of Jesus, ancient Israelite and the Celtic cross... 133
    The Book of Kells..135
Milesian 137
    Original Names of Ireland 147
    Origin of the name "Irish" 152
    Origin of the Name Gael and the Gaelic language 153
    Hebrew-Celtic language diverge 156
CHAPTER 14 - Jeremiah in Ireland...................................159
Milesian story summarized...159
Milesian etymology 160
The Bible story matches Irish History. 162
    Eagle and a Vine...163
    Three overturns 165
    Red Right Hand 166

CHAPTER 15 – Jacobs Pillar & Kingly Line. 169
Jacobs Pillar stone in the Bible 171
Lia Fail (stone of destiny) is an amazing origin 172
The Kings of Ireland 173
Throne of Ireland moves to Scotland 173
Book of Arbroath, 113 kings of royal blood, 1320 AD. 174
Throne of Scotland moved to England 175
In summary 175
CHAPTER 16 – White House, Scotland & England............ 176
Royal Coat of Arms 177
Birthright withheld due to sin! 178
British Empire (Israel's) Hay Day 1680-1900. 180
Army standard's Emblems Colors -Red Coats 181
British Bull Tribe 182
Phrases — Idioms — Proverbs, etc. 186
We need proverbs because they reflect who we are 186
British Bulldog spirit 201
CHAPTER 17 - Scotland - Hebrew 202
Bagpipes are from Israel 203
Did King David invent the bagpipe? 204
Scottish Cross / Flag 204
Kilt, Plaid or Tartan 205
CHAPTER 18 Welsh – Cymru - Hebrew 208
Relationship Between P-Celtic and Goidelic 208
Welsh Hebrew Cymry. 209
Britan, British, Britannia 211
Origin of Britanni (*Pritanī*) 211
The true origin of the BRITISH 211
Celtic words linking Brit to covenant 212
Welsh Gaelic is 80%+ HEBREW 213
CHAPTER 19 America 215
The name America and its origins 215
Amorica (*Armorica*) was used for a Celtic area. 217
America used 77 times in the Bible 218
The Jews call America the "land of the covenant" 218
Age of Discovery 15 and 16th Centuries 220
The White House 222
GI Joes 225
Yank and Yankee 230
The Great Seal of America. 233
13 Original United States 238
Origin of Gerrymandering — Political Shenanigans ... 240
Flags of the US and UK 241
The British obsession with the name Jack! 243

CHAPTER 20 - Prophetic fulfillments................................248
One Sheet Overview...250
References 252
Notes..299
List Of Figures...302
Index..319
About This book 327

Page Left Blank Intentionally

Introduction

I am British, born in Wigan, England, 20 miles from Manchester and 20 miles from Liverpool. My great-grandfather on my father's side came from Wexford, Ireland, and my great-grandfather on my mother's side came from Wrexham, Wales. My Celtic heritage goes way back, with a possible lineage of over 1000 years in both Ireland and Wales.

I was a very curious kid and liked to investigate things to see if they were really true. I checked out UFOs, Hypnosis, and Ghosts. I was very much into Karate and Bruce Lee in my teenage years. In my early career, I was hired by British Aerospace as an apprentice, and I later worked as a guided missile engineer. I did very well in college, coming top of my class in many subjects for years, and I feel I am a meticulous person when it comes to the truth. The reason I mention these things is that God was about to rock my worldview with a history that if anyone knew, surely it would be me! In my late 20s, I was living in California, in Culver City, California. One day, a book showed up on my doorstep titled "The US and Britain in Prophecy."

I asked my Irish girlfriend (later to be the mother of my 4 boys) where it had come from; she informed me that she had ordered it. I was shocked (to put it mildly), "The US and Britain were mentioned in the Bible, and this book claimed that we are Hebrew and the fulfillment of a promise made to the patriarchs Abraham, Jacob, Joseph, and David. How in the world can this be true? I have never heard of this story; it cannot be true; otherwise, I would have heard of it?" This sparked a night and day study. I had to find out if these things were true and how was it that I didn't know Jack!

This book is the culmination of my studies that started over 30 years ago and 40 years since I first became a Christian. I am sure you (as I was) will be as surprised and shocked to discover that not only are these things true, but that God said there was Zion in the Heavens that points to the truth.

God said that the sun, moon, and the stars were Tzions, Zions, (SIGNS H6725, H6726 צִיּוּן tsiyuwn, tsee-yoon, & yonder Jer. 31.35-36)! But why was it that I had never heard of it? In the

11

book of Daniel, he was given vision after vision, and toward the end of the book, Daniel wanted answers but was not given them. Daniel was asking, what's happening? What do all these Zions mean? (I am paraphrasing Dan. 12.9).

Daniel is told to just (Ye wLK) walk away (Ye waLK, H3212, יָלַךְ H1980, הָלַךְ hâlak, ha'wlak)'ǫ Because the words are sealed (שׂתם sâtham, s't'hm (stopped-s't'him) — aleph a guttural stop, stop am H5640, and khawt'ham, caught m, trapped חָתַם סָם H2856) until the time of the end. The same is reiterated in Revelation 10, where John is told to eat the little scroll, and the angel tells him the bitter-sweet truth of it, sealing the vision.

The vision included an angel that straddled the land and the sea; this is symbolic of Eber and the Hey bros (H5676). It means land beyond the river or ocean or sea; it also means to cross over. Notice in Revelation 10:11 that the last main message of the two witnesses was to be about many peoples, nations, languages, and kings. This is why I didn't know Jack about my history; God had sealed it until the time of the end.

This is what this book is about: revealing the many people, nations, languages, and kings of the Hey Bros. And even revealing that the language of the British is straight from the Bible; we were plucked up by our roots and regathered and made the greatest empire the world had ever known and the USA the greatest nation the world has ever known.

God has revealed so much information to me that I was not able to put it all in one book. The second part of the message will be in book two, "English is Hebrew," and will prove conclusively that not only do the Brits still speak Hebrew but that many of our everyday words were spoken by Jesus 2000 years ago. And other national symbols not previously discussed will be revealed when we look at the original Alphabet, which is over 3800 years old and the oldest in the world, yes, the Brits wrote the first alphabet! Please bear with me for the next three paragraphs; they are short and can be quickly read so that you can get to the real story of this book. That story starts in chapter one.

The need for God Do we really need God? He is not going to help us, is he? We evolved from a primordial soup without him, first an ameba and then eventually into very specific animals that can't interbreed between species, i.e., dogs can't breed with cats, and horses can't breed with cows; in fact, every creature has evolved into its own kind.

And isn't it great that the primordial soup gave us senses: sight, touch, smell, taste, and hearing?? Wow, the soup apparently could see beyond the swamp and identify our need to sense the world around us. When we consider this weird story that requires so much faith, it's truly hard to believe it happened that way, either that or blind trust in institutions that just flat-out lie to us.

I understand why many can be confused and deceived because most of us are like sheep and look to have someone explain things to us; this leaves us open to being manipulated and deceived. And this has been used against us throughout history, Martin Luther understood this, and this is exactly why the Reformation started. Martin Luther and others defied the anti-biblical tenets proposed by the Roman Catholic Church. Even though he was confronted with death, he held his ground. Today, we have many false teachings out there, even in the church!

Time is getting short. I feel it necessary to position the Bible and the plan of God in the context of this work. God made some amazing promises and many of his Bible promises have been fulfilled, and many last days prophecies are on the verge of being fulfilled. We are clearly in the last days; this is a time when God is opening the seals of Revelations, Ezekiel, Daniel, etc. The purpose of the Bible is to instruct his people in how to live our daily lives, for prophecy, for history, for encouragement, and as the Apostle Paul said, 'The word of God is profitable for teaching, for reproof, for correction, and for instruction in righteousness'(2 Tim 3:16). It is said by some that the Bible is 1/3 prophecy, 1/3 poetry, and 1/3 history (#9). Some say that 90% of that remains to be fulfilled. I feel that over 50% remains to be fulfilled, perhaps as high as 75% deals with the last days and what is and about to happen.

Where Are We on the Biblical Calendar

We are getting very close to fulfillment and the Second Coming; it is now that the Jews and the Covenant (British H1285, H376) tribe will come together, and Israel will once again recognize their role in history. It is now that the 3rd temple will be built, and the Jews will start their daily sacrifice; it is now that the Abomination that causes desolation will be revealed (the man of Sin). But how can we know for sure?

God ordained 6000 years for the earth and then the Sabbath rest for the people of God (Ex 31:15). Six days of work may be done, but the seventh is the Sabbath of rest, holy to the LORD: whosoever doeth any work on the Sabbath day, he shall surely be put to death. Those were pretty strong words back then, but here we have a 6-day on 1-day off cycle, God speaking of the children of Israel wandering in the desert [Psa 95:11, Lev 25:4, Heb 3:11, Heb 4:1-11 NIV]. So I declared on oath in my anger, 'They shall never enter my rest.' 'Here, God appears to be talking about rest from their wanderings, although he calls it a Sabbath rest; again, the prophet of Hebrews speaks about a Sabbath rest. He encourages us all to make sure we enter that rest; we know that the Sabbath comes around every week, and we can enter that rest once a week, but that is not what he is talking about here; also, we see that the children of Israel did enter the promised land yet Hebrews still says that the special Sabbath rest has not yet been attained (Heb 4:3).

The Sabbath rest he is referring to here is none other than the Millennium rest, and taking a quick look at history, we are about 6000 years into the plan of God. Therefore, the Sabbath rest is almost upon us! There are many scriptures that I could quote to back this up, but this is not the time. I suggest that God's plan calls for an almost full revelation before his coming because once Yeshua (YeHoWShaVH, your our savior, יְהוֹשׁוּעַH3091) is here, we can hear everything directly from him. We won't need the Bible anymore. God will reveal everything; therefore, it makes complete sense that God would reveal all his hidden secrets at the end of time and before his second coming, which, as stated earlier, is very soon.

Yahweh (h3050) wants all men to know his works and his ways. We are in the last days, and God is revealing his deeds to his disciples (as he said he would) and the world! Will he bring the Ark of the Covenant back out of hiding? He will speak to his two witnesses who will prepare the way for the Lord. He said of his servants He will turn the hearts of the fathers to the children, and the hearts of the children to their fathers, lest I come and strike the earth with a curse (Mal 4:6, Luk. 1:17). What is the real meaning of these terms? We will reveal the true meaning of this and many other aforementioned scriptures. Please don't just take my word as evidence. If you take the time to look for yourself, it's in the Bible; you will find everything I say in this book is true!

Put Your Money Where Your Mouth Is

In Hebrew, the word for "mouth" is פֶּה(*Peh*), and we often say: **"Put your money where your mouth is."** Isn't it remarkable how *Peh* (mouth) aligns with this idiom, both linguistically and conceptually? Coincidence, or something deeper? Stay tuned, because in this book, I present over 100 idioms that trace their origins directly to the Bible.

Now, let's raise the stakes. I am so confident in the accuracy of the claims I make in this book that I am willing to put my money where my mouth is—**literally.**

$10,000 Reward Challenge

I am offering **$10,000** to the first person who can conclusively prove the Bible is incorrect on any of the following points:

1. **The Kingly Line of David**: The kingly line of David, as prophesied in the Bible, is alive and well today, currently ruled by King Charles III. By extension, this supports the broader assertion that **We Are Israel**—that the British people of today are descendants of the ancient Israelites of the Old Testament.

2. **The Prophecies Fulfilled**: The British and American nations uniquely fulfill the biblical prophecy of becoming a "great nation" and a "great company of nations" (Genesis 35:11).

3. **Linguistic Roots**: Hebrew is the dominant root of the Celtic and English languages.

15

An Open Invitation to Scholars

I welcome any Pastor, Rabbi, Hebrew scholar, linguist, or historian to challenge these assertions. I am ready to debate these claims in any open session, at any university, church, or public forum. **I invite feedback, dialogue, and scrutiny.** Open discourse is the cornerstone of discovering and defending truth.

CHAPTER 1 -The British are coming-Covenant

God made some amazing promises to the Patriarchs, from Noah all the way to David. Promises like the greatest nation and the greatest company of nations (ever), along with the promise of a kingly line that will not fail while the sun, moon, and stars still shine. Incredible as it may seem, many of the terms we take for granted today were common thousands of years ago. Terms like White House, British, America, hello, and even haha, along with many other common day terms, Keep reading, and you will discover the proof!

Covenant, known as Brit

The Bible first mentions the term Brit as God's promise made to Noah and his children (Gen. 9.9, běriyth H1285 pronounced brit בְּרִית). The term means to cut, like the blood oath where two folks would cut their hands and mingle their blood for a promise (Gen. 9:11). In this instance, God says never again will life be cut off, as he did when floodwaters came on the earth, and the sign of his promise was the rainbow.

Was this term significant enough for all of Noah's sons to repeat it, Shem, Ham, and Japheth, along with their descendants?

It is clear from the Bible that the term was used anciently; even the Phoenician and Philistines would use the term Ba`al Briyth, meaning God (or deity h1170) of the covenant; it was also known as Lord of the covenant.

Eight times God told Noah that he and his children are covenanted. In fact, in Genesis 9 alone, the term Brit is used 7 times, starting in Genesis 9:9: 'And I, behold, I will establish my covenant (Brit h1285 ish h376) with you, and with your seed (ish=man in Hebrew) after you.' In saying these words, God made Noah and his seed covenant men; in Hebrew, you would call them British. But as always happens, the mantle or baton (Briton) is passed to the firstborn except when God specifically changes it, as in the case of Joseph.

Abraham The First Brit with Skin in the Game!

In 2300 BC, God made his covenant with Noah and his kids and, indeed, all flesh; the promise was never again to cut off all life with floodwaters. It appears that Noah died 350 years after the flood, circa 1950 BC (Gen 9.28), and Abram was born circa 2018 BC; perhaps Abram met Noah, and even Eber, since Urfa (Urartu #360) is close to the Caucasus (white) mountains and where the ark came to rest.

In Genesis 12, God starts to make some great promises to Abram (age 75) and tells him to leave his country, family (other Semites), and father's household and go to the land I show you. God again visits Abram in Genesis 15 and starts the covenant promise; this is repeated in Genesis 17. God repeats the term covenant (Brit) 10 times and tells Abraham he will be the first Brit Milah (Covenant of circumcision), the first Brit with skin in the game.

When God says something a couple of times, we should pay attention; when he tells Abram 10 times, you know he is paying attention, especially after he and the whole household get Brit Milah'ed! Abraham doesn't quite know how it's all going to pan out, but he knows that he is Noah's seed and the tenth generation from Noah, and Yah tells him ten times that he is the 'one' (H202, 3, 4) and he believes God and is credited as righteous.

It is clear from the Bible that the birthright (#359, 361) was passed by the firstborn son (Deu 21:17), and this was a promise to Abraham and the chosen seed! And one he took very seriously, one where nations and kings were promised.

Did you know that Jacob (also a covenant man) promised to build his church on a rock and instituted the tithe to support it? Did you know that the title Israel was given to Ephraim and Manasseh (not Judah or the Jews), i.e., the covenant people of Yah (Brit am Yah) would be the greatest nation ever and a great company of nations (again, the greatest empire ever)?

Do you know that in the synagogues on the Shabbat, they invoke this blessing: 'May God make you like Ephraim and Manasseh' (#11)? Why do they invoke this blessing? Because of all the promises God made to Ephraim and Manasseh, where is the fulfillment? Also, God said that if Israel sinned against him, he would pluck them up by their roots and replant them in a land where they would not be disturbed. He also said they would extend to the ends of the earth and supplant (Jack-up, Jacob) their enemies. God calls Ephraim and Manasseh a bull with horns like a wild ox (Unicorn); with them, he will gore the nations (Deu. 33.17).

This book is about revealing and bringing to light these scriptures and their fulfillment; we trace the two greatest nations the world has ever known and a kingly line that has existed for over 3000 years. We trace them back to their roots just as God promised!

The Bible's Amazing Promises

If God is real and who he says he is, then his word is real, and his promises are real. The ones spoken to the Patriarchs — Abraham, Isaac, Jacob (Israel), and David, should mostly be fulfilled by now. It's easy for God to fulfill his promises when he is fully in charge, but to fulfill his promises when dealing with stubborn, stiff-necked, bullheaded people who always want their way, not Yahweh's, combine this with the Devil in charge of the world, the social media, most of the radio, TV, news, and Hollywood (Prince of the power of the Airwaves Eph. 2.2), well, this then becomes quite a challenge. But as we will find out, God is up to the challenge!

God made some very specific promises to Abraham — God's promises to the patriarch and mankind start at the very beginning of the Bible and go all the way through the end of the Bible. God is the alpha and the omega, the beginning and the end.

In Genesis 12:10, the Bible records a famine in Canaan, and Abraham is instructed to go to Egypt. As he was entering Egypt, he told Sarai (later Sarah), "I know what a beautiful woman you are. When the Egyptians see you, they will say, 'This is his wife.' Then they will kill me but let you live. Say you are my sister (related) so that I will be treated well for your sake, and my life will be spared because of you."

What a stunner Sarah is! What kind of beauty does it take to make men go all googly-eyed and weak at the knees? She was at least 65 years of age, i.e., 10 years younger than Abraham (Gen 17:17), when this happened. Pharaoh took Sarai to be his wife (Gen

12:19). But God inflicted serious diseases on Pharaoh. What was it, herpes simplex 10? And when you have a harem, you spread the gifts quickly. I am sure Pharaoh thinks he is going to die, so he summons Abraham and confronts him about the white lie — she is his sister and his wife, but he fails to tell Pharaoh about the wife part. Well, God protected Abraham, and he was sent away with great booty, a bootyful woman, Sarah, and a bounty of money (aka booty).

God tolt Abraham that he would be his shield (Megan) and exceeding great reward, and it is paying off right here and again later, as we will see.

In Genesis 17, God revisits Abram and presents him with good and bad news (did God ask, "Which do you want first?").

The good news is God will soon fulfill his long-awaited promise, of a child, and now the bad news. Abram and all his household have to be circumcised. Ouch! Abram, now age 99 years old, and Yah reiterate his promise to give him a conditional covenant (Brit H1285). Again, it was the first with skin in the game.

Abraham and Sarah's HEY day.

Abraham, age 99, and Ishmael, age 13 (Bar Mitzvah), his household are circumcised; that has to hurt. God also gave Sarah the message and changed their names; they get a hey, the 5th letter of the Hebrew alphabet, which represents praise.

Abram goes to Abraham, Sarai goes to Sarah (he הָ Ps119:33), it was Sarah's and Abraham's "Heyday," the letter ה was also known as ha, so Abraham and Sarah both get a Ha, Ha, and the Bible reveals that both laughed when God told them they were going to have a child (Gen 17:17, 18:12). Not only that, but God says your son shall be named Isaac said to mean laughter but its slightly different, it means JOKE, (JiTS'CHaK Its Joke H3327 יִצְחָק) sometimes a sarcastic joke (mockery).

Isaac's pending birth is marred by conflict.

Isaac's birth is imminent; again, Abraham is 99, and Sarah is 90 years old. Pretty much their lives were over before they had the pleasure of having children together; God told them they would have a child within a year, and now more trouble is to befall them.

- Sodom and Gomorrah are destroyed (Gen 19)
- Lot's wife (no name) turned to a pillar of salt for looking back (Gen 19:26 longing for the life she was leaving.
- Abraham is again tested; he is hedging his bets when he tells another white (boy) lie to Abimelech, saying Sarah is his sister (family Gen. 20).

Sarah is still a drop-dead gorgeous woman in her 90s. This is so stunning! And guess who is going to drop dead (or think they are)? Abimelech, king of Gerar, steps in and tries to bed her, and as with Pharaoh, God visits (Megans-shields Abraham Gen. 15:1).

The troublemaker, Abimelech, is told in a dream by God, 'you're as good as dead.' talk about one bad nightmare, hello, not only did God threaten Abimelech, but his entire nation (Gen. 20:3-4). This was another 'drop-dead gorgeous' moment. Abimelech didn't just let them go but sent them on their way with a very rich reward (Gen 10:16).

Again, Abraham had a double booty, heyday! And finally, along comes Isaac (Yitschaq-laughter); that was one fun-filled year; I am glad they ended it on a high note with a lovely baby boy and laughter! Can I say, 'All's well that ends well?'

When Isaac had been weaned, Abraham had a big party to celebrate, but Ishmael was mocking Sarah and her son. Sarah had Ishmael, and Hagar kicked out and told not to come back (Gen. 21:8-10)! Ishmael (father of the Arabs) was eighty-sixed and was not the child of the Promise; this is the first time we used this term.

Abraham was eighty-six years of age when he had Ishmael, and thus, this child was eighty-sixed for mocking Sarah and the newborn Isaac!

Abrahamic covenant promises, summarized.

1. *I will make of thee a great nation* (British are coming) promise of greatness Gen.12.1-3), and I will bless thee, and
2. make thy name great, and thou shalt be a blessing:
3. I will bless them that bless thee, and curse him that curseth thee.

4. *In thee shall all families of the earth be blessed* (v3)
5. *For all the land which thou seest, to thee will I give it, and to thy seed forever* (Gen 13:15), walk through the land width and breath, — shoe promise (Deut 25:9, Ruth 4:7).
6. *I will make your offspring as the dust of the earth* (Gen 13:16).
7. *Do not be afraid; I am your shield* (Magen) *and exceeding great reward* (Gen 15:1).
8. *Righteousness was given to Abraham because of faith.*
9. *The seed of promise will be enslaved in a land, not their own 400 years* (Gen 15:13)!
10. *4th generation after taking possession of the land, Isaac, Jacob, 12 sons, Joshua, and children of Israel.*
11. *Covenant of Land* — From the river of Egypt (wadi El Arish) to the Euphrates River (Gen 15:18).
12. *Covenant of Circumcision* — a sign of the covenant on the foreskin that the seed might thrive (Gen 17).
13. *Abraham's request for Ishmael's blessing granted 12 rulers will come from Ishmael* (Gen 16 #1).
14. *Abraham was 86 when he had Ishmael, but Ishmael was eighty-sixed*, i.e., Ishmael was not the child of the Promise; this is the first time we used this term (#2. Gen21.9.10).
15. *Abraham had a son, Isaac, when he was 100 years old-Child of promise; through Sarah* (Gen17.15,21), *God will make Abraham fruitful* (^{H}Efrathee Ephrâthîy, double fruit^{H673} Ephraim, son of Joseph.
16. *And they blessed Rebekah, and said unto her, Thou art our sister, be thou the mother of thousands of millions* (eleph, H504; ox's head-i.e. Ephraim-Covenant tribe Brit-ish), *and let thy seed possess* (H3423 ירש yarash-Irish) *the gate of those which hate them* (Gen 24:60). Let's look at these promises again to see if they were fulfilled.

Isaac

The name Isaac, Yitschâq, yits-khawk'; (H3327) from H6711; laughter (i.e., mockery); Yitschak, again Jits chak, it's Jack.

Isaac was 40 years old (Gen. 25.19) when he married Rebekah after Abraham's servant found her while panning around in Paddan Aram (Armenia, as was the case with his mother Sarah); Isaac's wife was from the White House (#33), i.e., her brother was Laban, meaning white (Albon). Rebekah was barren, and Isaac prayed to God for her, and God answered him, and Rebekah became pregnant with twins. God told Rebekah that (Gen15.16):

- Two nations are in your womb.
- Two people from within you will be separated.
- One person will be stronger than the other (we know from the wrestling match with God that Jacob was JACKED).
- The older will serve the younger (Jacob's youngest).
- And Rebekah will be the mother of thousands of millions, (Gen 24:60).
- Thy seed possesses (H3423 יָרַשׁ yarash-Irish) the gate of those which hate them (Gen 22:17).

Yet years later, Isaac either forgot, or he played favorites (or played the fool) and was planning on giving his major blessing to the oldest; this was contrary to God's instruction.

And we see that Esau despised his birthright (Gen 25.34, 27.1,5,28-29) and gave it to Jacob for a bowl of soup, lentil soup!

Is there a clue of Isaac's name to tell him to give it to Jacob (It's Jacks)? Even his wife confirmed it. How many times, how many times do we need to be told? Isaac (Its Jacks) gives his Blessing to Esau, or so he thought (Gen 27.28-29):

- May God give you the dew of heaven, and the fatness of the earth, and plenty of grain and wine.
- Let people serve thee, and nations bow down to thee: be lord over thy brethren and let thy mother's sons bow down to thee: cursed be every one that curseth thee and blessed be he that blesseth thee.

Wow, did you see that Isaac (It Jack) tried to give Esau pretty much what God told him to give to Jacob! And clearly, this was God's gift via his father's blessings. Isaac did not appreciate God's promise and, in a sense, mocked it, as his Numero Uno Son did (Esau-Gen 25:34), and after Jacob (supplanter) took his birthright by divine inspiration (or deception?) via his mother, Esau comes in

23

from the field and asks for his blessing, but it's too late. Esau pleads again for a blessing, sobs, and cries. Isaac gives him a blessing, that's more like a curse, makes him the servant of his brother and says he will be away from earth's riches Esau Red (hairy red child #340), and again he sold his birthright for some red stew) and became very angry and was getting ready to kill his brother when their mother warned Jacob (Gen 27:41-2) to flee for his life. Isaac finally comes to his senses and blesses Yacob for real and tells him to go get a wife from the White House (Laban H3835 Gen 28).

Isaacs gives Jacob a 'for real' blessing:
- God Almighty bless you and make you fruitful.
- You become a community of people.
- Blessings of Abraham fall on you and your kin.
- Possess the land of promise (Gen 28:3).

Another reason to go to the white (boys) house is the seed of Canaan was corrupted with Nephilim, and God attempted to clean out all the fallen angels' offspring in the flood, but evidently, the wives of Ham (Gen 9:18), and maybe Japheth, had alien DNA, we know this because later the giants are found in Cannan, son of Ham.

In addition, Abraham and Isaac. Our fathers both had 'drop-dead gorgeous wives' so much so that both lied for fear of being killed! All the more reason to go to the "White House".

CHAPTER 2 - Jacob's Story & Birthright.

What does birthright mean? It is a term first used in the Bible in Genesis 25:31, where Jacob asks Esau to sell his birthright, which he agreed to, for a bowl of red stew.

The term "birthright" means firstborn or birthright. The term "firstborn" was first used to describe Abel's sacrifice, where he brought the firstlings of his flocks and their fat thereof as a sacrifice to the Lord.

The 'birthright' entails pre-eminence and authority (Gen 27:29; 49:3). In simpler terms, it involves a father who is wealthy and desires to pass on his legacy, his business, with the firstborn typically entitled to a double portion (Deu. 21:17, 1Ch. 5:1, 2).

When considering a kingly line, we can see how significant the birthright becomes, especially in relation to the legacy of promises made by God to our fathers and passed down through generations. We have examined the promises to Abraham and Isaac, which were designated to Jack per God's instructions to his mother (Gen 25:23).

Throughout Hebrew history, God occasionally sets aside the 'birthright' to demonstrate that His chosen ones are selected not based on human preference but on His divine authority. Consequently, Isaac was favored over Ishmael, Jacob over Esau, Joseph over Reuben, David over his elder brothers, and Solomon over Adonijah.

Jacob

Jacob's (Ya`aqob) real story begins after he leaves his father and his mother in search of a wife; he is troubled because his brother has sworn to kill him.

Jacob arrives at Bethel and takes a stone as his pillow. It is here that God visits him, and He reveals the plans He has for Jacob. The Stairway to Heaven prophecy (Gen 28:13) includes:
- Descendants, given the land he is lying on.
- Descendants are like the dust of the earth (erets).
- Descendants spreading out west, east, north, and south

(covering the earth).

- All people are blessed through you and your offspring.
- 'I am' with you — indeed, He is!
- 'I am' will not leave you, Jack, until I have done everything I am going to do — has He done it? Not yet, but I am sure He will.

When Ya'aqob woke from his sleep, he was afraid (# 24). How awesome is this place, none other than the 'House of God (BethEl) and heaven's gate'? Jacob makes a promise to build God's house on a rock and to tithe to support the church if God will be with him (Gen 28:20-21).

The White House

God led Jacob through the wilderness, a difficult and dangerous journey from Canaan to Paddan Aram Armenia, where Abraham was from Ur or Urfa and where Shem settled after the flood, about a 550-mile trip. At 2-3 miles per hour, with perhaps 8-9 hours per day, it probably took him around 24 days. And when he gets there, he rolls away the stone (Gen 29.2, 10), a Gadowl (H1419), Eben (H68), a great stone, from the mouth of a well, so Rachel can water her sheep!

Tears of joy, for Jacob meets the love of his life, and guess what, she is a Shepherdess; have his dreams come true? Hallelujah, praise the Lord! After meeting his father-in-law, LaBaN (Albion), Jacob commits to a seven-year promise to work at his promised father-in-law's house, THE WHITE HOUSE (h3837 white boy house), for Rachel's hand in marriage.

Seven years is a long time to wait, but he is in love, and time flies when you're having fun (Gen 29:20). Jack finally gets married. Hallelujah, Yahoo (3058 Yehuw' yay-hoo), it's time to be jubilant and party and consummate the marriage, but in the morning, when the veil is removed, and the light is on, he is married to the wrong woman.

'That's so Jacked up.', Seven years of work down the drain, time to talk to the boss and see if we can work this out. The good news, he gets two (women) for the price of one. Laban apologizes and says in our culture, the eldest is to be married first. 'That's your excuse for conning me?'

But now that you're married to my daughter Leah, you can have my second daughter Rachel (the drop-dead gorgeous, hard-working woman that you love). They marry straight away, and Jack agrees to work for seven more years. Seven years, good luck or bad luck, and no mirror broken — or maybe when Leah was looking into it?

There were mirrors. Even in those days, silver plates could be used. Was Leah not fond of mirrors? She was not good-looking; the Bible says she had weak eyes (Gen 29:17).

In addition, bronze mirrors were used at the time (Job 37:18), of Job and coincidentally, Job is believed to have lived in Urfa-Armenia.

Here are the wives of Jacob and their handmaidens that gave Jacob children — Rachel, handmaiden Bilhah, Leah & her handmaiden Zilpah after 11 children Rueben-L, Simeon-L, Levi-L, Judah-L, Dan-B, Naphtali-B Gad-Z, Asher-Z, Issachar-L, Zebulun-L, Dinah-L, Joseph-R, (and later Benjamin-R). A dispute breaks out between Laban's sons and Jacob. Basically, Jacob overstayed his welcome! And it's time to leave.

Some 20 years after he first arrived in Paddan Aram, he is ready to go home. But does he really have a home? Remember, Esau threatened to take his life (Gen 27:41), and now he's doing a runner from Laban, not telling him he's leaving, deceiving Laban, and Jacob's wives stole their father's Gods (Gen 31:19). Jacob had worked 20 years for Laban and made him very rich, and Laban kept changing the game plan; he kept changing the rules.

He would agree to one thing, then change it. This continued for a long time until God showed Jacob how to win! We can read the story in Genesis 30:25.

Jacob winning streak

Laban's flocks have greatly increased, and Laban knows its because of Jacob, and now he was Jack. What can I do for you? *"Name your wages, and I will pay you"*.

27

Jacob replies, don't give me anything; just let me take the spotted, streaked, and black sheep from the flocks, and they will be my wages! Laban agrees, and Jack is on his 'Winning Streak.' And my honesty will testify for itself... Any goat that is not speckled (streaked) or a lamb that is not dark-colored (brown or blackish h2345) will be considered stolen.

Jacob found a way to make the sheep and goats speckled and darker (#278) and, by doing so, became very wealthy.

Eventually, the attitude of Laban's sons toward Jack changed, and the Lord said to Jacob, go back to the land of your fathers and your relatives (but what about Esau?), and I will be with you.

He explains to Rachel (Gen 31.6) that her father has cheated him 10 times, and it was God, the Lord Almighty, who visited Jack in a dream and told him of his displeasure with Laban changing his wages and how the Jock could obtain a winning streak! He tells her its time to leave. God had instructed him to get out. *I am the God of Bethel, where you anointed the Pillar (Jacob's Pillar stone), now get thee hence and leave this place immediately and return to the land of thine kindred.*

If you have read the story, you will remember that Jacob put three days' journey between him and Laban, between his kids and Laban's, his flocks and Laban's. He was a farmer working out in the heat and sometimes cold of the day; often, wives were at home, and he sent word for them to come out to the field (Gen 31.4, and v16). So, Jacob did a runner with everything he had, and it took three days before Laban was told. This ended up giving Jack a six-day start on Lbn (#279). On the seventh day, Laban caught up with Jacob.

The Armenian (Aryan-German-see matrix) caught up with Jack in the country of Gilead (h280), and God warned Laban to be careful what you say to Jacob, but he still called him a thief and a deceiver, and what Laban said was so jacked up. How was Jacob to respond? He spoke his mind, and then Laban and Jacko set a Heap (Gael H1530 גַּל gal) as a witness (H5707 עֵד 'ed) between them, a pillar, a rock, a red line, or a line in the sand (#277) that neither of them can cross without a penalty, deadline, u cross and your dead, seems to be the meaning.

Interestingly, Bashan, the area where Gilead's located, is where Dan and a group of Manassites were later located (northern border of Israel-Machirites and h1569 Gileadites). More on this later.

And after this, an angel (Malak H4397) of the Lord met Jacob. It seems that God might have instructed him to send ahead to Esau and soften his heart (Gen 32:6). But Esau was already on his way to meet Jacob with 400 men. It looks like he's about to take him out. The book of Jasper (non-canonical) speaks of Laban's sons informing Esau and giving him a bad report, and this is why he was coming, apparently to kill his brother.

Jacob got scared, and he prayed to God; he was already anticipating the outcome and had decided to bring presents as a peace offering, staggering them with the hope of winning him over.

Jacob had intensely feared meeting up with his brother Esau and had been working out; he was very athletic and figured he could take his brother on one. In fact, he was Jacked; yes, he was the first Jock. He sent everyone on ahead of him, and he stayed the night alone, and a man came up to him in the dark and attacked him.

Try to imagine what must be going through Jacobs's mind. He steps away from the family and wants to get some quiet time with the lord and requests his help with Esau, and this figure shows up and wants to fight him. He must have thought, *"God what on earth is happening?"*

Jack got Hip & butt tap.

He fights all night, but it isn't until daybreak that '*It finally dawns on him*' who he's fighting with! The man (Jesus) uses his special powers to dislocate Jack's hip by tapping his hip/thigh/buttock area; it's a strange custom that many sports like Rugby, Baseball, American football, basketball, and volleyball, to signal approval, congratulation or encouragement. In fact, early Hebrews would use it as a sign to swear by (Gen 32:25). Notice in wrestling, a sign of *"I surrender is the body tap."*

29

Even though Jack was all 'Out of Joint,' he would not let go; he 'held on for dear life,' The man said let me go, for it is daybreak! Jack said I won't let you go unless you bless me. The man asks, what is your name? 'My name is Jacob, (deceiver), and Jesus answers and says your name will no longer be Jacob but 'Israel Sarah Elohim' (His Royal saw raw Elo him) because you have struggled with God and with man and prevailed!

Jacob named that place Peniel because he Saw raw Elohim and lived there. Additionally, there's the Apocrypha book of Enoch spoken of in the Bible. Both of these events were probably passed on by a strong oral tradition.

The process of swearing or making an oath clearly came from this practice. It was also a God bless sign.

Wrestling with God

Have you ever wrestled with God like Jacob did, wrestling with him in prayer? God likes this; he wants us all to be Israelites and to contend for the good, the betterment of humanity, to wrestle with God of humanity.

But what bad timing! Here he was, about to face his darkest fear – his brother coming at him with 400 men ready to attack.

Jacob was surely thankful to get a blessing, but he still had a lot of concern about meeting his brother. Even though God said he was with him, it doesn't take away all fear and anxiety. What must Jacob have been thinking? "I am a broken man. My brother (with 400 men) who wants to kill me is almost upon me. I'm still caught between a rock and a hard place, and now I'm worn out from fighting all night long, disjointed and in pain." Before the fight, he must have thought, *"It can't get any worse."* Think again!

Jacob limped away to meet Esau. He placed the long line of gifts for Esau with his handmaidens ahead, then Leah and her children, followed by Rachel and Joseph at the back.

Jacob showing his true colors.

Jacob was showing his true colors (like the coat of many colors). He was revealing to the rest of his sons who his favorite was.

In Genesis 33.4, they "kissed and made up." Jacob insisted on Esau taking the huge gift: 220 goats, 220 lambs, 30 camels and young, 40 cows, 10 bulls, and 30 donkeys, totaling roughly $300,000 in today's money.

Jacob made good on his promise with the gifts. I'm sure Esau thought Jacob had been a "jackass" in the past, but again all's well that ends well. Esau went on his merry way (Gen 33) with quite the parting gift.

The first place Jacob settled in Canaan was Sukkot (H5521-Scot-Gen 33:17 Booth-#293). After this, he moved on to the outskirts of Shechem and pitched his tent.

He bought a plot of land, set up an altar, and called it El Elohe Israel ("Hello to God from His Royal"); Israel means royalty (see matrix).

The Lady Di Problem

Jacob has 11 boys and one girl, and as Jack was settling into the land, his daughter decided to make new friends. She visited Shechem, but perhaps Dinah (H178 דִּינָה Di'nāh, Dinah) was as drop-dead gorgeous as her family line. The ruler's son wants to have his way with her.

Dinah, Jacob's daughter, gets raped. Jacob withholds it from his sons (for a while — they don't know Jack), but when he tells them, they get mad and eventually kill the whole crowd, all the males of the town. God appears to Jacob and tells him, "Get thee hence to Bethel" (Gen 35:1-5).

Jacob cleanses the people, they get rid of the foreign Gods, and then the fear of God falls on all the people around. Way to go, His Royal Brit (covenant of Israel).

Coat of Many Colors, and dream

Jacob made Joseph a coat of many colors (Gen 37:3). When his brothers saw it, they hated him and could not speak a kind word to him (they bullied him). Jack (again) 'showed his true colors'; he basically showed all his sons who his favorite was.

31

Joseph dreamt of sheaves of hay bowing to him. When Joseph told his brothers about his dream, they hated him even more! His dream of 12 sheaves of grain and 11 bowing to him (Gen 37:5-7) recalls the prophecy of the firstborn in Genesis 27:29, where the firstborn was to be lord over his brothers and nations. It seems like God is giving Joseph the birthright (Gen 27:28-29).

Joseph had another dream; this time, the sun, moon, and 11 stars were bowing down to him. This was the 'last straw' for the brothers! They couldn't take it any longer and started scheming. In Genesis 37:19, they say, "Here comes that dreamer. Let's kill him, then we will see what comes of his dreams." Reuben, the firstborn, tries to save Joseph by putting him in a cistern, but while he is gone, they sell him to an Ishmaelite caravan. You would think Reuben, the birthright son, would be mad, but he and Judah try to save their brother.

Joseph in Egypt

Joseph is sold to the Ishmaelites, descendants of Isaac's brother. Did they remember when they were eighty-six after a fight at the party (Gen 21:8,17-20)? Now, in a sense, they are helping Joseph fulfill his destiny. Joseph is taken bound to Egypt and placed on a camel loaded with spices (Gen 37:25,28) against his will. Was this the straw that broke the camel's back? Joseph held this grudge against his brothers for a long time; it was, you might say, the last indignation his brothers made against him, his 'last Straw.'

Joseph was handsome, the old English word FAIR (handsome, morally good Gen 39:6) was used by the Bible to describe him. In fact, he was so appealing that Potiphar's wife desired him greatly.

Seems like these rulers just take what they want when they want it in this society. Joseph was an honorable guy, and he would not sleep with his master's wife. His reward for doing the right thing was being thrown into jail. Now, this is really jacked up! Joseph hadn't done anything wrong, and it just went from bad to worse.

Joseph keeps faith through thick and thin.

But Joseph does not give up; he keeps the faith through thick and thin (lean years and years of plenty). He was accused of rape while being honorable to God and imprisoned for a crime he didn't commit, yet God was with him. The dreamer continued to dream and believe in God. He was not yet *living the dream*, but he was keeping the faith. Even in the bad times, can we say that about ourselves?

Sometimes life is jacked up, but if we keep the faith, we will receive our 'just deserts.

Years later, we see that Joseph was placed in charge of Egypt, and God blessed him. Joseph spent perhaps 4-5 years working for Potiphar and maybe 8 years in prison before being released and put in charge of all of Egypt. So, Joseph was 30 when placed in charge of Egypt (Gen. 41.46), very young for a ruler. But God had trained him well. The undercover boss in charge of the elite prison system already knew who he could trust and who he couldn't. The elites that came through his prison included the butcher, the baker, the candlestick maker (ha, ha), along with top bankers, lawyers, businessmen, and other Pharaoh officials.

Joseph's got a lot of work to do during the 7 years of plenty. Then, there were about 2 years of famine before Jacob instructed his boys to go to Egypt to get food for the family and live.

Joseph is in charge of Egypt at age 30 (Gen 41:46). At this point, some 13 years of hard work as a slave. Nine more years pass before he gets to see his father again (Gen 45:11).

Years earlier, when the children of Israel showed Jacob the coat of many colors with blood on it and torn to shreds, Jacob said some ferocious animal had devoured my son, and he wept and mourned for his son for a long time and would not be comforted (Gen 37:35). His children 'kept him in the dark'; (just as his fight with God) Israel *didn't know Jack* about what had really happened. He lost a favorite son, the firstborn of Rachel, and he lost the love of his life, Rachel, as she died in childbirth (Gen 35:18). He only had Benjamin to hang onto.

When Jacob learns that there is grain in Egypt, he asks his sons to buy some, and they stare blankly at each other. Were they thinking, 'Oh no, that's where we sent Joseph. God is paying us back!' But Jacob would not send Benjamin with them because he was afraid of losing him.

Israel's sons go to Egypt and bow down to Joseph. Joseph tests his brothers. Are they really repentant? Are they really sorry for what they did? (Gen 42:7). Joseph sees his brethren, but he makes himself strange unto them and speaks roughly unto them; and he said unto them, "Whence come ye?" And they said, "From the land of Canaan to buy food" (Gen 42:13).

And they said, "Thy servants are twelve brethren, the sons of one man in the land of Canaan; and, behold, the youngest is this day with our father, and one is not" (Gen 42:20). But bring your youngest brother unto me; so shall your words be verified, and ye shall not die. And they did so (Gen 42:21). And they said one to another, "We are verily guilty concerning our brother, in that we saw the anguish of his soul when he besought us, and we would not hear; therefore, is this distress come upon us."

Joseph put his brothers in jail for three days. On the third day, he brought them out and said, "Do this, and you will live: leave one of your brothers here, but you must bring your youngest back here to me" (Gen. 42.17)! They said to each other, "Surely, we are being punished because of our brother. We saw how distressed he was when he pleaded with us for his life — really, Joe pleads for his life, and they didn't care — well, Joe's going to "teach them a lesson." They did not know that Joe could understand them, i.e., he could speak their language.

Joseph's 'brothers from another mother' (Gen 42.v25) leave Egypt with their bags packed with grain. But dark rain clouds are forming. The kids have heavy hearts; they have to leave their brother behind and give Dad the bad news. More bad news for Dad is that the ruler of Egypt wants to see Benjamin.

The silver lining

At one place, they stop for the night, open the outer sack and find silver in the mouth! Again, their hearts sink. The metaphorical rain clouds in their hearts grow deeper. Is it possible the '*clouds have a silver lining*'? As they empty their sacks, they find *silver in the lining* of each sack. They are convinced that this is a dark, ominous sign that they will be charged with theft, lying, you name it.

They feel they are getting set up by the Lord of Egypt. Jacob says, "You have deprived me of my children. Joseph is no more, and Simeon is no more, and now you want to take Benjamin. Everything is against me!" Benjamin is Jack's last remaining connection to Rachel, the 'love of his life.' And, of course, God is also the love of his life. He loves God with a passion because he is in sync with God; he gets it; he knows God is good and the Devil is evil; he understands God is in charge!

Reuben, Israel's number 1, and Judah are responsible people and trying in a small way to honor God. Joseph takes Simeon and says Simeon will stand in pledge for their return with Benjamin. Was Simeon the main instigator in trying to kill Joe and then sell him to the Ishmaelites? When Jacob hears that the ruler of Egypt has imprisoned Simeon and will not release him until Benjamin shows up, his heart sinks.

Everything is against me (everything is jacked up). Now, the sons are feeling guilty and want to do the right thing. Both Judah and Reuben vouch for the safe return of Benjamin (Gen. 42:37, 43:8-10). They even offer their own sons, and Judah says, 'We could have been there and back twice' (are they finally learning their lesson). Jacob, at long last, sends them with a double portion and gifts for the man. And prays for a safe return. Again, it's always darkest before the dawn. Remember when Israel fought with God all night long, and at dawn, he saw it was God he was fighting with? We often wonder what life's all about and why we have to go through the challenges of life. I speak to this shortly.

Living the dream

When Joseph saw his brothers coming, he ordered the fatted calf to be slaughtered and a great feast to be made (Gen 43:16). Here we go again; they bow down to Joseph and present him gifts (Gen 27:28-29, 43:26). Joseph is *living the dream* — but there is more turmoil in store for the kids. This is like a Hitchcock thriller with more twists and turns than a roller coaster ride.

The brothers were frightened. They thought they were being brought to the rich man's house because they had the silver in their lining. They thought that "he is going to attack us, overpower us, seize us as slaves, and our asses" (is this where we got the phrase *'kick our asses'* Gen 43:18)? When they get to Joe's house, they speak to the steward and explain the silver in their lining problem. The steward says, 'The God of your fathers has given you the *silver in your lining*!

After a great banquet and feast where Ben is given a double portion, the children of Israel get ready to leave Egypt with their bags packed (Gen 44:1) with a variety of food products, which no doubt included wheat, barley, beans of all kinds, and other non-perishable foodstuffs. The Hebrew word used to describe their shopping bag contents is Okel (h400-could mean beans). They had not gotten very far when Joseph's steward caught them, interrogated them, and searched all the bags, starting with the eldest to the youngest.

When he gets to the youngest, they discover Joseph's silver cup. Could this be the origin of the idiom 'spill the beans'? Perhaps Ben's sack (silver cup holder) was carrying beans? And we developed the term "spill the beans" from this encounter? Of course, they didn't know what was going on, and they were so panic-stricken for the life of Benjamin. They go back to Joseph, who tests them one more time. Have they finally learned their lesson? Judah offers his life for Benjamin. Well done, Judah, for offering your life for a brother from another mother!

Yes, the whole show was very moving. The brothers did find their hearts and learned their lesson. Joe (and ultimately God) was a good teacher!

What was God doing here? If you wanted to build a bond of brotherhood that was so tight, not even the fear of death would separate them; it has to develop over time experientially, and this is what God did. Remember the saying, 'Blood is thicker than water?' This is our heritage that stretches through the generations because it's in our DNA; it's in our blood. That is what (I believe) was happening here.

Joseph reveals his true identity to his brothers. They are shaking in their boots with fear; they think they are all going to die. Joe reassures them and tells them it's God's will; what they meant for harm, God meant for good (Gen 45).

The boys are instructed to take wagons, go get the family, and not to worry about their belongings because the whole of Egypt is 'there for the picking' (Gen. 45:20 Pharaoh told them the land is yours for the picking). Israel was waiting with bated breath, not knowing what was going on. I am sure he prayed pretty hard while waiting for word to come back. When he heard the news, he 'got his second wind' (Gen. 45:27 Ruwach H7307, wind #28).

God then speaks to promises to Israel in a dream (Gen 46):

- Be not afraid; I will make you into a great nation in Egypt.
- Promise to bring them back to their land; so far, the land was not theirs!
- Joseph himself will close his eyes (keep him safe and secure during the sojourn in Egypt).
- Remember Abraham's promise, 400 years in a land not their own with at least 4 generations, then they come out.

Jacob meets his 'long-lost son.' It had been 22 or 23 years since Joseph's loss/death. All this time Jacob didn't know Jack; he had been kept in the dark (like his fight with God). Again, we could use the proverb, it's always darkest before the dawn. Jacob had been in the dark for over 20 years; what a relief to know that the promises of God were still alive for all his children, even his favorite.

Jacob, at long last, knew his son was alive! He saw him face to face (like when he met Elohim — it was a God moment), and they wept for a long time as they embraced. Israel said to Joseph, *"Now let me die since I have seen thy face because thou art yet alive"* (Gen 46:29).

Yo'saf, you're safe after 23 years, you're safe. I can imagine his dad kept repeating, Yo'saf, yo'safe, my son, my beloved son, Yo'safe (H3084 means to add, to save, metaphorically be safe). All the plans, all the dreams, all the prophecies, I went through hell and back, and now I see your face, Yo'safe, I can die. Well, he didn't die; his second wind kicked in; he renewed his strength, and he continued for another 17 years. The years of his pilgrimage were 147 (Gen 48.28). I have had him beat; mine is about 300 years old, or perhaps it just feels that way.

Many will say that we cannot understand the wonders or work of God till his work is finished, and often, it is difficult. We can see from the lives of the patriarchs that there is a purpose and a design.

I offer a quote by Corrie Ten Boom, a woman who helped perhaps 800 Jews escape the holocaust until she herself was interned.

Corrie Ten Boom

"Life is but a Weaving" (the Tapestry Poem)

My life is but a weaving Between my God and me. I cannot choose the colors He weaveth steadily.

Oft' times He weaveth sorrow; I in foolish pride Forget He sees the upper And I the underside.

Not 'til the loom is silent, And the shuttles cease to fly Will God unroll the canvas And reveal the reason why.

The dark threads are as needful In the weaver's skillful hand As the threads of gold and silver In the pattern He has planned.

He knows He loves, He cares; Nothing this truth can dim. He gives the very best to those Who leave the choice to Him. '

Story of Tamar

This story breaks my heart every time I read it; it is a story of a beautiful, Godly lady who was mistreated and ridiculed. She is given in marriage to Judah's son Er. (Can I suggest you blow the dust off your Bible and read the story in Gen. 38 and 2, Chr. 13?) But Er was wicked in God's sight, so he God put him to death. Onan (the destroyer) was told to marry Tamar, but he was also wicked. He just wanted to get his end away, spilling his semen on the ground because he knew her offspring would have Er's name (end) and not his, so God put Onan (the destroyer) to death.

Along comes Shelah. God had killed his two brothers for their evil. Was Shelah like his brothers, or was he Godly? A family normally gets their faith more from their mothers than their fathers. They are the ones nursing and raising them. Anyhow, Shelah had no guts. He was a right Sheila (Australian slang for girl). He would not fulfill his duties as the kinsman redeemer (Ruth. 1-4), so Tamar took matters into her own hands.

She heard that Judah was getting ready to go to Timnah to shear the sheep. Judah must have had a reputation. Because Tamar knew exactly what to do. Judah lay with his daughter-in-law (which fell to him as his son wouldn't do it). She became pregnant (but Judah didn't know it was his daughter-in-law). Pregnant at long last!

When Judah found out she was pregnant, he thought she had been whoring, and he decided she must die. Finally, Tamar had to reveal who the real father was. She had Judah's signet ring and staff as a token for future payment. When pressed, she said, 'The father is the one to whom these belong!'

Wow, Judah, you made a big song and dance about it and now it's come back to bite you! To be a laughing stock, the butt end of jokes, this is what came out of this encounter (Gen. 38.23).

He did the right thing morally (amen, to be a man- H543 אָמֵן 'âmên) good for him. However, it appears Judah did become the butt end of jokes, i.e., a mark for archery practice, properly a mound or other erection on which the target is set up.

The name Tamar also means erection (H8558); she set Judah up. Is this where we get the term laughing stock from?

Also of note is that Judah got his wife from Canaan, a group who had some Nephilim mixed blood. In a sense, God cleansed the bloodline with Tamar, fostering Judah's new children, Perez and Zerah (Gen 38.2).

The Red Hand of Zerah (Gen 38)

Tamar is about to give birth to twins, and the two boys tussled in her stomach, with one boy putting his hand out first. At this point, the midwife tied a scarlet cord to it (the red hand of Zerah), and then his brother came out.

They named him Perez (H6557), meaning breach or breaking forth, while his brother was called Zerah (H2226 — Zerach), meaning a ray of light or hope. Also, Zera and Zara = seed. God blessed Tamar with her twin boys-YAHOO (3058 Yehuw). Shout for joy; we have a couple of Jew boys; they were jubilant, and it was time to party (H6558 Partsiy par-tsee'329).

Interesting that the name Perez means to break forth, to scatter to go abroad, which is exactly what his twin brother Zerah did! Tamar is now the mother of the Jews, a great role model, diligent, long-suffering, and patient, awaiting her chance to create progeny, trusting in God.

Her first husband was evil. God loved her so much that he took him out. Her second husband was worse, Onan, the destroyer of the Er family line. She has twins, Perez is the prime promise holder, and Zerah almost came out first but came out last and was somehow held in contempt.

Zerah never really got over the breach; he felt he was cheated, even though his name means to rise, come forth, break out, arise, rise up, shine (compare Zara, seed H2232 זֶרַע)!

Later, we will see that Zerah, of the red hand of Judah, adopted his father's name, Er and broke out from the rest. In reality, when Judah stepped in as a surrogate and fathered Er's line, he no longer was the progenitor; the Kingly line was supplanted (Jacob) by Er, and he became the Heir (ER) of the Jewish race. Later we will see a tragedy unfold where some of the line is still in the land of Canaan, and we have a terrible Achan (h5912).

CHAPTER 3 Egypt, Joseph, and Moses.

Let's take a look at Egypt and see what clues God has left us:

Fig. 1Greater Israel-potential total landmass.

In Genesis 15:18, the LORD made a covenant with Abram, saying — 'Unto thy seed have I given this land, from the river of Egypt unto the great river, the river Euphrates (from the river to the sea).' The border of Israel went from Egypt (Wadi El-Arish or Nile) to Euphrates (see Fig. 1, Eze 47:19 & Num 34:5, #40). It is thought (by some) that Wadi El-Arish was considered the river of Egypt, not the great river of Egypt, which would be the Nile.

Archeological & Historic Evidence for Joseph - Egypt

Joe is a very well-known Bible figure; most of us know about his deep devotion to God and his mother, Rachel (whom Jacob loved). Joseph being born to Jacob in his old age made him Jacob's favorite, even though he was the 11th child, with Benjamin, his brother, being the last. Unfortunately, momma died during the birth of Ben (Gen 35:16-18).

Imhotep — Joseph

Again, to review the story, Jacob made Joseph a coat of many colors, which his brothers hated. After he told his first dream

41

of the sheaves bowing to him, his second dream of the stars-spangled banner with the sun and moon bowing to him was the last straw.

His brothers sold him to the Ishmaelites (Gen. 37:28) merchants. Then we have his work with Potiphar and God blessing him, and his reward was imprisonment. This gave Joseph (h3130) a quick and complete understanding of how business was run in Egypt and how to take advantage of it.

After a complete and thorough extensive training by God, he was ready for the Job. Joe was made the second in command next to Pharaoh and was so highly elevated in Egypt that a Pyramid was built for him.

Imhotep was spoken of by Manetho (#34); some think him to be Joseph, and I agree with this viewpoint. Imhotep (Joseph) also built huge granaries to store grain for the 7 years of plenty and 7 years of famine (Jacob and Joseph kept the faith through thick and thin 7 years of feast & seven of famine). He created an elaborate system of dispensation distribution that has only recently come to light.

In fact, it was found on an Island called Elephantine (#63), which itself has a unique story that we will cover later. Imhotep had a reputation for being a great teacher of medicine — the forerunner of modern medicine who also invented the art of building with hewn stones; he likewise was considered a priest, and Pharaoh Djoser gave him the title of chief of Egypt under the king (Gen 41.41-45). He ruled in Saqqara, near Memphis; the famine stele (#63), written 1000 years after the event (333 BC), details these facts, and while it had some items that were corrupted, it mostly mirrors the description written in the Bible.

We should understand that history often gets blurred hundreds and thousands of years after the event; even so, there often remain salient points to authenticate their accuracy and plausibility. I hope you will feel that I have used good reason, judgment, & biblical hermeneutics to develop a plausible outcome. In fact, I feel that the body of evidence is so overwhelming that even a mere novice (or 5th grader) can reach the same conclusion as I do. Please check out the movie 'Patterns of Evidence! (#64).

Joseph is said to have built a residence in the city of Rameses II, but archaeologists couldn't find a city or trace till 1970 when a farmer found the remains of a remarkable statue of Rameses II (#65), he was one of the most important kings of the New Kingdom and lived in Pi-Rameses (Nile delta — Goshen).

The discovery made people think they were on the verge of finding evidence of Joseph and Israel till they realized it was 300 years too late. However, digging deeper, they discovered the city of Avaris, and although most of the buildings were Egyptian, there were some areas that had a definite Semitic presence in terms of burial, artifacts and style of building.

An Archaeologist called David Rohl (#282) did an outstanding job reporting the facts. It is clear archaeological evidence of the biblical story of Israel in Egypt.

Joseph Promoted to Lord of Egypt

During Joseph's rule of Egypt, the Israelites lived in luxury on the fertile plain of Goshen. It is worthy to note that Joseph controlled all trade, borders, and ports. They found a Palace in Avaris and a vandalized statue which is stocky with red hair and white skin like the Celts; also, the Bible says he was well built and handsome (Gen. 39.6). Even the Hebrew name for handsome is English, or is it that the English name is Hebrew LOL so we have come full circle. Seriously though, in another section of the book, I develop this language connection between Hebrew and English.

The Hebrew word for handsome (Strong's H3303) ya'pheh) pronounced yaw-feh', meaning beautiful, means almost the same in English as ya-your and feh-fair, meaning beautiful. I believe this is where we get the English term 'fair' (#47). We actually get Ya, yeh ye, your, and yes from Yah Hebrew name for God and in English means to agree with God or just agree Yes.

The red, white and blue multi-colored coat is a guess at what was thought to be the original, as only a small fraction was left to evaluate. Also, his facial features were very different from what is portrayed in this reconstruction; as mentioned earlier, Joseph was

43

very handsome and strapping. David Rohl reconstructed the Colonnade of Joseph's Palace, which had twelve columns and a Pyramid tomb which was empty as it should be because Joseph instructed his children to take his bones with them. I am assuming that Jacob's bones had already been taken?

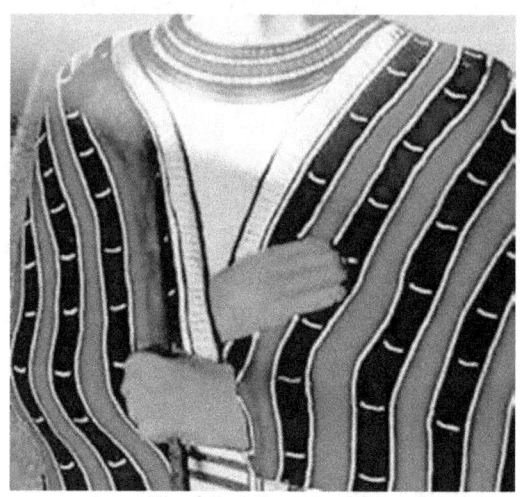

Fig. 2 Imhotep-Joseph

Image Courtesy: Imhotep-Joseph. Credit David Rohl

The Joseph's Hay Day

Joseph was promoted to be in charge of Egypt after his dream of the bales of hay bowing to him; the Israelites enjoyed great success living and thriving alongside the Egyptians; it is even thought that Joseph was the first one to show the Egyptians how to cut stone and build a pyramid. This clearly goes against all (or most) of the Egyptologist's false dating methods as mentioned above.

We can see from the Bible that Joseph was an outstanding figure who was so smart that he excelled everywhere while working for Potiphar and then again when working in the prison system. Finally, he was put in charge of all of Egypt. Pharaohs were not stupid.

They would not put someone in charge if they didn't have overwhelming evidence of their capability, and when one of Pharaoh's trusted associates came forward and vouched for Joseph, he was accepted and promoted to Lord of all Egypt, and he started *living the dream*, and had his *Hay day*.

Let My People Go Pharaoh 13 Times

The years roll on, and we get a Pharaoh who doesn't remember Joseph; we Israelites are now oppressed slaves and cry out to Yah (h3050) for mercy and deliverance. Yah raises up Moses (H4872) who is brought up in Pharaoh's household as a son of Pharaoh himself. Moses asked Pharaoh 13 times to let God's people go — most of us know the story – Pharaoh's heart was hardened, and he was stubborn and would not listen even though God provided miraculous signs.

God was making a huge point here; this was the city of Satan, they worshiped all the Satanic deities they could also engage in open sexual acts and all kinds of perversion (whoring), and God's point was – you have all this technology, knowledge, and Satanic witchcraft power, okay, let's have a test.

We can see all the miracles that God performed, and the Egyptian sorcerers were able to mimic the first two, the snake and turning water into blood, but look what happened, the fact that they were proud of being able to mimic God's miracles came back to bite them, Moses' snake ate the Egyptian one and the Nile river stank, fish died and was the catalyst for many of the next plagues (Ex 7.19-25), the second plague came back to bite them worse, it's the only plague that God didn't reverse. They didn't repent and ask God to heal the water of the Nile.

After the next plagues, Moses was asked to pray to God and have him take them away, which he did, but then Pharaoh used fake promises and Moses' goodness against him, and as soon as Moses prayed for the calamity to be gone, Pharaoh was back to his same old liberal democratic tricks (chapter 7-13).

In chapter 11, we have God clearly making a distinction between Egypt and Israel, and of course, chapter 12, the Passover, which we have almost forgotten, in fact, most of the feasts of the Lord we have almost forgotten, if not for our brothers the Jews (Hos 10:11), they would be lost to obscurity.

CHAPTER 4 — The Exodus.

After the final plague, which was provoked by Pharaoh himself, Pharaoh's heart was softened, and he summoned Moses and said, "Up and leave quickly and go and worship. Take your herds and flocks and 'Also Bless Me'" (Ex 12.31-33). Even he understood the power of a blessing from a holy person. Things always seemed to improve for him after Moses interceded with prayer.

Another interesting detail is that we baked bread without leavening. This process prevented the cakes from rising and resulted in flatbread. At the time, it probably didn't taste or feel right. Did the phrase *'You can't have your cake and eat it too'* The phrase is supposed to mean "you cannot simultaneously retain possession of a cake and eat it, too", that is even closer to what happened, we cooked bread without years and were driven out before being able to eat it (Ex 12.39).

On a brighter note, we did acquire a significant amount of plunder from the Egyptians (Exo 3:18), but consider 400+ years of slavery where we made Egypt great, this was a well-deserved reparation, not one that was 3 or 4 generations later, where none of the incumbents contributed to the problem, if reparations are due it should be the party responsible!

In Exodus 12.37, the Israelites journeyed to Succoth. Earlier, Moses stated his original intent was to journey into the desert for three days and celebrate a feast with the Lord. God knew Pharaoh would not let them go until the last plague had hit them, and when it did they got out for good.

As said earlier, Israel left in the night, and we can surmise that around 1-3 days (Exo. 8.27) later, they arrived at Succoth (Gen 33:17). But where was Succoth (a Hebrew name)? Some show it right next to Goshen (Fig 7 later this section), but that would not be a three-day journey, and it would not be wise to gather the troops so close to Goshen.

We can see in Genesis 33:17 that Jacob journeyed to Succoth (h5523) and built himself a house and made booths (H5521) Sukkot for his cattle; therefore, the name of the place is called Succoth. This is in Israel proper, as Israel was heading back from Paddan Aram, so this would be northern Israel, Succoth near Shechem, in the territory of Gad. But when did we settle in Succoth in Egypt?

El Arish — Sukkot Etymology

The name Sukkot is Hebrew, meaning booth, tent, or temporary dwelling. So why do we have it listed in Egypt? At what point did we establish this location and why, or was there another reason for calling it Sukkot? Sometimes names get put to a place after the fact, i.e., it was not until Dan occupied Laish (Jud. 18.29) and renamed it that it became Dan, yet Moses in Genesis 14.14 talking about Abraham rescuing Lot chased the attackers to Dan.

This indicates that the Bible was never stagnant but was rewritten. Many times, where spelling was changed names were changed, but the essence remained the same. We do this today; when discussing ancient history, we would use the modern name and spelling.

There are said to be four places named Sukkot (#42), 1 in Egypt and three in Canaan. Even the Babylonians, when they came to Israel, named a place of idol worship a brothel 'Sukkot ben-ohth" booth for daughters (2Kin 17:30).' I believe these names are significant because we take them with us on our journeys, i.e., El Arish and Sukkot.

El Arish was named after its unusual lush grove of palm trees, with no (clearly the wadi feeds underground) apparent water source. Of course, the locals have made palm huts for thousands of years there; even the Aussies were impressed and carried the name back to their land (#70, 81). Also, during the 1st World War, El Arish became the center of operations for the British. So, it's been a strategic military outpost for many millennia.

The city grew around a Bedouin settlement near the ancient Ptolemaic outpost of Rhinocorura (#74). In the Middle Ages (5th to the 15th century), pilgrims identified the site as the Sukkot of the Bible (booths are made from palm branches). 'Arīsh means 'palm huts' in Modern Standard Arabic.'

I will show that it was not only in the Middle Ages that it was believed that Arish was Tharu and next to Sukkot, but there are many other references.

Palm trees are important religious symbols. In the Bible, the people of Jerusalem greeted a triumphant Jesus by laying palms in his path just one week before his death and resurrection, a tradition now known and celebrated as Palm Sunday, the week before Easter.

Palms are mentioned dozens of times in the Bible; in Judaism, palms represent peace and prosperity. God says I have written you on the Palm of my hand; we named the palm of the hand and the palm tree because they look alike (#72, 73). The mother of the Jewish and Irish/British-kingly line is Tamar, which means Palm tree in Hebrew; it is also a phallic symbol (H8558).

Four Proofs for the Location of Tharu — El Arish

I have 4 references that all believe or prove that Succoth was Tharu, and Tharu was located very close to El Arish.

- Ron Wyatt (Respected biblical Archaeologist) says that Moses had to organize the tribes in a staging point, and this was Tharu, aka 'Succoth had to be a place large enough for this tremendous amount of people and flocks to assemble. A place called variably 'Tharu,' T'aru,' and 'Takut' fits the description of Succoth perfectly.'
- Josephus writes about this in his 'Antiquities of the Jews,' Book II, Chapter 10. As a military man, once again, Moses knew 'Tharu,' and it was here that he organized his largest 'army' ever for travel. From here, they traveled to Etham, modern-day Eilat, on the northern border of the Red Sea (Gulf of Aqaba).
- According to Exodus 13:18-20, the locality from which the Israelites journeyed after departing Egypt was Sukkot. The name Sukkot means 'palm huts' in Hebrew and was translated as El-Arish in Arabic. It lies in the vicinity of El-Arish, the hometown of the Jewish commentator Saadia Gaon, who identified Naḥal Mizraim with the wadi of El-Arish. (#66)

- Also, the Map Madaba found in Jordan shows that El Arish was the fort town, holding a huge prison, fort, and border town, protecting Egypt's right flank. As part of the trade route 'Way of the Philistines' and 'Way of Horus.' The Madaba Map, which is perhaps the oldest known map of Israel 542 AD, is from Madaba, Jordan, although it is said to be perhaps a copy of The Onomasticon and the Exodus route. by Eusebius, 325AD

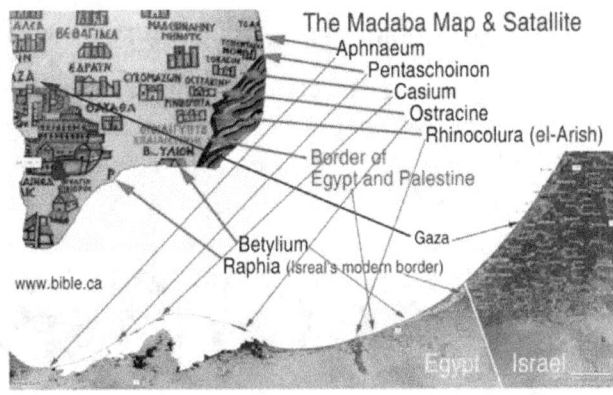

One of the most important things the Madaba map shows is that the border of Egypt was at the Wadi El-Arish. This is the historic border between Egypt and Israel from 1446 BC, the time of exodus, to 70 AD, when the Israel of Jesus time was destroyed. In modern times, the border has been moved 44 km northeast to Raphia at the eastern edge of the Gaza Strip. You can see from the Madaba map that the border is between Bitylium and Rhinoculura (Arish).

Fig. 7 Madaba Osticon map

The Bible clearly shows that the border between Egypt and Israel was just north of the Wadi al-Arish (Gen. 15:18; Josh.15:4,47). The Wadi Al-Arish is the southern/eastern border of the promised land.

This proves that the modern Sinai Peninsula was under the control of Egypt and considered Egyptian territory, just as it is today. Since we can prove the Sinai Peninsula was 'Egyptian,' this also proves that Mt. Sinai cannot be where Queen Helena chose it to be in a dream in 325 AD, at Mt. Musa, beside the St. Catherine's monastery. Mt. Sinai was not in Egypt. The Bible says that Mt. Sinai was located in Arabia, not Egypt (Gal 4:25).

49

The Onomasticon tells us that Bitylium was 20 km south of Raphia. 'Bēthphou (Bathaffu). Where a tribe of Judah was located, a village fourteen miles beyond Raphia on the road to Egypt. It is the border of Palestine.' The Onomasticon and the Exodus route. by Eusebius (325AD)

The Great Edict of Horemheb, the law shall be executed against him, in that his nose shall be cut off, and he shall be sent to Tharu. (James Henry Breasted, Ancient Records of Egypt, 1906 AD, Vol 3 p 50-67, #83, 1300 BC).

Archaeologist Claims: Tharu, Sinai (Biblical Succoth?)

Archaeologists claim to have identified the fort as Tharu 'The ancient military road, known as 'Way of Horus,' once connected Egypt to Palestine and is close to present-day Rafah, which borders the Palestinian territory of Gaza.' — Associated Press.

Figure 4: Inscription courtesy Associate Press

Apparently, this inscription (Fig. 4) mentions Tharu. Tharu has sometimes been identified with biblical Succoth (the setting for the legendary first stop by the 'Children of Israel' after leaving Rameses). This depends on the particular reconstruction of the route from the books of Exodus and Numbers.

The news stories haven't gotten onto this angle yet. They will, though... Succoth had to be a place large enough for this tremendous amount of people and flocks to assemble. A place called variably Tharu, Taru and Takut fits the description of Succoth perfectly.

'Over a century ago, Max Müller recognized the importance of Tjaru [Tharu] in ancient Egypt and realized that it must have played a role in the movement of the Israelites; he declared that 'no town of the eastern Delta frontier has a greater importance than Tharu [i.e., Tjaru], which was not only its largest town but also the principle point for the defense of the entrance to Egypt, therefore also for the military and mercantile roads to the East.' He also felt that the route of the exodus could not be fixed with any certainty until Tjaru was positively located.' — James K. Hoffmeier, Israel in Egypt: The Evidence for the Authenticity of the Exodus Tradition, 1997:184.

Alternative theories place the ancient Tharu homeland closer to Goshen, near present-day Qantara. However, this placement weakens the idea of a secure border. Following the collapse of Egypt after the Exodus, the Hyksos kings, who had ruled Egypt, likely retreated to a more defensible position at Qantara, as Ramesses II (who reigned much later, around 750 BC) wouldn't have been a factor. This aligns with the Hykso's arrival following the destruction of Egypt's army and economy, estimated around 1430 BC, after the 13th Dynasty (as per the new timeline, Fig 4).

Therefore, based on the available evidence, a border/fort complex during the Exodus would be more likely located at El Arish (Rhinoculura). Placing the border town at Qantara would be akin to placing a crucial border checkpoint hundreds of miles away from the actual border, offering minimal protection. The Bible's description of the palm hut city of El Arish as the border aligns best with the strategic needs of the time.

Military Fort, Naval Base & Prison, Succoth-El Arish-Tharu.

We assume that military guards were everywhere in Egypt. The Israelite population was massive and difficult to control, with over 1 million people, some estimated upward of 2-3 million. Moses could not have taken the slaves and prisoners of Egypt without authority from Pharaoh, which he revoked on many occasions; it was an enormous task evacuating 2,000,000 people, giving them the news that they were ready to leave, then — no, we were not leaving.

How did the Egyptians keep order with an ever-increasing unhappy Israelite slave population? Undoubtedly, rules infractions were dealt with severely; this is depicted in the movie 'The Exodus' with Charlton Heston portraying Moses, as he tries to protect a slave who is assisting the moving of a huge stone (Exo 2:11). Anyhow whenever a person committed a crime or a slave worker rebelled they could get sent to Rhinoculura, its where we get Rhinoplasty, i.e., nose job and the Naos obelisk?

El Arish in Egyptian means palm hut, aka Succoth in Hebrew (#44). Tharu is the Fort/Prison, and as we have mentioned earlier Great Edict of Horemheb links it with Rhinoculura(#75). They cut the nose off the prisoners (not nice), 'cut your nose off to spite your face.' The phrase means, "Don't be stupid; think about it before you do it. Is the risk worth it?" Did we get it from Egypt a connection again long lost? (#45). I feel that perhaps large numbers of Hebrews were imprisoned at Tharu (Psa 79:11, Psa 102:20) and that, along with a good staging area and the last border crossing point out of Egypt, would be good reasons why Moses would initially re-group there.

The Bible says this is where God intervenes. He directs Moses (Derek H1870 Exo.13.17,20) not to cross the border and take the Philistine road, even though it was (I believe) right next to them (H7138 — qarow, cf. Gen. 19.20 #69). Only after leaving Succoth did God lead them by a pillar. In some ways, he is still leading us by a pillar today (Gen 35:14, Exo 13:21, II Kin 11:13-14), i.e., Jacobs Pillar, and the item of veneration and the covenant (Brits) promise of God, also Jesus said on this Rock (Pillar-stone), I will build my church.

The El-Arish shrine (which means God of the Arish [Irish]), which, in addition to confirming that Pharaoh was killed in the Red Sea, also corroborates another event of the Exodus; it suggests the Hyksos kings were Semitic (# 60) It also states how Pharaoh chased the Queen Mother, Tefnut, some say the royal princess that once raised Moses, as she was leaving with the departing Israelites. The Talmud (Sotah 12a) also states that the princess left in the Exodus, marrying the Israelite leader, Caleb, son of Yefuneh.

The Bible says Caleb was the young man who went to spy out the land of Canaan and actually came back with a good report (Num 13:30), so Moses's mum could not have married him. Also, there is no mention of an earlier Caleb. In addition, Moses was over 80 years old when he led the Israelites out of Egypt! His mother would have been 100, give or take. Does this seem plausible, perhaps a daughter or, more realistically, her granddaughter? The story is intriguing because of its similarity to Irish history, which we will cover shortly.

Additional evidence of the Exodus comes from the Papyrus Ipuwer (#62), which states that the Hyksos kings were Semitic and came in and took control of Egypt after their destruction, caused by the plagues of God and the destruction of their army. Apepi, A Hyksos king, probably in the 14th Dynasty (1300 BC), has a large serpent inscription attributed to him; this seems out of place with other Egyptian paintings. Could this suggest a Danite influence? Also, the Hyksos kings ruled from Avaris (Goshen) and buried their dead in a Semitic way and were attributed with Semitic names. There is also a Hyksos scarab, which appears to have the early Celtic swirls or snakes on it! (#46).

Rhinoculura — Tharu — Cut Nose Off

On the next page, I show numerous images of the ruling class from ancient Egypt with their noses cut; what are the reasons for this? The first is obvious and perhaps speaks of vandalism, but why? Some list the reason as white boys not being able to take a different ethnic group as being superior (in some way). But does this hold water? Many of the ancient Egyptians were white with red hair and Semitic features (#332), i.e., noses, etc., so maybe a better reason would be to hide this fact.

My personal belief is that it's revenge from family members or released prisoners who had been disfigured by a barbaric act of cutting their noses off!

Figure 3 Neferure and Senemut Noses cut off

Image Courtesy: Neferure and Senenmut ("Captmondo," CC BY SA 3.0), Great Sphinx of Giza (Diego Delso), Head from a female sphinx (Brooklyn Museum), statue of a Man Public Domain), and Senusret III (Public Domain).

This view seems the most plausible since the only item often vandalized is the nose; notice the ear lobes, eyes & chin are still intact.

New Chronology of Egypt

Most Egyptologists created a sequential chronology for the familiar dynasties, although some archeologists think this is wrong, and this new chronology matches the Bible timeline very well. Remember that there are upper and lower Egypt like there were two Kingdoms in Israel, the northern ten tribes (Samaria) and the southern 3 tribes of Judah. Likewise, Egypt had a similar setup. In addition, they would have co-regents as (Israel did) and even when King David was king, we had problems when Absalom rebelled and tried to steal the kingdom (2Sa 15:10).

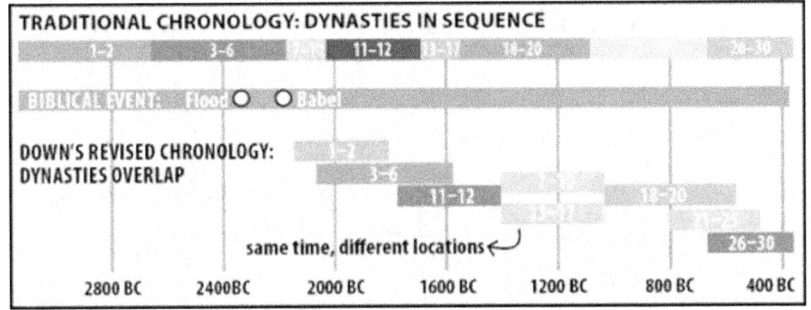

Figure 17: Patterns of evidence – (#32).

David Rohl. Israel Finkelstein, Kent Weeks, Bryant Wood

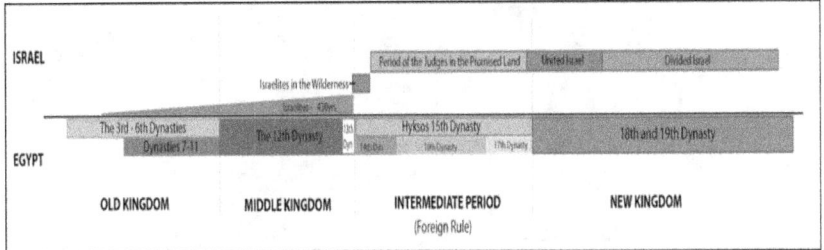

Figure 18 Another different David Downs Egyptian chronology

55

CHAPTER 5 - The Exodus -New Route.

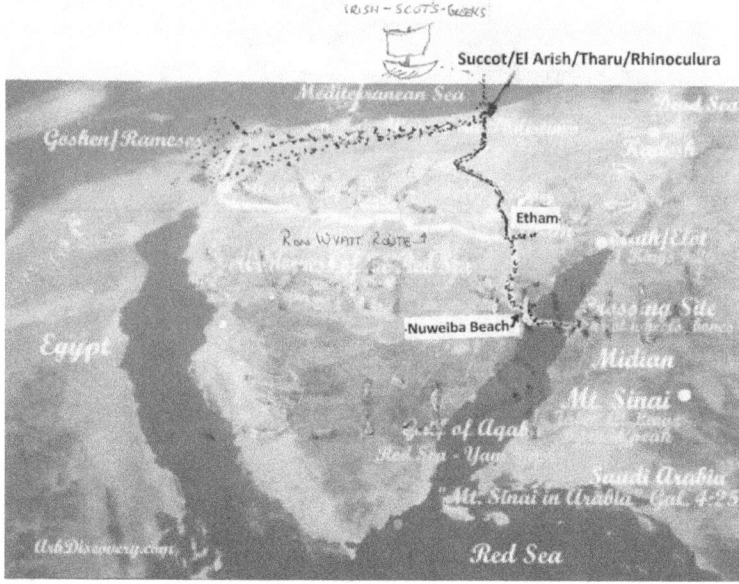

Figure 7 Succot -El Arish New Exodus route

Important to note that God did not start leading Israel by a Pillar of cloud by day and post of fire at night till after they had regrouped at Sukkot (Ex 13.17-20) and after they had organized and picked up (and many say dropped off) folks at Tharu (El Arish-port) then God instructed Moses, not take them through Philistines country. Yes, they were right on the border of Philistine and Egypt at the Wadi El Arish, as shown at the beginning of this chapter.

From Pillar to Post

Some say the true origin of this saying has been lost. It means a lot of people being forced to go from one place to another in an unceremonious or fruitless manner, occasioning much frustration and anger in the process — sounds like us when we were coming out of Egypt and with a lot of whining and complaining, with God leading us with a Pillar of cloud by day and a Post of fire at night (don't shoot the messenger — also from the Bible, #82).

The next few scriptures speak volumes. The words "pillar" and "post" are interchangeable, so for clarity, I have translated the second pillar to post. It will help us appreciate the origin of our idiom/proverb. (Exo 13:20) And they took their journey from Succoth and encamped in Etham, on the edge of the wilderness. v21 And the LORD went before them by day in a pillar of a cloud, to lead them the way; and by night in a post of fire, to give them light; to go by day and night: v22 He took not away the Pillar of the cloud by day, nor the Post of fire by night, from before the people. (Exo 14:1) ¶ And the LORD spoke unto Moses, saying, v2 Speak unto the children of Israel, that they turn (back) and encamp before Pi hahiroth, between Migdol and the sea, over against Baal Zephon: before it shall ye encamp by the sea. v3 For Pharaoh will say of the children of Israel, they are entangled in the land, the wilderness hath shut them in.

Let me translate – the Israelites are running about like headless chickens from pillar to post, and now they are trapped between 'The Devil and the Deep Blue Sea.'

Pi-HaHiroth, which is modern-day Nuweiba Beach (Fig 7)

7), is about halfway down the Red Sea, a circuitous route penned in with mountains on each side till they finally came to what appears to be a sandbank overlooking the Red Sea. The Red Sea is estimated to be 50 feet deep at this point; the Israelites thought, 'We are done! Pharaoh and his army are behind us (Devil), and the Red Sea (Deep Blue Sea) is in front of us with nowhere to escape.' (N10) Even our idioms remind us of our past! God said he would gain glory through Pharaoh. He uses a Hebrew term (H3513 – kabad 331), which gives honor to Moses' mum. God is sneaky. Go(o)d.

What I find interesting about this event is that the whole land of Canaan knew what happened. Forty years later, when God leads Israel to the promised land, they are terrified because of what God did at the Red Sea and within Egypt, so God did get glory through this event, and our idioms speak volumes about our history and our connection to the Great One!

Here, we are terrified at the Red Sea again, 'caught between the devil and the deep blue sea.' We cry out to God and Moses, who says don't worry, wait and see the deliverance of Jehovah (#76). Moses then goes on to say the Egyptians you see today will never see again, but secretly, Moses was afraid. Yes, even Moses was afraid and cried out to God (Ex. 14:13-15). 'He put a brave face on' (his face shone after meeting with God-Exo 34:35). God told him to raise your hands and stretch out his staff; this he did all night long.

Clearly, Moses and the children 'Held Out' for a long time. God drove the sea back, and the following day, Moses, still 'holding out,' walked the children through the Red Sea with a wall of water on each side (just as God said).

At the other side Mosheh was still holding out, and at the end of the last watch of the night, i.e., at daybreak.

'It's always darkest before the dawn.' God told Mosheh to stretch your hands (#79) over the sea and bring the water together over the Egyptians. 'Clap your Hands together.' We still use this as a sign of congratulations today, signifying the event of Moses when he clapped the Red Sea over the heads of Pharaoh, a type of Devil, i.e., Satan's and their army (Psa 98:8, Psa 47:1). Let the floods clap their hands: let the hills be joyful together.

Here today, gone tomorrow

Remember what Moses said (Ex 14.13): 'Do not fear! Stand by and see the salvation of the LORD, which He will accomplish for you today; for the Egyptians whom you have seen today, you will never see again forever. V27 So Moses stretched out his hands (#79) over the sea, and the sea returned to its normal state (Ps 98:8) at daybreak, while the Egyptians were fleeing right into it; then the LORD overthrew the Egyptians in the midst of the sea.

'Here today, gone tomorrow.' Remember the works of the Lord O Israel! We are his children, here today, gone tomorrow. As Moses said, Pharaoh's army was 'Here today and Gone tomorrow' never to be seen again!

God promised, "He will turn the hearts of the fathers to the children, and the hearts of the children to their fathers, lest I come and strike the Eretz (earth) with a curse" (Mal 4:6; Luk 1:16; Luk 1:17). This means we need to remember our roots and tell our children who we are! We are Israel! Baal Zephon was on the opposite side (Ex14.1-31).

What God did at the Red Sea was Awesome. He tricked the Egyptians into following us through the Red Sea. God, through a strong wind, pushed the water off a shelf that had existed between the Red Sea from Egypt to Midian, a plateau if you like. Ron Wyatt found it and documented it, and others have verified it along with Pharaoh's gold-plated chariot remains. We have many detailed accounts of what happened when they reached Midian, i.e., Baal Zephon. And we have Moses & Miriam's account — Do we remember the awesome works of God!

Exodus Ron Wyatt's Route, Sukkot, El Arish —

As mentioned earlier, I believe Sukkot (Tharu) is El Arish, and Wyatt's route can be seen in Fig 7 (#80). The Egyptians did have watch-posts all through the Sinai Peninsula and most likely would have had one here to keep an eye on ships coming up the Gulf of Aqaba. It is historically documented that they flashed messages from watchtower to watchtower using reflected sunlight by day and fire by night. In fact, that may well be how Pharaoh knew exactly where Moses and the people had gone.

However, it's hard to hide a large group of over 1 million people, so I don't think finding them was the difficulty, but certainly, having watchtowers and a form of Morse Code would help reduce the lead time. The question has been asked: 'Isn't this site for the crossing too far? Wouldn't it have taken them a long time to get there?'

Well, in 1967, Moshe Dayan marched his troops from Nuweiba (the crossing site) to Suez City (near ancient Tharu/Succoth) in six days. And they camped at night. The Israelites were told to use only unleavened bread for seven days — indicating that they would be traveling quite briskly without time to camp for seven days.

'Seven days thou shalt eat unleavened bread, and on the seventh day shall be a feast to the. And thou shalt show thy son in that day, saying, this is done because of that which the Lord did unto me when I came forth out of Egypt.'... (Exodus 13:6,8)

The Israelites didn't stop and camp every night, as Moshe Dayan's troops did — they traveled both day and night:

59

'And the Lord went before them by day in a pillar of a cloud, to lead them the way; and by night in a post of fire, to give them light; to go by day and night:'... (Exodus 13:21)

I can imagine how it looked to God: a large rabble (mixed multitude) moving fast, carrying all their goods, and not knowing where they were going. They weren't able to get organized until they had crossed the Red Sea. Numbers 1 counts the people, and Numbers 2 organizes them in a strict order.

'Ye have seen what I did unto the Egyptians, and how I bore you on eagles' wings, and brought you unto myself...' (Exodus 19:4).

And let us not forget that God fed us all manner of goodness during our 40 years of dessert with water from the rock and Manna, a wafer bread-like material that tasted like honey. Yes, we know where our bread is buttered (Exodus 16:15)! And when the children of Israel saw it, they said one to another, *'It is manna: for they wist not what it was.' And Moses said unto them, 'This is the bread which the LORD hath given you to eat'* (Exodus 16:31).

Israel on the March — The Cross

Israel marched in the form of the cross, and God instructed Israel to march with their standards (Num 2.2). In Isaiah, God said, 'When the enemy comes in like a flood, I will raise a standard against him.'

What is that <u>standard</u>? It is a distinctive flag or other conspicuous object displayed from a position in battle to serve as a rallying point for a military force. Fig. 8b depicts what the tribes looked like from on high, they appear to march in the form of a cross with their standards flying in front of the lead groups, a wheel inside a wheel.

Why is this important? Well we can see the living creatures in Eze and Rev are the

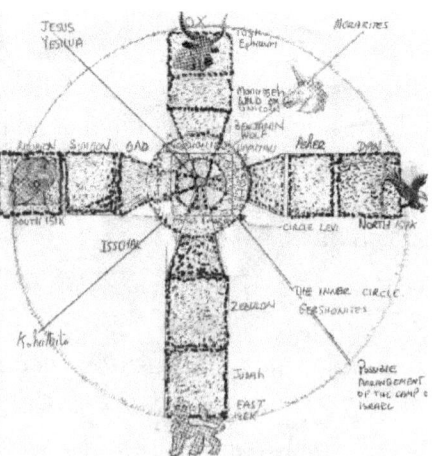

Figure 8b Cross in desert-living creatures

Lion, Man, Ox, and Eagle. These were depicted here in numbers and represent the lead tribes of Israel.

Fast forward to today and the new covenant, the symbol/standards of a spiritual Israel, i.e., a Christian, is the cross. It is raised up as a standard against Satan/Evil. I will cover this in greater detail in the next chapter.

CHAPTER 6 - The Tribes & Their Emblems.

Symbols, Blessings, and Promises.

Ween Israel was on the march, they were instructed to assemble with their standards flying (Numbers 2:2). These banners represented their families and served as a sign or token of the covenant or promise made by God through their father, Jacob.

Following I list what most see as their symbols.

Jacob, as he was approaching death, gathered the children together and Prayed and Prophesied over them, we picked up the prophetic utterances for Jacob in Genesis 49:10.

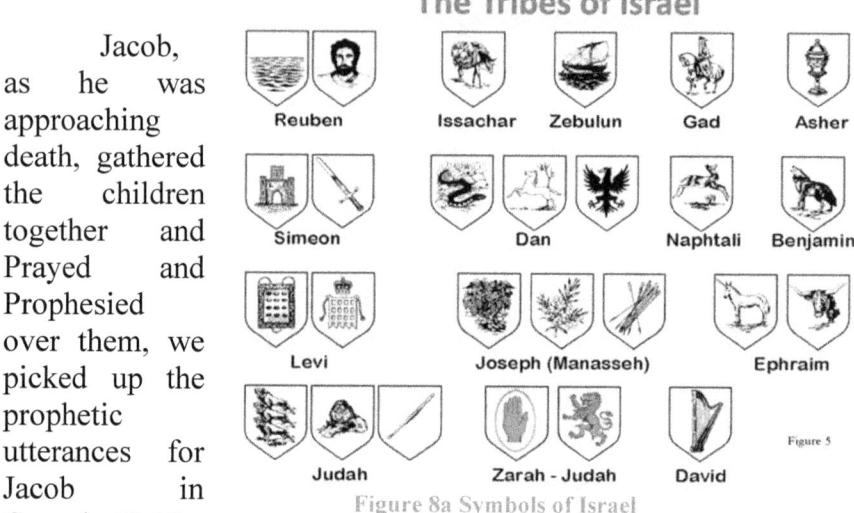

The Tribes of Israel

Figure 8a Symbols of Israel

Where did the standards come from? Let's investigate the origins, focusing on four of the main tribes for this section.

Rueben

Reuben is the firstborn (believed by many to be from France). He is the Head and lead in Hebrew. This is RESH, and where we get RACE from (see matrix). He is the first sign of Jacob's strength, excelling in honor and power, then Jacob adds, turbulent as water. The standards for Rueben are man's head (Resh), the honor is symbolized by the lily of the valley, a three-pronged leaf (normally shown without the flower) and used as a sign of honor (emblem), indicating high rank or royalty and commonly known today as fleur de lis, another symbol is water, (Gen 49).

Reuben took the lead in trying to protect Joseph when his other brothers wanted to kill him (Gen. 37.21).

Judah

Judah was the fourth-born child of Jacob, and he also tried to save his brothers from killing Joseph (Gen 37:26). They sold Joseph to some of their distant great uncle's children (the Ishmaelites), Isaac's brother from another mother. Do you remember who Ishmael is? He is the one who was eighty-sixed (Abraham's age when he had Ishmael) after they threw a big party and a fight broke out between Ishmael's family and Sarah's family; they kicked them out and told them 'don't come back' (Gen 21:8-10).

In Genesis 49:8-11, there is a very interesting prophecy about Judah, where Jacob says the following: "Judah, your brothers shall praise you. Your hand shall be on the necks of your enemies; your father's sons shall bow down to you. Judah is a young lion— my son, you return from the prey. Like a lion, he crouches and lies down; like a lioness, who dares to rouse him?

Symbols of Judah, Lion, three lions, and staff or scepter; see British coat of arms for details.

Joseph — Ephraim — Manasseh

There are incredible things prophesied for Joseph. We can see in Genesis 48:17 where Jacob does a switcheroo and crosses his arms like the Scottish cross; he then places his right hand on Ephraim's head (the youngest), and Joseph tries to switch his hands, and Ya'aqob (Jacob) says 'no, my son, I know what I am doing; he too will become a great nation. Nevertheless, his brother will be greater than he, and his descendants will become a group of nations.' Then he blessed them, saying (Gen. 48:18-20, 49:22, Deu 33:17), *"In your name will Israel pronounce this blessing: 'May God make you like Ephraim and Manasseh' — a phrase repeated in every synagogue to this day! (#333).*

Joseph is a fruitful vine, a fruitful vine near (abundant water) a spring, whose branches climb over a wall. With bitterness, archers attacked him; they shot at him with hostility, but his bow

63

remained steady, and his strong arms stayed supple because of the hand of the mighty one of Jacob (Gen 49:22).

Jacob was strong as an ox; he was jacked and passed his birthright onto Joseph. Also, note the British Longbow, i.e., military superiority. And, of course, the military strength of America today, the protector of the world (all nations blessed by your seed).

Joe, a fruitful vine

- Planted near abundant water (spring, rain, rivers, lakes, etc.).
- A vine protected by natural borders (wall, i.e., place of safety) spreads over the wall — and marches to new lands.
- The Almighty will be our help and sure reward.
- The enemy will attack but cannot defeat the Joes because his Bow remained strong as Yah supported them (G.I. Joe's, Brits, and military might).
- Blessing of sunshine and water/rain from the heavens above.
- Blessings of the deep that lie below fish, minerals, coal, oil, underground water, etc.
- Blessing of the womb and the breast, good, healthy, strong, intelligent children.
- Choicest gifts of the ancient mountains, minerals, iron, copper, silver, gold, etc.
- Favor of him who dwells in the bush! (Bull and Bush). In majesty, he is like a firstborn bull; his horns are the horns of a wild ox (unicorn-speaking of Ephraim and Manasseh).
- Joe's children will subdue the nation even to the ends of the EARTH (see matrix); they will be the prominent power in the whole earth (note 11, Deu. 33:17).

We can see from the old bull and bush prophecy Moses (מֹשֶׁה Mosheh) is invoking his experience where he met God for the first time (אֱלֹהִים 'Elohiym hello him Exo. 3:6). God would not give his name; hence 'Hello Him.' Moses then asked, "Who shall I say has sent me?" Elohiym replied, "Tell them hayah hayah (hello hello h1961 הָיָה hayah) sent you." Oh, Yah, hello, he has a sense of humor, and we are Brit'ish; we Ben His Royal a long time.

Back to the bush, Moses was a man of immense learning; he was raised as a prince of Egypt, but later in life, he developed a faulty tongue and a speech impediment (Exo. 4:10). He even complained to God about his slow speech; it's where we get the term, "Don't beat around the bush, hurry up and say what's on your mind!

In England, the term "Bull and Bush" is a colloquial term referring to the average man on the street, but it strikes me that there was a deeper symbolism. We can see the blessing that Moses gives to the tribe of Ephraim, where there appears to be deep affection for them. From Balaam's prophecy in Numbers 24:8, we learn that God brought them out of Egypt, and they have the strength of a wild ox (Unicorn); they devour hostile nations and break their bones to pieces.

This must have been very discouraging to Balak, who tried to get Balaam to curse Israel but ended up getting himself a black eye in the process. After the prophecies from Balaam, we get the prophetic message from Moses:

"And of Joseph he said, Blessed of the LORD be his land, for the precious things of heaven, for the dew, and for the deep that coucheth beneath. And for the precious fruits brought forth by the sun, and for the precious things put forth by the moon, and for the chief things of the ancient mountains, and for the precious things of the lasting hills, and for the precious things of the earth and fulness thereof, and for the goodwill of him that dwelt in the bush: let the blessing come upon the head of Joseph, and upon the top of the head of him that was separated from his brethren.

His glory is like the firstling of his bullock, and his horns are like the horns of unicorns: with them, he shall push the people together to the ends of the earth: and they are the ten thousands of Ephraim, and they are the thousands of Manasseh" (Deuteronomy 33:13-17).

This passage represents a special blessing for Joseph, who was separated from his brothers for about 23 years. When he finally

65

met his dad, Jack, and was reunited with him, he threw his arms around his neck, and they both wept for a long time. All the while (I believe), Jack was saying, "Yo'saf, my son, yo'saf, my beloved son, you're safe!"

The symbols of Ephraim and Manasseh were the Ox and Unicorn. We also know that the rainbow was a covenant symbol of Israel. These are still ingrained in our DNA today.

Dan is known as a judge (policeman) and lawgiver.

Regarding Dan, Jacob said

"Dan shall judge his people as one of the tribes of Israel. Dan shall be a serpent, by the way, an adder in the path, that biteth the horse heels so that his rider shall fall backward."

Dan, as a judge, is standing in for God, who has, on occasion, drawn an analogy between himself and an eagle. God also, when escorting Israel out of Egypt and looking after the young tribe, depicted himself as an eagle (Ex 19:4 Due 32:11). Dan was a pioneer; he leaped from Bashan, and he abode in ships (see chapter 13). There appears to be a good reason for Dan to adopt the eagle symbol (Genesis 49:16-19, Exodus 19:4, and Deuteronomy 33:22).

Dan's emblem/symbol/standard is the eagle, often depicted with a snake in its clasp. Additional symbols associated with Dan include the white horse and scales, symbolizing purity and judgment (another symbol of God).

The Cross of Jesus (Yeshua) in Ancient Israel

Israel's army on the march — Raising a standard — Here is another amazing thing — God instructed Moses to number and organize the tribes (Num 1:2, see next pages for cross of Jesus). God tells Israel to march in a specific formation that appears to form the shape of a cross. It is not completely clear how they were set up around the tent ohel (hotel—H168 לְהֹאֵ) of meeting with Dan to the north, Reuben to the south, Judah to the east, and Ephraim/Manasseh and Benjamin to the west. How amazing is that, the exact Christian symbol of Yeshua (Jesus H3442)!

The Bible uses a term meaning gat circle H5939), but then the Lord says the positioned in three, and the alignment starts without the tent of meeting (hotel, English hotel).In Numbers 1:53, God says, however, that the Levites shall camp around the hotel, suggesting that the rest of the tribes will be positioned differently. The alignment of the tribes starts with Judah (and the tribes with him) setting up to the east; at this point, the location of the Tabernacle has not been determined. Next, Reuben and his tribes are set up toward the south. After these data points have been established, Yah positions the ohtel (Num. 2:1-17).

This would mean they were to be set up in the form of a cross (see the illustration next). Amazingly, the exact form of the now sacred symbol set up over 1400 years prior to the event, with the shekinah glory positions i

n the center, with a halo about him, a consecrated holy priesthood (Levi). The Hebrew feminine for circle is çᵉbîybâh (H5439, see babe). We are the bride of Christ; a woman shall encompass (H5439, Jer. 31:32) a man.Judah would have the longest leg, symbolic of providing support for the testament (Pentateuch) and the savior, Ephraim, Manasseh and Benjamin, the shortest, and as such, on top. See the following picture.

There is,however, a phrase that rings in my head, and that is the inner circle, a term that today means a small group ofpeople who advise and have the ear of the ruler, in this case, Yaw. This term suggests an outer circle, whichI think can still be achieved by the Levites in general, and a small number that form the inner circle: Aaron,Miriam, Moses, and the sons of Aaron. Moses, of course, talks directly with the boss, Elohim Jehovah.

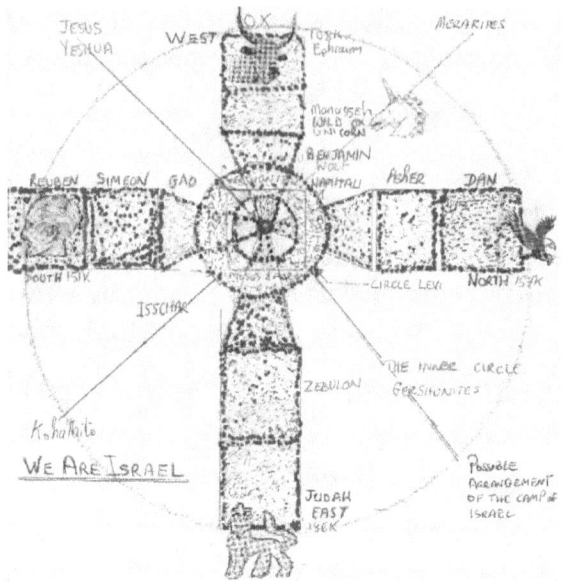

Cross Of Jesus Numbers Fig 8b

9th c. Celtic cross
from Kells Monastery
with Ox, Man, Lion
and Eagle Fig.

Again, the astonishing thing here is that almost nobody, including the current-day Priest, Rabbi, and Clergy, realizes and understands the significance of God's words here! It is important to God and a key to unlocking the Bible. Not only does God position, strategically, the tribes and ensure that they are a distance away from the Tabernacle, with the Cohen (priest) protecting them from God.

The significance of this symbolism cannot be overstated. J. Vernon McGee, in his "Through the Bible" radio program, said that the symbolism of the living creatures is one of the most important in all the Bible.

In summary, the living creatures of Ezekiel and Revelations are the tribes of Israel with their standards. Replacement theology suggests that the church replaces physical Israel. This book shows that the church is Israel, and in them, God continues to acknowledge them and honor his promises to the patriarchs. *"I will never leave you till I have accomplished all the plans I have for you"* (Gen 28:15). Jacob is Israel and the apple of God's eye, the centerpiece, the bull's eye.

CHAPTER 7 - Priest to Kingship

Israel Asks for a King

When Samuel grew old, his sons were tasked with the job of looking after the priesthood and ruling in his stead, but his sons did not walk in his ways, so Israel asked for a King (1Sam 8:1-5); God warned them that their King would want taxes and make the people slaves (1 Sam. 8:13-18). Remember, we had 10% for the Priesthood (Gen 28:18-22), and now an extra payment. The day will come when you cry out for relief from the burden the king has placed on you, and I will not hear you (1Kin 12:4). Your father put a heavy yoke on our necks; now please lighten it. After getting good advice from the elders, Rehoboam chose the advice of younger men and caused the division of Israel (1Kin 12:16). This is exactly what God told Solomon would happen if he fell away from worshiping God correctly (1Kin 11:11-13).

The only time Israel (as stated in the Bible) was the United Kingdom was under Kings:- Saul, David, and his son King Solomon, around 1000 BC. King David and Solomon.

Kings of Israel

The United Kingdom of Israel started around 1050-930 BC. King Saul (from the tribe of Benjamin), David (from the tribe of Judah, but from Ephrata-Bethlehem-Ephraim), and Solomon (Judah) each ruled for forty years, a total of 120 years. After Solomon's death, the 'United Kingdom' was divided into two distinct entities with different royal lineages. God himself told Solomon that the nation would split into two separate pieces because Solomon caused the people to worship many pagan Gods.

"And the LORD was angry with Solomon... And had commanded him concerning this thing, that he should not go after other Gods; and he did not keep that which the LORD commanded. 11. And the LORD said to Solomon, 'Since this has been done by you... I will surely tear the kingdom from you and will give it to your servant (Jeroboam). But I will not do it in your days, for David your father's sake, but I will tear it out of the hand of your son" (Rehoboam, 1 Kings 11:9-12, HBFV, see also verses 29 to 39).

Kings of the Northern Kingdom of Israel

Date	Name	Years Ruled	
1050 — 1010	Saul	40	
1010 — 970	David	40	
970 — 930	Solomon	40	

Date	Kings of Israel	Years Ruled	Rating
930 — 909	Jeroboam I	22	Bad
909 — 908	Nadab	2	Bad
908 — 886	Baasha	24	Bad
886 — 885	Elah	2	Bad
885	Zimri	7 days	Bad
885 — 880	Tibni *	5	?
885 — 874	Omri military skills*	12	Extra Bad
874 — 853	**Ahab and Jezebel**	**22**	**Worst**
853 — 852	Ahaziah	2	Bad
852 — 841	Joram	12	Bad mostly
841 — 814	Jehu	28	Bad mostly
814 — 798	Jehoahaz	17	Bad
798 — 782	Jehoash	16	Bad
793 — 753	Jeroboam II (c.r. 793-782)	41	Bad
753	Zechariah	6 months	Bad
752	Shallum	1 month	Bad
752 — 742	Menahem *	10	Bad
752 — 732	Pekah *	20	Bad
742 — 740	Pekahiah *	2	Bad
732 — 723	Hoshea	9	Bad

2 Kin14.23,26-heavy suffering in Israel

Pul, king of Assyria, invaded 1 Kin 15:19, a brief mention in Scripture; nothing else is known about Tibni. After his death, Omri became the sole king of the Northern kingdom in 880 B.C. Pekah began as a ruling rival of Menahem in 752 B.C.

This rivalry lasted ten years (2 Kings 15:17) until Menahem's death in 742. From 742 to 740, Pekah and Pekahiah maintained rival thrones (2 Kings 15:23), with Pekah beginning his sole rule of the Northern kingdom in 740 BC with his assassination of Pekahiah. Pekah's reign ended when he was assassinated by Hoshea in 732 (2 Kings 15:30).

Kings of Judah After Solomon 970-930

Date	Kings of Judah	Years Ruled	Rating
930 - 913	Rehoboam	17	Bad mostly
913 - 910	Abijah	3	Bad mostly
910 - 869	Asa	41	Good
872 - 848	Jehoshaphat (c.r. 872 - 869)	25	Good
853 - 841	Jehoram (c.r. 853 - 848)	8	Bad
841	Ahaziah	1	Bad
841 - 835	QUEEN Athaliah	7	Devilish
835 - 796	Joash	40	Good mostly
796 - 767	Amaziah	29	Good mostly
792 - 740	Azariah (Uzziah) (c.r. 792 - 767)	52	Good
750 - 732	Jotham (c.r. 750 - 740)	16	Good
735 - 715	Ahaz (c.r. 735 - 732)	16	Wicked
715 - 686	Hezekiah	29	Best
696 - 642	Manasseh (c.r. 696 - 686)	55	Worst
642 - 640	Amon	2	Worst
640 - 609	Josiah	31	Best
609	Jehoahaz	3 months	Bad
609 - 598	Jehoiakim	11	Wicked
598 - 597	Jehoiachin	3 months	Bad
597 - 586	Zedekiah	11	Bad

All dates are 'B.C.' Dates and date ranges for Israel and Judah rulers taken from The Mysterious Numbers of the Hebrew Kings by Edwin R. Thiele.

*C.R. stands for co-regency.

Warnings to Judah Before Final Captivity

Was it too little, too late? Josiah started a reformation within Israel; not only was the land completely corrupt, with shrines to many Gods, but God's temple was in bad shape. Josiah was 8 when he became king and died when he was 39 years old.

At age 16, he began to seek God, and at age 20, he began to clean up the filthy towns, the shrines, Asherah poles, carved images, cast idols, and remove the Baal (Baa el'zeebub) alters in his 18th year.

He set out to repair the Temple of the Lord (622 BC) it was then that High Priest Hilkiah found the book of Moses (2Ch. 34.8-9,14). Not only were they not going to church, but they had even lost the Book of the Law, the Pentateuch, and the books of Moses. Josiah did not have a clue how far they had fallen from grace!

Josiah, the king, didn't know how bad it really was. When he heard the words of Moses, he tore his robes and inquired of God. Guess where he went? He went to a woman, a prophetess, to inquire of God (2Ch. 34:22-28). Josiah's servant returned to him; I could just hear him telling the king: I have good news, and I have bad news; which do you want first?

God says, 'Well done, good and faithful servant, I have heard your cry and seen your tears, but this land is too far gone, and I am done with it. You will soon die a peaceful death and will not see all the trouble I will bring to this place (Note 11).

God is moving behind the scenes, and in Josiah's 13th year circa 627 BC (age 21 – 8+ 13, i.e., age 21), Jeremiah is called as a kid and instructed to speak to the people (Jer. 1).

Was the high priest, i.e., the Kohen Gadol Hilkiah, he was a close confidant to Josiah, as I am sure Jeremiah was. It is also possible that Hilkiah the High Priest was Jeremiah's father (Jer. 1.1?). Jeremiah was just a kid v6 when he was called, perhaps as young as Josiah was when he became King?

I think It was a little too late. God had already made his mind up, and the plan was being acted out despite Josiah's brave and valiant efforts.

We can see the Anger of God as he sets to remove Judah from his sight........to some, this doesn't seem right because they, don't understand why God could do such a seemingly horrible thing as desecrating his sanctuary and cast Israel and now Judah out of his sight (world view).

What happened in Israel and Judah was child sacrifice, and pagan worship, lies, bribes, corruption at all levels of society, which is what happens when you take God out of the picture when he is removed from the people's hearts and minds when the High places are desecrated when temple worship is just a show, and people's hearts are not in it.

God warns the Children of Israel not to worship Molech, and then the Bible speaks of all the times that they do, starting with Solomon (1Kin. 11.5) and repeatedly they kept doing it despite God's constant warnings (Jer. 32:35).

God Says: 'They have built pagan shrines to Baal in the valley of Ben-Hinnom, and there they sacrifice their sons and daughters to Molech.

Clearly, God had to act. A loving, caring God had to do something (Jer 52:3) and act as he did; he cast them out from his presence. 15 times in the Bible, God speaks on the fact that he had to cast Israel out of his sight and give her a certificate of divorce (#10).

CHAPTER 8 - Judah's Fall – Jeremiah.

Who are the main Prophets at the time of Judah's demise? One was Jeremiah, who started Prophesy in 627-570 BC while still a boy (some suggest as young as 13-17 years of age), Ezekiel, who probably preached 593-571 BC, and Daniel 605-539 BC.

1st sacking of Jerusalem was in 606 BC, and Daniel was taken at this time, i.e., 3rd year of Jehoiakim 609-598 (Dan 1:21).

2nd sacking of Jerusalem was during the reign of Jehoiachin 598-597 BC. Only 10,000 people were taken during this time (2 Kin. 24:11-12). There would be a third and a fourth and final destruction of Jerusalem still to come.

3rd sacking of Jerusalem — 597 BC. Jerusalem falls at the hands of Nebuchadnezzar of Babylon. Nebuchadnezzar captures Jehoiachin and takes him as a prisoner to Babylon. Zedekiah is set up as a puppet king over Judah (Jer. 24:1).

4th and final destruction of Jerusalem — 586 BC. King Nebuchadnezzar lays siege to Jerusalem. He destroys the city and burns the temple. The destruction of the temple starts on the 9th of Ab (Hebrew month) and completes on the 10th. The 9th of Ab will also be the day Jerusalem's SECOND temple (Herod's temple) will be completely destroyed in 70 AD; what a coincidence, it must be a mother nature or karma thing (#335)!

Again, Daniel was taken in the first wave, 606 BC. Ezekiel was taken in the second wave of captives. Jeremiah is never taken captive by the invading armies (or if he is, he will be released).

The book of Jeremiah is especially unique because Jeremiah was the son of Hilkiah (Jer. 1.1), and during Josiah's reformation, Hilkiah the kohen(H3548 כֹּהֵן) gadowl(H1419 גָּדוֹל) (High Priest) found the book of the law during, the Bible says Jeremiah's father Hilkiah the priest came from Anathoth and does not clarify if the two Priest are the same, although I feel it highly likely.

Jeremiah's Commission

God identifies Jeremiah as a special child, one that the Spirit of God had known (in dwelt) even before he was born (Jer 1:4). Yah has a very special job for him.

Jeremiah says he can't even speak yet; really, he was so young when God called him (Jer 1:6) that he can't even speak? Perhaps his public speaking was a problem. He was nervous, but the calling and Jeremiah's age were important; God had a huge task for him.

"Today I appoint you over nations, and kingdoms to uproot and tear down to destroy and overthrow, to build and plant" (Jer 1:10). God's plans were so important and took so long that he needed someone very young to accomplish this task. When we look at the order of the text, God says he will pluck before he destroys and he would build before he plants, these are very important points and items to keep in mind coming up.

Israel Driven from God's Sights

The Eternal has already taken Samaria out and now is about to do the same to Judah, and God is using Jeremiah to uproot and tear down; who is he going to uproot? How can God do this and still keep his promises to the patriarchs and the promise of the kingly line to David and plant them in a place of safety for the tribes, a place where evil people will not disturb them? The Israelites know these promises were for the future because God had already given David peace from all his enemies, yet he spoke in a future tense through the prophet Nathan (2 Sam. 7:1,9-16).

Well, it looks like God's got a real task on his hands to keep these two promises: You will never fail to have a man sit on the throne and Israel, at the same time uprooting the kingly line of Judah, while deporting the rest into captivity and cast from Gods presence.

Let's take another look at this term, 'cast from God's sight or presence,' We know that the tabernacle and holy of holies, i.e., the ark, was the place where God resided 'And let them make me a sanctuary, that I may dwell in their midst' (Ex. 25:8,22). So, in essence, to be cast from his presence means to be sent away from Jerusalem; we note that even when Israel was taken into captivity in

Assyria, God still watched over them and disciplined them (2Kin. 17:24-25).

I believe that there is also another meaning here in the name Israel and Judah. The LORD said, I will remove Judah also out of my sight, as I have removed Israel, and will cast off this city Jerusalem which I have chosen, and the house (Temple) of which I said, my name shall be there.' Essentially, being cast from God's sight means being hidden from the world; the connection between Israel and God and the chosen people will be hidden and sealed until the time of the end.

Israel and Judah will lose their homeland, they will cease to be called Israel, and Samaria's role will be completely hidden, while some of the Jews retain their ethnic identity but lose national status.

Where Did Jeremiah Take the Remnant?

What we learned from the previous section was that God's promise to David was unconditional and that he would fulfill his promises, as in (Gen. 49:10; Jer. 33:17-22) the Scepter shall not depart from Judah or a ruler's staff from between his feet until Shiloh come, the Davidic line will accomplish this. Also, all of the known Kings of Israel and Judah have been deposed, killed or deported either to Assyria or Babylon.

After the final destruction of Jerusalem and the removal of Zedekiah (Jer. 39:5-8), a small remnant, mostly the poor folks, are left behind, while the rest of the folks are either in or being taken to Babylon, even Jeremiah himself was taken (Jer. 40:1-4) but is released by word from the King of Babylon.

Gedaliah is put in charge of Jerusalem but is quickly killed along with the Babylonian guards (Jer. 41.1-2), and this is done by Ishmael, a member of Royal Blood; this goes against God and the rulers of Jerusalem, so we know that will not end well. As a result, we see Ishmael runs for his life and escapes.

In Jeremiah 41:10, Ishmael takes everyone captive, including the king's daughters; then along comes Johanan, and he attacks Ishmael, who then flees. Then Jeremiah gives advice to Johanan (Jer. 42:7,43.6), who again, against God's will, decides to take everyone to Egypt.

Then Jeremiah prophesies that Egypt will be destroyed by Nebuchadnezzar (Jer. 43:8-13), but he still takes them to Egypt… after Jeremiah 44, the book goes backward in time, and the trail appears to disappear. What happened next?

Did Jeremiah get out of Egypt? We can pick up the trail in Ezekiel 17 (NIV), *"The word of the LORD CAME TO ME: Son of man, set forth an allegory and tell it to the Israelites as a parable. Say to them, 'This is what the Sovereign LORD SAYS: A great eagle with powerful wings, long feathers, and full plumage of varied colors came to Lebanon. Taking hold of the top of a cedar, for he broke off its topmost shoot and carried it away to a land of merchants, where he planted it in a city of traders."*

What does an Eagle mean? God said he brought Israel out of Egypt on eagle's wings, symbolic of God doing the work and accomplishing his goal, and we know that the Eagle is a symbol of Dan who is a merchant!

Powerful wings and long feathers mean it comes from a distance, with varied colors. We know that Joseph had a coat of many colors, and multicolor is a symbol of Joseph a Brit (Israel-Dan, Judah, Levi, Joseph, others). Also, color was a symbol of authority; the higher the rank, the more the colors, especially purple.

On top of the cedar, we can see that the king of Babylon was symbolized by a tree, and Daniel interpreted the dream it meaning high, the kingly line, taken to a city of traders where Dan (th'ar(sh)ish), Zarah and ultimately the Brit's are.

V5' "He took one of the seedlings of the land and put it in fertile soil. He planted it like a willow with abundant water, V6 and it sprouted and became a low, spreading vine. Its branches turned toward him, but its roots remained under it. It became a vine and produced branches and put out leafy boughs."

V22' *"This is what the Sovereign LORD SAYS: I MYSELF WILL TAKE A SHOOT FROM THE VERY TOP OF A CEDAR AND PLANT IT; I WILL BREAK OFF A TENDER SPRIG FROM ITS TOPMOST SHOOTS AND PLANT IT ON A HIGH AND LOFTY MOUNTAIN".*

23 *"On the mountain heights of Israel, I will plant it; it will produce branches and bear fruit and become a splendid cedar. Birds of every kind will nest in it; they will find shelter in the shade of its branches".*

24 *"All the trees of the forest will know that I, the LORD, BRING DOWN THE TALL TREE AND MAKE THE LOW TREE GROW TALL. I DRY UP THE GREEN TREE AND MAKE THE DRY TREE FLOURISH. "I the LORD HAVE SPOKEN AND I WILL DO IT."*

Did you get that God will take a tender sprig (female) of royal lineage to the mountain tops of Israel (Ireland / Britain aka #347) sacred mountain top), a city of merchants? God promises to take the kingly line somewhere. Where do you think he took it?

Astonishing Promises of God Reiterated

In the midst of saying that he will cast Israel and Judah from his sight, God makes this astonishing promise: 'The descendants of Israel will NEVER cease to be a NATION before me, and call's the sun, moon, star's and earth (erets) as witness only if you can measure the foundations of the earth or the heavens can be measured, will I reject all the descendants of Israel.'

God said I will watch over them to build and plant (Jer. 31:28); he calls Ephraim an unruly Calf, *is not Ephraim my dear son in whom I delight, I have great compassion for him… "set up road signs, put up guideposts, take note of the highway, the road you take return O Virgin Israel return to your towns" (Jer. 31:9, 18-21). "Because I am Israel's father and Ephraim is my first-born son* (the covenant [Brit] goes to the firstborn). *Hear the word of the Lord O nations; proclaim it in a distant coastland, he who scatters Israel and will gather them and watch over his flock like a shepherd.* He who commands the sun and moon and stars says…*will the decedents of Israel ever cease to be a nation before me" (Jer. 31:35-37, Ps. 19).*

Waymarks pillars, high heaps

Israel had a habit of setting up pillars, heaps (Gen. 28.22, 31.13, 45, 52, 35.14), signposts, memorials, tombstones, and even

God led Israel by a pillar (Ex. 14.19) of cloud and a post of fire, and as we see above God instructed Jeremiah to set up Pillars.

'Set thee up waymarks (see yonder-H6725), make thee high heaps (Tamar-erection-pillar h8564) set thine heart toward the highway, even the way (direct me-derek h1870) which thou wentest: turn again, O virgin of Israel, turn again to these thy cities.' (Jer. 31:21). Again, God is turning our hearts back to him, our roots and our origins (Mal. 4.6). Three prominent Hebrew connections, Tamar in Britain, the river Thames (anciently Tamar), river Tamar in Devon (tin mining area), and Tara (Tea as Thame, is a Tamar diminutive) the ancient seat of kingly lines (two thousand years) and power.

"I know the plans I have for you, declares the Lord, Plans to prosper you and not to harm you, plans to give you hope and a future!" (Jer. 29.11). Lest we forget, the Lord is the same yesterday, today, and forever (Heb.13.8). Believe it, it's true!

God made a solemn oath to Jeremiah to set up the kingly line somewhere, and today, I am showing you where it was. And as witnesses, we have the sun, moon, and stars!

As C.S. Lewis said …..God leaves us no alternative here; either he is a liar, or his word and promises are true! And if they are true, then we need to look for fulfillment! We will revisit where Jeremiah goes later.

What did the Israelites look like?

Jeremiah describes the princes of Israel, 'Her Nazarites were purer than snow, they were whiter than milk, they were ruddier in the body than rubies, their polishing was of sapphire' (Lam 4:7). Here Jeremiah is talking about their countenance, not their spiritual state.

I think it safe to assume that milky white skin and ruddiness, red hair and freckles were pretty common in Israel, and blue eyes like a sapphire.

As we saw from Abraham, Isaac, and Jacob and their 'Drop Dead Gorgeous' women, they were different. They had unique features, like blonde hair and blue eyes. These were different from the natives of the land, and that is why they stood out. They came from the hills of Armenia (the white house), and as we have shown, the area was a known place for these features.

I am not saying that one ethnicity is better than another. I am just saying they stood out, like Solomon's honey babe was dark, and he loved her because she was unique and different in Israel (Song 1:6). She was dark; whether she was tanned or not, she had dark skin, the Bible says, not white. King Solomon, however, loved many foreign women besides Pharaoh's daughter — Moabites, Ammonites, Edomites, Sidonians and Hittites (1Kin. 11).

They were from nations about which the Lord had told the Israelites, "You must not intermarry with them because they will surely turn your hearts after their Gods." Nevertheless, Solomon held fast to them in love. He had seven hundred wives of royal birth and three hundred concubines, and his wives led him astray.

Prophetic fulfillments are Key to Finding Israel.

See Chapter 21 for prophesies concerning Israel and their fulfillment.

CHAPTER 9 – Egyptian trade & migrations.

While Joseph was in Egypt (as mentioned earlier), he would have been in control of trade, ports, military operations, the Army, the Navy etc. And the Hebrews could have a hand in anything they wanted, providing they were good at it; all they needed to do was to talk to their brother from another mother.

Joseph controlled Egypt around 1885 BC, and as we can see from Fig 8 below, mining operations started just before Joseph's tenure, and undoubtedly, Joseph got involved and helped perfect their techniques. We can see from God's commission to Moses that two tribes were already very proficient in working metals, precious stones and woven fabrics (Ex. 34:10). All who are skilled among you are to come and make everything the Lord has commanded.

Figure 8

Additionally, they present offerings of silver, gold and bronze (Ex. 35:22, 24-29). The Israelite women were well-versed in spinning fabrics (v30). Uri, son of Hur, the white Jew boy (Ben Hur son of whiteness H2353, #33), whom God had previously filled with the gifts required, was now a well-known artisan in gold, silver, bronze, stonework as well as dyeing cloths & embroidery. Israel's primary colors were blue, scarlet (red) and white; yes, that's red, white and blue. Since white was considered the natural color of cloth without pigmentation, it did not need the skill to create the desired color, but clearly, from Uri's family name, he was well versed in white cloth also.

Gold Mining in Ancient Egypt

By the end of the reign of Thutmose I (1520 BC), all of northern Nubia had been annexed. The Egyptians built a new administrative center at Napata and used the area to produce gold and incense. The Nubian gold production made Egypt a prime source of the precious metal in the Middle East. The primitive working conditions for the slaves are recorded by Diodorus Siculus, who saw some of the mines at a later time. One of the oldest maps known is of a gold mine in Nubia, the Turin Papyrus Map dating to about 1160 BC; this map is also one of the earliest characterized road maps in existence.

We also have the story of King Solomon's mines, which comes from the golden days of Israel, yes Israel was teaming with gold under King David, and we had a United Kingdom, where peace and prosperity reigned, and it continued under Solomon, even King Hiram of Tyre presented Solomon with gold, cedar and fir trees (1Ki 9:11).

A vast amount of Gold was brought from Ophir (1Kin. 9:28). Even the Queen of Sheba (Ethiopia or perhaps Nubia) had a very great train, with camels that bore spices, and a lot of gold, and precious stones (1Kin. 10:2), Moses wife was Ethiopian a Cushite (Num. 12:1).

Gold, just as today, is as precious as in the ancient world. We remember the Gold Rush of California, the 49'ers, that brought mostly the white boys to the West Coast in droves? Back in the gold rush days of the 1850s, San Francisco was awash of people in tents. It looks like we have come full circle; San Francisco needs another wash!

Israel set out early to treasure hunt or escape.

If this were a crime scene and a detective were analyzing this, they would look at the following:

- **Motive** — What would be the reason for leaving, tough conditions, slavery, hard work etc?

83

- **Means** — We know that Egypt traded with all nations roundabout, and we can be sure that the Israelites functioned in many capacities. We can see later in Jeremiah's day that Israelite soldiers fought for Egypt as mercenaries (Jer. 46:21).
- **Opportunity** — This is a tough one; perhaps early on during Israel's time in Egypt, they did have many opportunities to escape, but the bible suggests long after Joseph's death, a Pharaoh arose who did not remember Joseph (Exo. 1:8 Acts 7:18), and as light servitude turned us into hard servitude. The motivation to leave increases.

1st Breakaway appears to have taken place between Jacobs's death and the tightening of the thumb screws after Josephs's death 1859-1600 BC.

Below are listed some important dates in Israel's history.

1859 BC	The Burial of Jacob	Genesis 50
1806 BC	The Death of Joseph	Genesis 50:26
1800 BC	Jacob's Family Stays in Egypt	Exodus 1
1700 BC	Israelites Multiply in Egypt	Exodus 1:6
1600 BC	Israelites Oppressed by New King	Exodus 1:8

As we had said before, Joseph was in charge of all of Egypt, and his brothers (with a little bit of effort) could get involved with any endeavor they wished.]

1st breakaway.

Geek mythology (quasi-history) says that Danaus, son of Bela, made the first boat to leave Egypt and set up a colony in Argos (#51). We know that at this time, Dan was in Egypt with Joseph, and Dan's mother was Bilhah (Bela-Gen. 35.25). It also states that his brother was the King of Egypt (Joseph). Many believe that the tribe of Dan and the story of Danaus are one and the same (#368).

After Jack's death, Dan and his brothers clearly got scared (Gen. 37.2). Dan, with a friend Cadmus, may have done a runner later to return after being reassured. There is a lot of evidence to support this.

Hecataeus of Abdera 600 BC (#52, 98, 107) quoted by Diodorus Siculus 50 BC. Says the Egyptians expelled all aliens (this thought to be around 1450 BC or earlier), the most distinguished followed Danaus and Cadmus into Greece, but the majority left with Moses, and stating that the ancient Greeks came from Egypt and Tyre, see also section on Athens in this book.

Josephus, Antiquities of the Jews 94 AD, Hecataeus of Abdera 600BC, Diodorus Siculus (50BC) Homer, and Iliad, all of which show a connection between the Greeks and Hebrews.

In Aeschylus' Suppliants (6th century BC), Danaus and his daughters are represented as a 'seed divine,' exiles from Egypt, fleeing from their brother Egyptus; since…they feared an unholy alliance, they appear to have passed through Syria and perhaps Sidon into Greece. Compare also Petavius Cir. 1630 AD. History of the World (#337), and Sir Walter Raleigh Cir. 1586 AD. From the Bible, we gather that there 5 major migrations into Greece and Britain.

If Dan took off for Greece, then how come we still have the tribe of Dan coming out of Egypt? Well, Judah left his brothers early and got a wife from the Canaanites (it didn't turn out well Gen 38:1, Gen. 46:12. Judah later came back to the flock and was part of the group that came to Egypt with Jacob.

It is quite feasible that part of the tribe did migrate to Greece, and part of it stayed behind; the Danites (Irish) took God literally when he said to go forth and multiply; it was one of the commands that they enjoyed fulfilling ☺.

2nd breakaway took place 1806-1600BC between Joseph's death and the Israelite oppression under a new Pharaoh (1 Ch. 7:21-22). In 1 Chronicles, we see that a contingent of Ephraimites went out from Egypt on their own to Gath (the details are also recorded in the Apocrypha book of Jasher Chap. 75 # 59). In the chronicles, it says the sons of Ephraim went to take Gath and failed and were killed!

Jasher 75 (N12, 1685 BC) confirms that a son of Ephraim with a contingent of men "went forth from Egypt, with valiant men, thirty thousand on foot, and attacked Gath, but were killed.".

Joseph saw the 3rd generation of Ephraim's and Manasseh's children; it appears that the 7 generations of children from Ephraim were the group who attacked Gath(1Chr. 7.21).

3rd breakaway circa 1426BC was during Israel's wanderings in the desert after the Exodus.

When in the Wilderness, the bible states that they said, "And they said one to another, let us make a captain, and let us return into Egypt." (Num. 14. 1-4, Neh. 9.17). The indication is that many folks did rebel and leave. In fact, it appears that God also caused a plague to rise up and caused them to fall in the desert. He also scattered them and their descendants throughout the nations (Psa 106:26-27; Eze. 20:21-23).

| 1445 BC | People Murmur at the Spies' Report | Numbers 14, 15 |
| 1426 BC | Korah's Rebellion Timeline Link | Numbers 16 |

Census before and after 40 years in the desert in 1446-1406 BC:

Census Number			
1	Dan	62.7	64.4
2	REUBEN	46.5	43.7
3	ASHER	41.5	53.4
4	Levi	?	23k
5	Ephraim	40.5	32.5
6	Manasseh	32.2	52.7
7	Judah	74.6	76.5
8	Benjamin	35.4	45.6
9	Gad	45.7	40.5
10	Naphtali	53.4	45.4
11	Issachar	54.4	64.3
12	Zebulon	57.4	60.5
13	Simeon	59.3	22.2

Clearly, while some tribes increased in number during the exodus wanderings there are notable reductions. It would not be easy to wander around the wilderness of sin for 40 years without either becoming tough, dying or leaving for an easier life. God used this period to toughen Israel up; as the saying goes, when the going gets tough, the tough get going, and apparently, the weak takeoff, Simeon took off!

4th Breakaway 1235BC. When Jabin, King of Canaan, afflicted Israel-Dan abode in ships and Asher in his seaports (Jud. 5.17). This is when Deborah and Barak, Judges 4, fight for Israel, as prophesied earlier, God was scattering Israel to the far reaches of the world, yes Dan, Naphtali (1Kin. 7:14, Zebulon and Asher. As we have mentioned before, the th'arshish navy (only) would travel for years at sea, Israel would set up a foreign seaport for collecting merchandise, and many Israelites would have a trading post, as we did with the USA in the early days (see Chapter 16).

In summary, we have the following:

- 1st — cir. 1859 BC. Jacob's death (Exo. 1.8).
- 2nd — cir. 1806-1600 BC, between Joseph's death and Israelite oppression under a new Pharaoh (1 Chr. 7.21-27).
- 3rd — cir. 1420 BC. Whilst Israel was in the Wilderness.
- 4th — cir. 1235 BC. When Jabin, King of Canaan, afflicted Israel-Dan abode in ships and Asher in his seaports (Jud. 5.17).
- 5th — cir. 869-753, and 721 BC Final migrations at the time of Jeroboam II (1 Chr. 5.17).

5th Breakaway — The whole of the tribe of Dan and Zebulun (Gen 49.12-ship merchant) seems to have left Canaan prior to the time of Jeroboam II (1 Chr. 5.17), and they do not appear in this genealogy. Was this geology written 793-753BC? We know that Samaria was taken into captivity in 721 BC, but the skirmishes and attacks started much earlier, and Dan, being a northern border tribe, would be perhaps the first tribe to be under attack from the north, i.e., Assyria and Damascus? We know that it was prophesied that Dan shall leap from Bashan.

During Ahab's reign (874-853 BC), we had three years of drought and severe famine in the land (863-860 BC), before this the good king in Judah, Asa, made a pact with Ben Hadad, who, in turn, sacked Ljon, Dan and Naphtali; this would be circa 869 BC (1Kin. 15:20, 2Kin. 15:29, 2Chr. 16:4), under this type of oppression, it is highly probably that the Tribe of Dan (along with Naphtali) started there jump from Bashan before 869 BC, and it intensified when the rainmaker came.

The Ruling Class

Despite the effort of God to discipline Israel, we continued our destructive tendencies; "The ruling class" could sustain much of the punishment, but we, the people who, like sheep needing a good shepherd, would suffer the worst.

Jesus (Yeshua) had great compassion for the people and had very strong words for the ruling class (Mat 23:15 Isa 33:1), i.e., Kings, lawmakers, Captains of Industry, Pharisees, Sadducees, Lords, Chieftains etc.

I would estimate that toward the end of Jeroboam's reign, Dan, Zebulun, Ashur, and undoubtedly a large percentage of other tribes left Israel; some migrated to Judah while most headed for Tarshish, as we will soon see. This was Britain, home of Cassiterite tin ore. Along with Britain and Cassiterite, we were in Greece, Italy-Etruscans, Spain, Norway, Denmark & Sweden. They are all locations that God drove us to in the early years.

The Aram (Garman-GERMAN), kingdom was from the mountains of Lebanon to the Euphrates River and was part of the Neo-Assyrian Empire (911-605 BC).

The Assyrians were Semites, and God used them to discipline Israel. The northern tribes would be hit the hardest first, and as conditions got harder at home, the tribes would start to migrate; they knew what the word of God said, that he would drive them to the ends of the world where they would gore the nations.

"I said I would scatter them and blot out their memory from mankind" (Deu. 32.26). Their origin would be blotted out until God was ready to reveal them, and speaking of Joseph's birthright son's Ephraim v33.17

In majesty (Israel His Royal Highness), he is like a firstborn bull; his horns are the horns of a Unicorn; with them, he will gore the nations even to the ends of the erets. Our wonderings around the world are most easily traced by looking at the tribe of Dan; as God said, "Dan will be a serpent by the roadside, a viper along the path." A serpent, as it travels, leaves a trail (Gen. 49.16), and again God says set thee up waymarks, high heaps, signpost (Jer. 31:21-H1567, H8564 Tam-roor-erection, and Zion's, sign post-H6725).

Jonah-Aran-Nineveh, 761-760 BC.

God was getting the Assyrians ready to take Samaria out! He instructed the prophet Jonah to give them a message exactly 40 years before Samaria's sacking (721-720BC); why did Jonah do a runner – The Assyrians were the enemy of Israel, and everyone knew it, Jonah didn't want to help the enemy avoid the wrath of God, so he fled!

The People of Tyre

Hiram, king of Tyre, was a great architect. The Freemasons trace their heritage to him. The Greek historian Menander states that Hiram built the temple of Hercules and that of Astarte. Hiram was a close friend of Israel's and the key architect of God's Temple (1Kin. 5.6 #338 h2438חִירָם Chiyr'am).

The English word HIRE comes from Hiram (Proto-Germanic *hurjan), co-incidence. It means to hire someone for wages, Hiram was a household name among the ancient builders and was paid very well for his service Solomon gave him towns as payment. There were two Hiram, one king of Tyre and one his chief architect (

The Phoenicians had a very strong pact with Israel. In fact, we held joint merchant (and probably military) exercises for many years. Again, our seafaring enterprises stretched far and wide, and Dan was at the forefront of these endeavors.

Dan's continued serpents trail

We can see from the Bible that Dan renamed a place after their forefather; when they attacked Laish, they renamed it Dan; we also know that Dan will leave a trail as a serpent does. The way Dan will leave a trail is by the use of their name, Danube, Danai, Danmark (Denmark), and Dardan of Homer's Iliad; we can see the naked warriors with a horse shield, another symbol of Dan (Gen. 49) Also the symbol of Troy and the Trojans was an eagle with a serpent in his talons, which appeared on the left hand of the Trojans, again Danite symbols the Horse, Eagle and Snake.

In Iliad Homer, it shows a coin with Hercules fighting a Lion (Jud. 14.4-6). Samson was a Danite, and as I stated elsewhere, the similarities between Samson and Hercules are striking. Throughout the Iliad, we have many pictures that appear to suggest Israel; we have an eagle, a man and woman, an Ox, and a Lion, all are depicted around a Greek God. We have repeated many times throughout the Iliad Dardania, Dardanus and Dardan, clear utilization of derivations of Dan, Danites, Dun, and Don, and as we trace the Tribe of Dan, the use of these terms will become more evident.

In the book 'Dan the Pioneer of Israel" Colonel Gawler catalogs the places Dan and the Phoenicians went; these include Don-gola (Greece), Caly-don (Attica), Eri-dan, Make-don, Danube, Danastris (now Dnieste), Danapris (now Dnieper) Dan-zig. Latham's Ethnology of Europe p. 157, suggests the traveling about of Danai is the tribe of Dan.

The Bible and Josephus speak of the nobility of Tyre being of mixed blood from Ur and Israelite stock (#339). This is important as they are in the same family line as Abraham, Isaac, Jacob, and their wives.

Again, in Ezekiel 27:6, "Of the oaks of Bashan have they made thine oars; the company of the Ashurites have made thy benches of ivory, brought out of the isles of Chittim" and In Ezekiel 27:12, "Tarshish was thy merchant by reason of the multitude of all kind of riches; with silver, iron, tin, and lead, they traded in thy fairs." Notice the area known as Tarshish has the rare tin, along with silver, iron and lead; we can add to that total gold as Britain has all these in rich abundance (#370) and is said to be the reason the Romans invaded Britain. Ezekiel goes on to say that Dan is also a merchant and trader (Eze. 27:19).

Clearly, the Phoenicians and Israelites were close-knit. In fact, as we show elsewhere, the Phoenicians were Hebrews and originated (like Abraham did) from Armenia! We Hebrews were very talented in language, architecture, and writing and we spread it through the world together with the Phoenicians (#338).

Kittim-Chittam

Observe Kittim — Earlier in the book of Jeremiah 2:10, we read, "cross over the coast of Kittim (H3794) and look, send to Kedar, (Kittim aka Chittam appears to point to island people in the west, sons of Javan) and observe closely," because Gods people (Israel) now live there (#13).

This is an interesting statement; let's look at it closely. Kittim is singular, and hardly used, possibly a general term for all islanders, and Kedar could be talking about a son of Javan. Also, when we put this in with a prophecy from Balaam that Asshur will be attacked (Num. 24:24). *"And ships shall come from the coast of Kittim, and shall afflict Asshur, and shall afflict Eber, and he also shall perish forever."*

A map of Israel shows that Dan occupied Joppa and Asher occupied Acco and Tyre, we know Tyre was primarily occupied by the Phoenicians (Sidonians) and was really a part of Israel. It is clear from the prophecy that Asher was attacked by ships. In addition, this strongly suggests that Dan's territory extended to the port and was a seafaring nation. Dan was also in Tyre (2Ch. 2:14-55), and Debra's prophetic statement, "Why did Dan remain in ships? Asher continued on the sea shore, and abode in his breaches" (Jdg 5:17). Also, Balaam mentions that Jacob seed shall be in many waters! (Nub. 24:7).

A People Prophesied to Invade Israel from Islands

A people invaded Israel from the Islands of the Sea (Jdg.5.17). This seems to indicate Tarshish trading ships. Kitti (Chittim also notices H2845; Chittite) one location was thought to be Cyprus, a hub for the Phoenician merchant trading; another was off the southern coast of Spain, and yet a third is a present-day Britain; whoever they were, they were totally wiped out by Asher and Eber (other tribes of Israel, according to the prophecy) and we took over their land.

Also, God repeats this in Isaiah 23.1: "The burden of Tyre. Howl, ye ships of Tarshish; for it is laid waste so that there is no house, no entering in from the land of Chittim, it is revealed to them."

According to ancient tradition, Chittim (Kittam) means Island in the far west (#13) and (I believe) refers to England and Ireland, i.e., Britain. Remember, earlier in Jeremiah 2, God gives us a snapshot of what happened to Israel and in verses 9 and 10, he tells Jeremiah and us where to go and where to look for Israel and the children's children.

God says he will continue to contend with us in the Isles in the coastland of Chittam (later Britain) and tells Jeremiah to pass over to the Isles of Chittim! And as we saw earlier the ancient name of England was Chittam (#13).

This appears to be a clear message to Jeremiah as to where to take the kingly line of Israel to a secure nest set in a rock. A place that already has the children of Israel; we will revisit this in Chapter 14 — Jeremiah found in Irish history.

CHAPTER 10 – British-Hebrew links.

Ancient Jews Spoke Gaelic

There have been many books by well-respected, learned people who have stated that Hebrew and the Gaelic language come from the same roots.

"The Jewish Telegraphic Agency," on July 11, 1934, said that the Jews spoke Gaelic based on scripture. This article goes a little further by stating that the Jews spoke Gaelic, and it was published in a prestigious Jewish Magazine.

"A theory has been advanced here in the Evening News to the effect that Gaelic was the language of the ancient Jews in Palestine".

I analyze the concepts in this article later in chapter 18; I do not think a few Gaelic words provide substantial evidence; however, when taken with the rest of the body of this work, it is significant.

Th'Ar(s)hish — Irish Connection

The Tarshish connection is very interesting. One; analysis of the Hebrew root suggests that it is the location of the stone! Location of Jacobs Pillar stone?

King Solomons's navy was called Tharshish 'For the king had at sea a navy of Th'arshish (note.8) with the navy of Hiram: once in three years came the navy of Th'arshish, bringing gold, and silver, ivory, and apes, and peacocks.' and undoubtedly tin (1 Kin 10:22 H8659). You could circumnavigate the globe in three years, and I am sure they did.

Ezion Geber is a port in the Gulf of Aqaba, near the original Red Sea crossing of the children of Jack. Th'arish navy would go south and east from this port. They used Tyre and Joppa, Acco, and Dor for the Mediterranean and Western voyages.

As said earlier, some think Tarshish is located in southwest Spain, but many believe that it was Britain. Britain and Ireland were very difficult for the ancient people to get to; anything west of the

Pillars of Hercules was not on most maps, and venturing into the unknown scared people (see map at the start of this section 500 BC).

Pillars of Hercules – Embellishment of Samson

Hercules and pillars of – Samson, who was a Danite (the tribe of Dan, i.e., Irish), had long hair and was very muscular; even today, an Adonis, a strong, muscular person, would be depicted with long hair. Samson killed more people in death than he killed while alive; he brought the temple down by pushing out two huge support columns (Pillars) and caused the whole temple to collapse on its occupancy. We also have the Pillars of Hercules that enclose the Mediterranean Sea. It is considered by many that Hercules was the embellishment of Samson, and this by the tribe of Dan; both had the following in common:

We also have the Pillars of Hercules that enclose the Mediterranean Sea. It is considered by many that Hercules was taken from the story of Samson. Both had the following in common:

- Mothers were barren till visited by angels.
- Both are exceedingly strong.
- Both tore a lion apart with their bare hands.
- Both had a thing with pillars; Samson killed more in death than in life by pushing two pillars apart; we have the Pillars of Hercules (Strait of Gibraltar), a trademark sign.
- Both appear to have had long hair (#350).

There are many more similarities -They appear to be one and the same person.

Solomon Tin – Cornwall England connection.

We have British Historians who say that Solomon got much of his tin (needed for bronze) from England. Also, the Greek historian Herodotus, in the 5th century BC, talks of the metal trades with the 'isles of the west,' calling them Cassiterites of Tin Islands (Cassiterite being an ore of tin).

In addition, Diodorus Siculus (100 BC Roman historian) spoke of voyages beyond the pillars of Hercules during the 7th and

6th centuries BC. The Phoenicians sailed the Hippos, a long-range, sea-going vessel that could remain at sea for over 1 year.

Harry Bourne, in his article 'Canaan to Cornwall, says that the quotes of ancient historians (as listed above) and the 'cassiterites' (tin ore) did not refer to Cornwall but rather Armorica/Brittany, where the tin was stored for pick up, he says the Tin was mined in Cornwall and then transported to inlets (small ports) for pick up, also the ancient Annals of Ireland state that some seanchaí (Poets and Storytellers) say Milesians came from this area (#256) others assert they came from the Ebro river, Zaragoza area.

2 Fig. Phoenician-Hebrew navy

Notice the snake symbol (Dan) and
two of the colors of Joseph on the second ship.

As we have mentioned previously, Kittim Island in the far west was Britain and Ireland. In fact, it is common knowledge that the Phoenician trade did extend to Britain. England had a strong tin

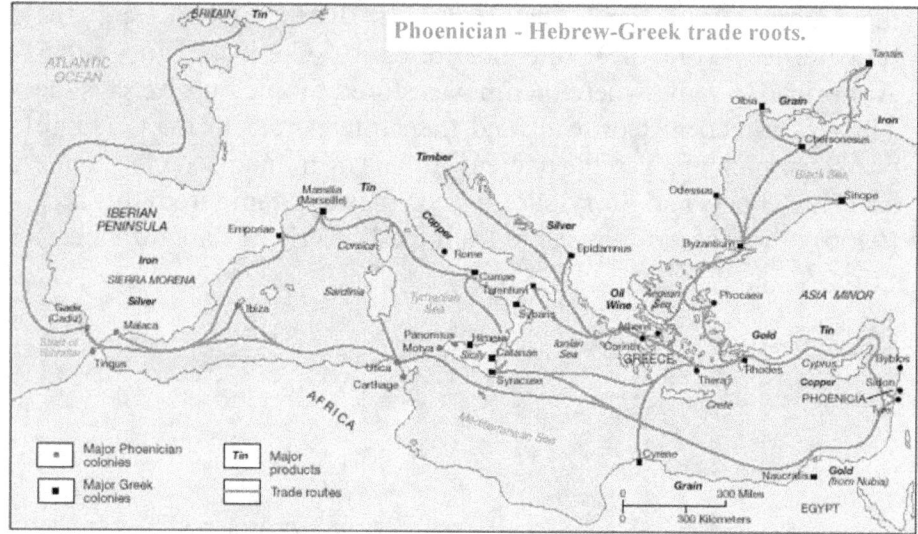

Greek and Phoenician Colonies and Trade. The Western Mediterranean was first colonized by Phoenicians and Greeks who together controlled trade throughout the region.

trade, and it is said that Ireland was covered by trees (so logging would be huge). Also, it was said that vast hordes of copper, iron, tin, and leaden ore were found in Ireland (#95.)The tin trade in Cornwall was huge and supplied Solomon's building of the Temple (#96).

Phoenician — Israel

We can see from the following map the Phoenician trade routes (this was a name given to sea people), and we will show that this is exactly where Israel went.

Metallurgic evidence linking Solomon to Britain.

The Tin Ingots:

Tin ingots discovered in shipwrecks off the coast of Israel date back to around 1300-1200 BCE, during the Late Bronze Age.

The composition of these ingots has been analyzed, and the isotopic signatures match those of tin ores found in Cornwall and Devon in the southwest of Britain.

The presence of Cornish tin in Israel indicates a well-established trade network stretching from the British Isles to the Eastern Mediterranean. This network likely involved the Phoenicians and Hebrews, who were known as skilled sailors and traders and who had extensive connections across the Mediterranean.

There are references in historical and biblical texts suggesting trade relationships involving tin. For example, the Book of Ezekiel mentions the trading of tin with the city of Tyre (Ezekiel 27:12). Tyre, a major Phoenician city, could have been a hub for redistributing tin to other regions, including Israel.

Some researchers propose that the tin trade was active during the time of King Solomon, whose wealth and international connections are detailed in the Bible. The idea is that Solomon's kingdom might have engaged in trade with the Phoenicians, who sourced tin from Cornwall.

In addition to the tin ingots, other artifacts such as pottery and shipwreck remnants have been found along the Mediterranean coast that further support the theory of extensive trade links between Britain and the Levant.

The discovery of these tin ingots is significant because it challenges the notion that ancient civilizations were isolated. It illustrates that complex trade routes existed long before the advent of more formalized global trading systems. The trade-in tin was vital for the production of bronze, which played a critical role in tools, weapons, and art during the Bronze Age.

The connection between Cornwall and the Levant is also consistent with traditions and legends about Phoenician traders visiting the British Isles, particularly in search of tin. This aligns with accounts from historians like Herodotus and Strabo, who described the tin trade in the ancient world.

In summary, the discovery of tin ingots from Cornwall in Israelite shipwrecks provides concrete archaeological evidence of an ancient trade network linking the British Isles with the Eastern Mediterranean, emphasizing the importance of tin and the interconnectedness of ancient civilizations.

I have many more connections. Please see my book, English is Hebrew.

CHAPTER 11 Birthright not to Jews.

Birthright and lost ten tribes

The birthright gift of a great nation and a great company of nations, along with the title covenant people or Israel, was typically given to the firstborn, e.g., Rueben. However, we know Jacob passed over him and instead gave it to Joseph. Joseph was not and is not a Jew. He was the father of Ephraim and Manasseh, who led the northern ten tribes of Israel.

I know even Pastors and Rabbis, for the most part, don't know this.

The Jews did receive an allotment in the Promised Land, as determined by God (Josh. 15) from the desert of sin (zin) to Edom (Autum-red) and onto Benjamin, the territory of Judah as large as any in Israel, perhaps with the exception of the Manasseh (Am Macir-Manasseh #268). The Jews also were promised the kingly line, along with being the father of Yeshua (Jesus Gen. 49).

Gen 49.8 Judah, you are he whom your brothers shall praise; Your hand shall be on the neck of your enemies -
Keeps the oracles of God, the Bible

Your father's children shall bow down before you. We all bow before the King/Queen.
9 Judah is a lion's whelp...(young lion).
From the prey, my son, you have gone up.
He bows down, he lies down as a lion;

And as a lion, who shall rouse him? Three Lions, (see British coat of arms).

10 The scepter shall not depart from Judah, Kingly line promise
Nor a lawgiver from between his feet, Until Shiloh comes;
And to Him shall be the obedience of the people.
  Lawyers – Judges, and the king of king's promised.

11 Binding his donkey to the vine, And his donkey's colt to the choice vine,
He washed his garments in wine,
And his clothes in the blood of grapes.

12 His eyes are darker than wine,
And his teeth are whiter than milk. Specific prophesy about Yeshua

Judah's territory was imposing (see map following). Only Manasseh was bigger.

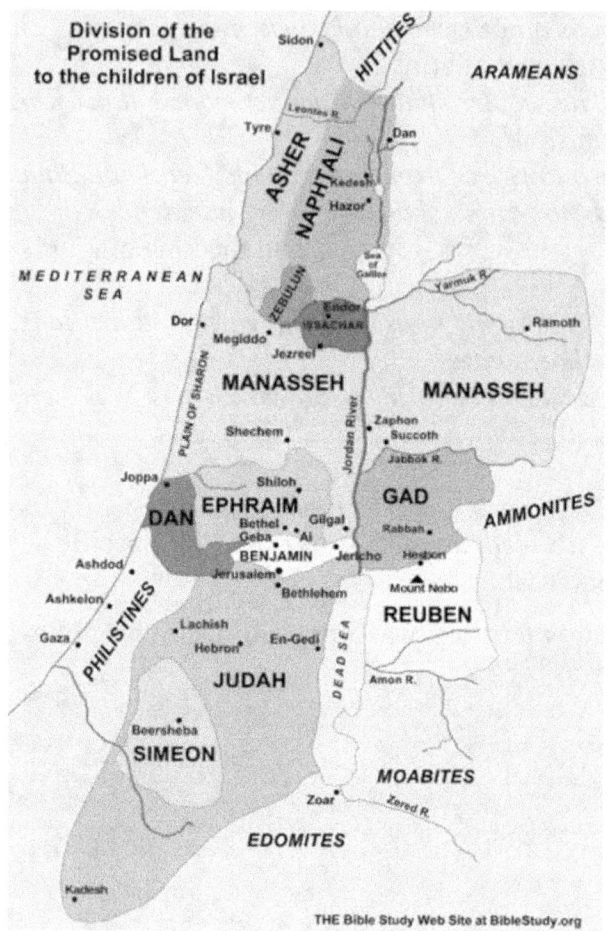

Division of the Promised Land to the children of Israel

THE Bible Study Web Site at BibleStudy.org

Assyria

Where did the house of Israel go? To answer this question, we must look at Assyria.

Assyria has existed as a nation from early times 2600BC and continued until about 625 BC. In its earliest days, it was the city Asser, which later expanded out into the fertile crescent, an area including the Tigris and Euphrates rivers (#227).

From 900-625 BC, the Assyrians (upper Mesopotamia) and Babylonians (lower Mesopotamia) warred with each other; this was disastrous for Babylon, and in 728BC-Pileser III of Assyria became King of Babylon (AKA Pul) and from then till 625BC, (except for periods of open insurrection), Babylon remains part of the Assyrian Empire Babylon.

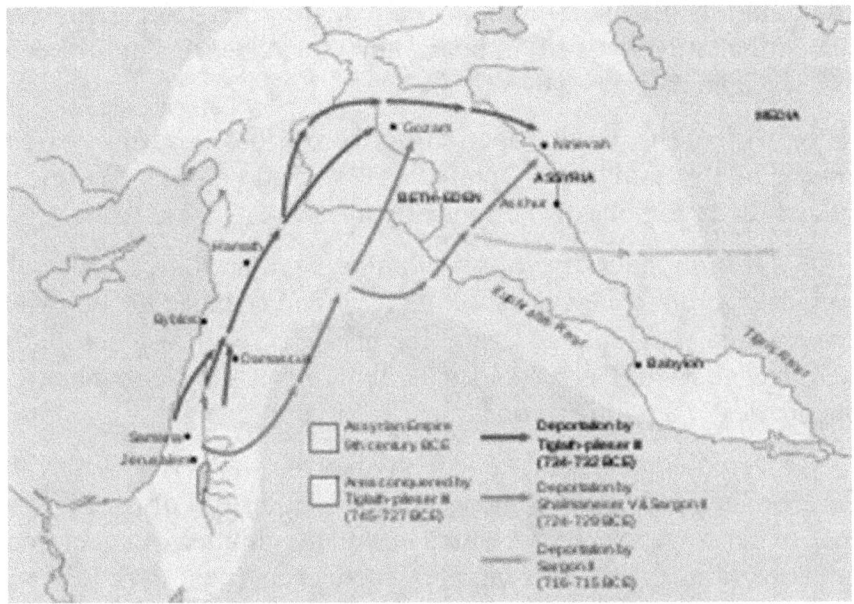

Deportation of Jews by Assyrians-courtesy Wikipedia

As stated earlier (Chap. 7), in 723-721 BC, Samaria, the capital of the Northern Ten Tribes, fell to Assyrian King Shalmaneser V, and the Israelites went into Assyrian captivity, I also pointed out (Chap. 9), that the Neo-Assyrian empire was subjecting Israel to tribute, this caused hardships and caused many Hebrew migrations through the Mediterranean and beyond.

Sins of Jeroboam-main reason for Israel's demise.

Jeroboam is mentioned over 100 times in the Bible and is almost always bad; Solomon liked Jerry and gave him charge over the ten northern kingdoms (1Kin. 11:28), although he still reported to King Solomon. After this, Ahijah the prophet met Jerry (1Kin. 11:31), and he said, *'Take thee ten pieces: for thus saith the LORD, the God of Israel, Behold, I will rend the kingdom out of the hand of Solomon, and will give ten tribes to thee'* This happened because of Solomon's, change of heart toward God, his many wives cause Solomon to worship false Idols (1Kin. 11.4, 9-13), and to set up graven images of them.

Jeroboam's name in English means יָרׇבְעָם Yârob'âm, yaw-rob-am, did you get it Jerry was 'yaw rob am' he stole the ten northern tribes from Solomon – although when God gives you something you can't steal it, but Solomon and his sons didn't see it that way and the name stuck!

It is also true that the ten northern tribes were taken from God. Yaw Rob Am took it upon himself to re-organize the political, cultural and religious affiliations of Samaria.

He introduced new holidays that were not based on God's holy days, brought new laws, set up Idols and changed the political, cultural and religious landscape for his own political gains. Jerry was the first to Gerrymander, which means to rearrange the boundaries of a political constituency for your own gain!

Jeroboam did something really bad; he was given a gift from God, but he used earthy logic to hold onto it instead of trusting the rock of our salvation. Jerry wanted to stop the children of Israel from going to worship at God's temple in Jerusalem (next to Solomon's palace), so he set up Baal worship at Bethel and Dan. We can see nothing new under the sun (Ecc. 1:9).

Yes, he set up the golden calves to remember the horrible event after the giving of the law on Mount Sinai (aka Mount Horib[ble]!). The golden calves were appealing to the vanity of the tribe of Joe, being the calve tribe and the children, being like sheep, just followed along, "Follow my leader." God expects us to follow our leaders, be respectful, and do as we are told, right? Well, not exactly; we are to follow a leader only if he is in the will of God, and if he isn't, then we don't follow them — there are many examples of this, but not a topic I will develop here.

What Ya Rob Am was doing greatly displeased God, and as a result, Jerry's son became ill, and Jerry sent the misses to inquire of God; she was disguised and pretended not to be Jerry's wife, but the prophet was told ahead of time and said the boy would die, and be mourned and given a proper funeral, albeit the last one that Jerry's family would have. The boy was a good lad; only the good die young, and perhaps because of his goodness God spared him the heartache and pain of seeing his family disrespect God and the trouble it caused (1Kin. 14:12).

This was the beginning of the end for Israel; things just went from bad to worse. It was a political environment where there was a breakup of the family, law, and values.

When we take God out of the equation, something will come in and fill the void; the devil (#388) finds work for IDOL hands. This was the setting for some very bad kings in Israel. Ahab and Jezebel came from this practice, and Ephraim and Dan were leaders in this debauchery. We can see that Israel had a habit of putting rule upon rule, precept upon precept; this has the appearance of right but often does nothing to stem the evil caused (Isa. 28.10). A similar practice is being done by modern-day Israel (the USA and English-speaking world).

This seems to be the end of the story for Samaria (#227). God casts Israel (birthright tribes) from his sight and issues them a certificate of divorce 721BC. We can see this in 2 Kings 17.18, 22-23 (it is thought that this was written around 580 BC).

Assyria's Demise

We know that after Assyria took out Shome 'r' own (Samaria), they didn't last very long, less than 100 years after Samaria's submission, i.e., (721-100 BC) 625 BC, and Assyria is no more. As we can see, when the going gets tough, the tough get going, and most of the tribes packed their bags and skipped town. We know from past chapters that the whole tribe of Dan and Zebulun was AWOL before the Assyrian assimilation.

Babylon Neo Babylonia Chaldean Empire – 625-538 BC

Starting 625 BC till its complete downfall circa 602 BC, Assyrian was under constant attack. The capital city of Nineveh was attacked and finally sacked by the Babylonians.

Neoplasia and his ally Cyaxares, King of Media, destroyed Nineveh in 612 BC and divided themselves the Assyrian Empire. Later, Nebuchadnezzar (Nebu) attacked and subdued Pharaoh Necho at Carchemish in 605 BC.

Through the victory of "Nebu" over Pharaoh at Carchemish, Judah became subject to Babylon (#227). Nebu took Jerusalem twice in 597 and 586 BC but failed to capture Tyre. Remember, Tyre and the Phoenicians are from the lineage of Eber (Hebrews).

They predominantly are a mixture of the tribes Dan and Benjamin along with descendants of Ur (Abraham's birthplace), with others undoubtedly thrown in, i.e., Zebulon and Asher. Nebuchadnezzar besieged Tyre for 13 years but failed to capture it; perhaps he needed a navy.

I guess the seaport continued to operate? It is said that in ancient times, Tyre had a fortress out at sea; it also traded with locations over 1 year's journey from their ports; remember Solomon's navy was gone at sea for 3 years; there are very few places in the world you cannot get to following the trade winds, in fact in the 15 century it would only take 6 weeks to 3 months to sail from Europe to America. I believe Th'arshish circumnavigated the globe in 1000 BC, but that story is for another time.

God did prophesy the destruction of Tyre, and he did prophesy that Nebu would attack it and besiege it. Much of Ezekiel 26-28 covers this, Tyre being proud, arrogant, conceited and with a complete disdain for God. This speaks of Tyre as a physical entity and Satan as the spiritual entity (Eze. 28.1-2,11-19).

Babylon Nabonidus and Belshazzar, Co-regent's 555-538 BC.

Nabonidus reigning in conjunction with Belshazzar, do you remember Belshazzar (Belsha'tstsar h1113 — Belt) from the Bibles? We can find him in Daniel 4.3: Belt' had the gold goblets brought in that his father Nebu (Nebuchadnezzar) had brought from Jerusalem and he toasted to his Gods using the real Gods goblets, 'wow' then from nowhere the fingers of a hand appear and wrote on the plaster wall.

The belt was at the time plastered (yes, he was plastered a British term meaning drunk [Dan 5.1-2]). He was so frightened that his face turned pale, he went as white as a ghost (after seeing the ghost, he turned white) and his knees knocked and he collapsed. The king called for all his wise men, but nobody could interpret the dream, that was until they remembered Daniel (Dan. 5:25).

And this is the inscription that was written: *MENE, MENE, TEKEL, UPHARSIN.*

This is the interpretation of each word:

- **MENE:** God has numbered your kingdom and finished it;
- **TEKEL:** (Job 31:6; Ps. 62:9; Jer. 6:30) You have been weighed in the balances and found wanting (notice are a symbol of justice being the scales is straight from our history):
- **PERES:** Your kingdom has been divided and given to the Medes and Persians.' That same night, his life was taken (*The writings on the wall!*)

We don't mess with the creator if we know what's good for us; respect and honor him!

Medes and Persians 538-332 BC Darius and Cyrus.

In Daniel 5:30, the very night Belt was getting plastered, someone should have told him to belt up, and things might have been different. Anyhow, his life was taken, and Darius the Mede took over the kingdom. Langer's book of world history says that in 538 BC, Gobryas, a general of Cyrus the King of Persia (#227), took the capital without a fight that same night.

In Daniel 6, we can see the liberal democrats of Persia sought a way to trap Daniel, so they schemed and devised a plan to get Daniel killed, for him praying to his God – you know, the one, the God of our fathers Abraham, Isaac and Jacob. Guess what?

They succeeded, and King Darius wrote a decree that could not be broken, and Dan had to be thrown into the lion's den; as luck had it, the lions weren't hungry (what a break), and after an agonizing sleepless night for Cyrus and at first light of day "It's always darkest before the dawn" (God likes this term) he rushes to the lion's den and in an anguished voice cries out to Daniel.

Daniel replies to Darius, "God sent an angel to shut the mouths of the lions," so Dan was lifted from the den, and those evil liars / God-haters with their wives and children were thrown in, and all of a sudden, the lions were hungry again! What bad luck for the Liberals ☺.

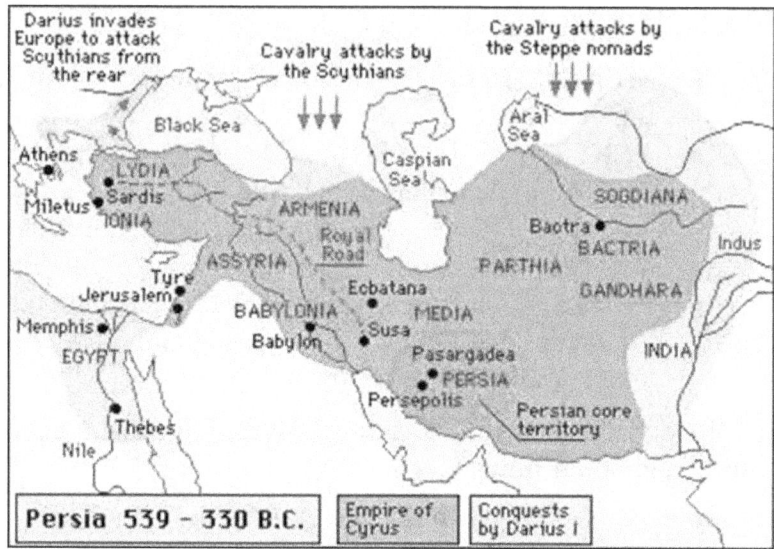

Darius issues a decree, that all the people in his kingdom must fear and reverence the God of Daniel – that's a nice turn of events.

Daniel fasts often and prays for Jerusalem and his people 3 times a day in front of an open window so everyone can see him. He can see the great kingdom of the Persians and the Medes. The thought must have crossed his mind the vastness of the empire was huge, many times greater than the promised land to Abraham, Isaac and Jacob, and we can see from his prayers he wanted answers: why is it that we have a smaller nation than the others, was this one of his questions?

God answers; God takes Daniel through time and says there will be many kings and many kingdoms, but almost like a Hitchcock thriller, there's a twist, and we can see from Daniel 7.17-18 that there are 4 kingdoms that will arise (none of which are Hebrew or Jewish, what happing here?) and then (v18) the saints of the highest will receive the kingdoms and possess it forever and ever. Yes, the possession of the whole earth (Erets) will go to God's servants, and God and David will rule the earth from Jerusalem, but before that happens, there is much more for Daniel to learn.

We won't take the time to analyze Daniel at this time other than this one pertinent scripture (Dan. 11:30), where he talks of the last Days, Daniel says: "For the ships of Chittim (western coastlands) shall come against him: therefore he shall be grieved, and return, and have indignation against the holy covenant: so shall he do; he shall even return, and have intelligence with them that forsake the holy covenant.

Let me summarize: We again have Chittim or Kittim (ships of the western coastland, Isles of the sea with the holy covenant! (NIV)). This is symbolic of America, Great Britain etc.

Again, this is where Jeremiah was told to take the kingly line! There are just so many instances relating Tarshish, Kittim and Chittim to the British and people of God that it must be clear by now that "We are Israel."

Scythia

From the area where the Assyrians and Babylonians took Israel came a mysterious group of people called Scythians. The histories of the British and Irish nations have waves of people coming to them from Scythia. Who are these people? The Encyclopedia Britannica says this:

Scythian, also called Scyth, Saka, and Sacae, member of a nomadic people, originally of Iranian stock, known from as early as the 9th century BCE who migrated westward from Central Asia to southern Russia and Ukraine in the 8th and 7th centuries BCE.

The Encyclopedia Britannica says that the Scythians came for Iranian stock. How do they know this? Did they do a DNA sample of a large bunch of people? It's like saying Americans are from Africa, Asia, Germany or Russia, all of which are true to a small degree. But that does not tell the whole story.

Wikipedia says the following: The relationships between the peoples living in these widely separated regions remain unclear. The term 'Scythian' is used by modern scholars in an archaeological context to display attributes of the 'Scytho-Siberian' culture, usually without implying an ethnic or linguistic connotation. The term Scythic may also be used in a similar way, 'to describe a special phase that followed the widespread diffusion of mounted nomadism,

107

characterized by the presence of special weapons, horse gear, and animal art in the form of metal plaques.' Their western most territories during the Iron Age were known to classical Greek sources as Scythia.

Literary Evidence

Map of the Roman Empire under Hadrian (ruled AD 117–138), showing the location of the Scythae Basilaei ('Royal Scyths') along the north shore of the Black Sea.

The approximate extent of Eastern Iranian languages and people in Middle, Iranian times in the 1st century BC is shown in orange. It is said the Scythians first appeared in the historical record in the 8th century BC. Herodotus reported three contradictory versions as to their origins. However, accounts by Herodotus of Scythian origins have been discounted recently; although his accounts of Scythian raiding activities contemporary to his writings have been deemed more reliable. Moreover, the term Scythian, like Cimmerian, was used to refer to a variety of groups from the Black Sea to southern Siberia and central Asia. They were not a specific people, but rather a variety of peoples none of which were indigenous to the area.

Even Herodotus had a hard time putting his finger on the origin of the term Scythia or Scythian. It's clear that the Hebrews were in this neck of the woods and migrated south and west; what is also clear is the complete connection with culture, language, traditions, idioms, proverbs, emblems, signposts, and waymarks, as God calls them.

We know these things because history records that elements of the Scythians came to Britain and are said to be part of the

Milesian and Danite journeys, and as empirical history records, they not only spoke the same language but merged peacefully with the current inhabitance of Britain, in fact, the Picts who the Venerable Bede says came from Scythia, were given wives from the Scots, who were in Ireland and Scotland (#303).

There is ample evidence to support that the freed Hebrew slaves of both Assyria and Babylon made up portions of the nomadic Scythians. Bear in mind that the Israelites were tent dwellers, Abraham, Isaac, and Jacob, and during our 40 years of wanderings in the desert, even God dwelt in a tent till Solomon built him a temple. There are many writers who have done detailed research on the Scythian, Cimri, Hibernian, Danaoi, Sacae, Omri, Khumri, Galatae, and Abiri (#250), and ties these to the Hebrews, but it's beyond the scope of this book to deal with these issues, yet even a cursory look at this subject uncovers striking evidence to support the Scythian-Hebrew connection.

Some say the origin of the name Scotland is from the names Scythian, Scyutha, and Scutta. We will analyze this further in a later section.

CHAPTER 12 - Greece

The ancient Greeks are well known for their learning, art, philosophy, medicine, science, astronomy etc.

Greece is said to have been populated by numerous people at various times. We have the Proto-Greece civilization starting around 2000 BC. Later replaced by the Mycenae civilization 1600BC, Wikipedia says, 'the Mycenaean Greeks borrowed from the Minoan civilization its syllabic writing system (i.e., Linear A) and developed their own syllabic script known as Linear B, providing the first and oldest written evidence of Greek. The Mycenaeans quickly penetrated the Aegean Sea and, by the 15th century BC, had reached Rhodes, Crete, Cyprus and the shores of Asia Minor.

Around 1200 BC, the Dorians, another Greek-speaking people, followed from Epirus. Traditionally, historians have believed that the Dorian invasion caused the collapse of the Mycenaean civilization, but it is likely the main attack was made by seafaring raiders (Sea Peoples) who sailed into the eastern Mediterranean around 1180 BC. The Dorian invasion was followed by a poorly attested period of migrations, appropriately called the Greek Dark Ages, but by 800 BC, the landscape of Archaic and Classical Greece was discernible.

Mycenaean Art with Eagle Crown

The Greeks of classical antiquity idealized their Mycenaean ancestors and the Mycenaean period as a glorious era of heroes, closeness of the Gods and material wealth. The Homeric Epics (i.e.,

Iliad and Odyssey) were especially and generally accepted as part of the Greek past, and it was not until the 19th century that scholars began to question Homer's historicity.[65] As part of the Mycenaean heritage that survived, the names of the Gods and Goddesses of Mycenaean Greece (e.g. Zeus, Poseidon and Hades) became major figures of the Olympian Pantheon of later antiquity.

Here are a few pointers – It is said the Mycenaeans borrowed from the Minoan, who in turn came from Crete. Crete is a stronghold of the Phoenicians; it's really not that hard to put two and two together. We have language, religion and culture. Religion, being the God of Abraham, Isaac and Jacob, along with the Gods of Samaria, i.e., a whole host of pagan deities, including Bull worship.

In fact, when we look at ancient bull worship, we can see exactly where we went: Egypt, Samaria, Crete, Assyria (Iran), Greece, and, of course, the Celts. Minoan culture not only had bull symbols and most likely worshiped them but also a snake Goddess with what appears to be an eagle on her head. Also, birds were placed on the sarcophagus, which some say were eagles, but certainly, the eagle was celebrated in their culture; bull speaks of Ephraim, and snake and eagle Dan.

As we have already spoken to, advanced medicine is said to have originated in Egypt by Ruler Imhotep (Joseph) and most definitely got transferred to Greece; recently, a port was found in Egypt called Heraklion. It was a main trading port going back at least 1200BC, and perhaps was active at the time of Joseph and definitely Moses time; it traded with the Greeks and many other nations and was written about in Greek literature, clearly an Egyptian-Greek and possibly British connection going back to ancient times.

Greek Alphabet

The Greek alphabet is said to have been derived from the Phoenician, and as we have already shown, this is Hebrew (see English is Hebrew). The alphabets of both descend from the paleo-Hebrew alphabet, and their order is largely preserved (less well so in Greek):

Phoenician	=	*Hebrew*	=	*Greek,*
Ālap	=	Alef	=	Alpha,

Bēth	=	Bet	=	Beta,
Gāmal	=	Gimel	=	Gamma,
Dālath	=	Dalet	=	Delta,
Hē	=	He	=	Epsilon,
Waw	=	Vav	=	Digamma

We can see a strange occurrence with the letters from Phoenicia that get flipped in Ionia and Athens, Etruscans and Minoans. This is like a mirror image; could the reason for this come from the printing of posters? It was not uncommon for the ancients to write in both directions (#20). In school art class (when I was a kid), some 450 years ago, we (I look good for my age) were asked to make a stamp out of a potato, dip it in paint and stamp away! I believe we had the manual (and leg) operated printing press for eons. In fact, the process of printing is putting in a series of letters into the order that you want and then the plate gets inked, and you can stamp away. Printing multiple sheets of one page (#21), this process of producing posters for events would help solidify the language and would help to put it into the learning establishments. We will also see that printing was used in Ancient Israel. We have already seen the seal that Judah had back in 1800BC. This clearly establishes printing was in use from very ancient times, and they would print onto a wax seal, more about this later.

How about perhaps the most renowned of Greek words, "Academy," this is said to be from the Italians; the one main problem with that the Italians came after the Greeks; the Greek word Academy is also said to originate from Plato's Academy which is said to have been founded 428 BC (#16). The great institutes of learning for the Greek said to have come from Athens i.e. Grove of Akademos (#17), AKA Hekademos or Hecademus.

The name actually comes from Hebrew, "Hakar-Aka," means to study or inquire and "Damah" means meditate. Hence the name "inquire" and "mediate," H1970 hakar-haw-kar (Aka) H1819 damah — daw-maw, to compare, to think, to meditate, to plan, so when we put the two together its Aka Damah Greek Akademos — once again another Hebrew connection!

Athens — Cecrops — Calcol — Darda

"According to the "Harmsworth Encyclopedia," Cecrops ("Calcol" of I Chron. 2:6 and "Chalcol" of I Kings 4:31 — and brother of Darda, #55,135,249) was the mythical founder of Athens and its first king. He was thought to have been the leader of a band of Hebrew colonists from Egypt. Historical records tell of the westward migration of the descendants of Calcol along the shores of the Mediterranean Sea, establishing "Iberian" (Hebrew) trading settlements. We have many settlements in the Ebro Valley in Spain." From Spain, they continued westward as far as Ireland." (Note 15) This appears to be similar to the story of Danaus and Cadmus, who come from Egypt to Greece link.

Miletus

Miletus, a city-state on the coast of the Aegean Sea in Ionia (modern-day Turkey, also Iona means dove in Hebrew h3123 [and Jonah's name], Javan h3120 is said to be the father of the Greeks), which had served as the center of the Ionian rebellion that sought freedom from the Persian Empire. The first ancient Greek philosophers, Thales, Anaximander, and Anaximenes, were all from Miletus, and so they are known as founders of the Milesians School.

They were primarily invested in cosmology, the order and interaction of the elements, and observation of nature. In the ancient world, cosmology and science were primarily passive observations; as we are about to see, these were also Hebrew.

We have already seen that the Phoenicians were Hebrew and that they spread through Greece, in fact, the founder of the Academy of Miletus was Phoenician/Hebrew born.

Thales of Miletus

What is the Etymology of the name Mile or Milidh or Miletus? There is a Hebrew word that could match male or female in Hebrew, meaning full, either actually like a full stomach or pregnant or figuratively such as fulfilled as in prophecy fulfilled (#252)? Thales was the first member of the Milesian School, which was not a formal school in a building but a label applied to the three interrelated thinkers from Miletus.

Thales is believed to have lived sometime between 620 and 550 BCE based largely on his prediction of a solar eclipse in 585 BCE. According to Diogenes Laertius, a historian who chronicled the lives of Greek philosophers, Thales was a Phoenician born to Phoenician noble parents who emigrated to the area that became known as Miletus. He became famous for his accomplishments, as shown by a line from Aristophanes' comedy "The Birds" and "The Man's a Thales!" Unfortunately, none of his writings survived. Other sources say he wrote two treatises on astronomy, but if he did, they are now lost to history.

Theater Seats in Miletus

The evidences attest to the presence of a Jewish population in Miletus in the first century, the theater benches are decorated with animal legs and paws along the aisles. Nearby, one of the seats has a Greek inscription that reads "to the Jews." This, along with the Phoenician/Hebrew Thales, shows strong evidence of a Hebrew/Jew origin for Miletus in Greece. The etymology (being name origin) of Mile or Miletus shows a direct connection to our fathers Abraham, Isaac and Jacob and the Hebrews.

Lacedaemonians of Greece

The Lacedaemonians/Spartans of Greece were Hebrews we can see by their letter to Onias, the high priest of the Jews Cir. 180 BC (#31. #87).

"We have met with a certain writing, whereby we have discovered that both the Jews and the Lacedemonians are of one stock and are derived from the kindred of Abraham. It is but just therefore that you, who are our brethren, should send to us about any of your concerns? as you please. We will also do the same thing, esteem your concerns as our own, and will look upon our concerns as in common with yours. Demoteles, who brings you this letter, will

bring your answer back to us. This letter is four-square, and the seal is an eagle with a dragon in his claws."

The relationship is both claimed and acknowledged, and the seal of the letter of the Lacedaemonians is an eagle with a dragon (flying snake) in its claws, the symbol of Dan (#87). The Lacedaemonians were living in Sparta, Greece, and we have all heard of the Spartan's power.

We have covered this earlier; there are many who believe the Danai (Argive #372) of Greece is tied to the Lacedaemonians and is Hebrew. Gladstone tells us the Tuatha de Dananns of Ireland came from the Danai of Greece. (#373)

Greek-Ireland connection

O'Flaherty (a noted Irish Historian) says Danann's started to flourish in Ireland at the time Troy was being destroyed in Greece (Ogygia p118). This would place them around 1200 BC. Annual of the Four Masters (p18) says that Balor Benien, who was a giant and had an evil eye, was also general of the Formerians and was slain by a stone, thrown from a device called tabhall (sling), and he was of the original tribes of Ireland and killed by the Tuatha De Danann. This story is used to frighten children at bedtime; it is most remembered on Tory (#18 Troy) Island opposite Donegal (Dan Eagle). This is of ancient antiquity in Ireland and none other than a corruption of the story Da'vid and Goliath (carried by seancha poets and storytellers).

You may remember in the original story, the general of the Philistines taunted Israel, and no one would come out and fight the giant (1Sam.17.33,42), till a freckled red-haired young boy came out at him with a slingshot and the God of Abraham, Isaac and Jacob! Goliath cursed David by his Gods, David responded you come against me with sword, spear and javelin, and I come against you in the name of the Lord God Almighty of the armies of Israel. "Shem Yehovah tsaba Elohim ma'arakah Yisrael." David killed Goliath, cut his head off with his own sword, and took his spear, javelin and sword to his own tent. There are four treasures of the Tuatha De Dan:

- Dagda's Cauldron is of Unknown origin, possibly an artifact captured from a fight with Canaanites.
- The Spear of Lugh is Most likely the spear from Goliath
- Lia Fáil (The Stone of Fal) – stone of destiny – Jacobs Pillar Stone.
- Claíomh Solais (The Sword of Light) Possibly the sword of Goliath?

The sword's keeper is usually a giant (gruagach, fermór) or hag (cailleach), who oftentimes cannot be defeated except by some secret means. Thus, the hero or helper may resort to the sword of light as the only effective weapon against this enemy. But often, the sword is not enough, and the supernatural enemy has to be attacked on a single vulnerable spot on his body (just like Goliath).

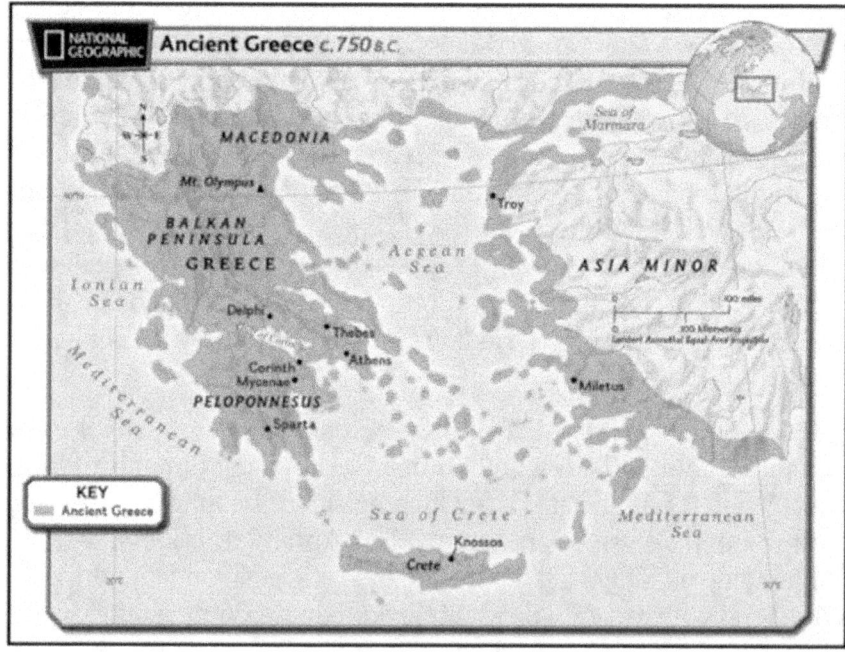

Sometimes the Irish Annals tell us that Danann came from Macedonia, Greece & emigrated into Boeotia in Achaia, and into Athens, and after studying and perfecting their magic art there, they passed over into Scandinavia, and the northern parts of Europe, viz. into Norway, Sweden, and Denmark (mark of Dan), where they inhabited Falia, Goria, Finland, and Muria. From thence, they departed and settled in the North of Britain and resided at Dobar and Irdobar until, at length, landing in the northern parts of Ireland, they conquered and dispossessed (Yarash h3423ס. סֹ שׁ the Fir-bolg, O'Flaherty goes on to say the Danann's and Milesian's are from the same father and all speak the same language (Ogygia-p6) which he calls Scotic.

Looking at the map of Ancient Greece, we can see the locations of Miletus, Troy, Macedonia, Athens, and Sparta, all of which are linked to Ireland, and the tribes of Dan and Miletus (Milesian-Zorite-Jews) and with clear ancient references to each other and are Hebrew!

CHAPTER 13 – Ireland-Irish-Hebrews

Ireland

Ireland has a history that is said to predate the flood. Its earliest inhabitance is said to be from the sons of Japheth, i.e., Magog (#167); Keating goes on to quote a history that he (apparently) feels is false about the daughters of Cain, i.e. Cain's daughter came to Ireland before the flood –if all were to perish during the flood how is it that we have a history of Ceasair (Cain's daughter), and why does her name sound like the kings of the holy roman empire? It makes no sense. Much of ancient folklore, myth and legend often does not make sense; however, I will utilize a technique needed to unlock the truth; I will analyze the collected jumbled mass and compare it with the facts and truth, as detailed in the Bible and ancient history. When we do this, I think you will find it makes perfect sense.

The Irish had storytellers, poets that were employed by the kings, chieftains and noblemen; they would retell their poetry and history, these they called Seancha; it is said the Irish didn't have written laws and histories, but the Bards (Seancha) would keep it in verse, poetry and song – It is possible that the Irish did have writing in ancient times, history records the Ogham script, a system of writing that was in use for a long time but no ancient manuscripts have survived. The oldest manuscript known today comes from the 5 Century AD. They are said to be two works of St Patrick that are repeated in the Book of Armagh.

The 5th century AD does not take us back far enough; it's clear from Irish history that they leaned heavily on an oral tradition as ancient Israel did, but where are all the ancient documents spoken of by the Irish historian? Many of these documents were purposefully destroyed, some by St. Patrick, others by Cromwell, and I am sure others. The ancient bards were masters of the law, language, and poetry. Unfortunately, over time, the traditions were not maintained, and errors were introduced.

The Bardic history, as attested to by Keating, the four, and O'Flaherty, shows that the strict bardic (Seancha) traditions have given way due to the entertainment value of salacious, unverified, and often shocking stories. These stories are perpetrated by a high official who wanted to mask the truth and muddy the waters.

Here we have an example from Keating's General History: Three hundred years after the deluge, It is a tale of truth, as I reckon, All holy Ireland was desert Until Partholón came.

"All holy Island was desert," 1st question I have is what is meant by the term desert? I cannot believe it means no trees because the island was full of trees, as stated by O'Flaherty, so this is a miss-spelling, and they mean deserted, and who was there to witness it? Moreover, it's hard to believe that almost 6000 years ago, someone would call the Island "All Holy," why would an uninhabited Island be called "All Holy"?

As mentioned previously, the truth gets corrupted, and events that occur at one-time interval get mixed with other events from another time interval. Ireland does have a reputation for being holy and blessed by God. We can see that from O'Flaherty's book Ogygia, which is said to be an ancient name of Ireland and means sacred Isle, or Ancient Isle. (#168).

This, along with many references in the Annals, lends credence to this thought. In this book, we will look at the Etymology of Ireland (roots of names and words), how it is that Ireland was known at one point as a "Holy Island," how it became venerated and how it was that they had people dwelling there that could recount the event from creation!

The old Irish Chronicles are full of folklore, myth, and legend in the midst of which some truth exists. In order to extract the truth, we need a map, something we can trace that leads us back to the truth. I will show an unambiguous connection between Israel, Dan, Judah (Zerah), Joseph, and Britain. We will be comparing like for like, i.e., side by side, the traits, habits, language etc., that reveal the true origin.

Did the Irish come from Magog?

First, we must look at the credence for statements in the Irish Annals where it is said the Irish come from Magog (#341).

The table of nations from Genesis 10 clearly says that the island of the sea shall be the progenitor of Japheth. And God said of Japheth, God shall enlarge Japheth, and he shall dwell in the tents of Shem; and Canaan shall be his servant (Gen. 9:27). And the sons of Javan; Elishah, and Tarshish, Kittim, and Dodanim (Gen. 10:4). Again, we can see these names Tarshish and Kittim!

By these were the isles of the Gentiles divided into their lands; every one after his tongue, after their families, in their nations (Gen. 10:5 #374). According to God, the ancient Islands now called Brittan were called Tarshish and Kittim. According to the Irish Annals, the original inhabitants were the Fir Bolg, who had dark skin and an aboriginal look.

The sons of Japheth mixed with Shem (Gen. 9.27) and became Gomer and Magog; these are the sons of Japheth who live in Russia (and elsewhere). I will not take the time to analyze this in detail; you can see from the Table of Nations that the early distribution of Meshech and Magog was in Russia, also see (#15).

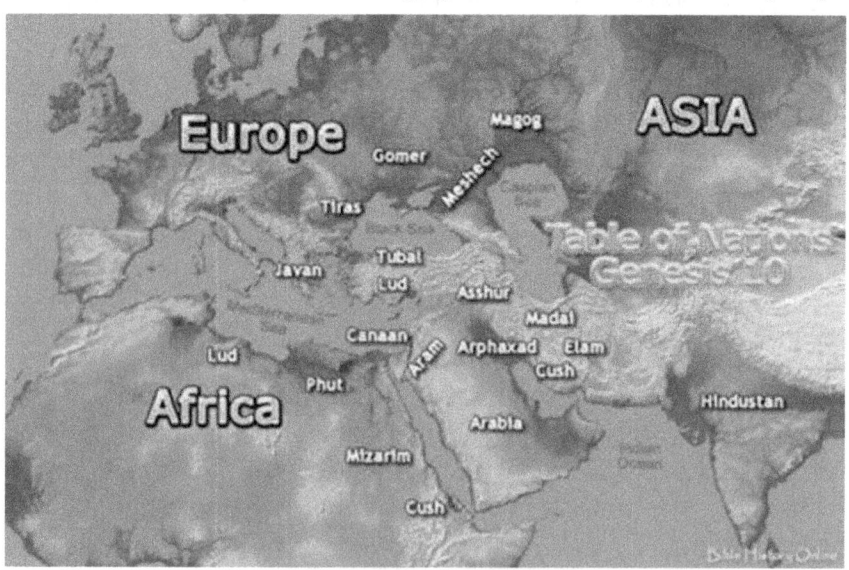

Courtesy bible-history.com

Map – Table of Nations

We can see from Genesis 10.4-5 that the islands of the sea are inhabited by Javan (Great Britain and Ireland), so Javan's sons should occupy these Islands. Javan is a son of Japheth and a brother of Magog.

The Ethnographic division into races

The ethnographic division into races is not a popular topic these days since the false history of *evol*ution is promulgated in schools and learning institutions.

Meyers Konversations lexikon of 1885-90 is listing:

1. **Caucasian** races (Aryans, were Assyrian and now German), Hamites— North Africa, Semites -Hebrews, Midian, Moab, Meshesh, Meshesh is also Javan)
2. **Mongolian** races (northern Mongolian, Chinese and Indo-Chinese, Japanese and Korean, Tibetan, Malayan, Polynesian, Maori, Micronesian, Eskimo, and American Indian),
3. **Negroid** races (African, Hottentots, Melanesians / Papua, 'Negrito', Australian Aborigine, Dravidians, Sinhalese)

There were three main types or strains of humans that came from Noah's children,

Most historians, anthropologists paleontologists *of 100 years ago* would agree; however, the Bible and everything God (good) has come under intense attack, and Liberal (just like Jerry-Jeroboam) are trying to erase the past and create a new history (does this sound familiar, it's what happening today in the USA).

It still remains that we have three distinct human types, Caucasoid, Negroid, and Mongoloid; Also, recent news has stated that the early inhabitance of America was from the same stock as the Aboriginals in Australia. And were of the Mongoloid stock (Japheth), BBC News | Sci/Tech | 'First Americans were Australian. This clearly is the description of an earth people type race as mentioned by O'Flaherty, so the Original inhabitance of Ireland (like Australia, USA, and Britain) were from Japheth – Mongoloids. Javan's sons are clearly not Irish.

Irish – Russian

3Red Square Saint Basile courtesy Wikipedia

While I agree that Javan/Magog were the original inhabitants of Ireland, the question today is: Are they the origin of the Irish, and did they come from Russia?

As the ancient testimony of Ireland seems to say, this to me, is the least plausible suggestion ever; when we look at the Irish, they are drawn to Russia very seldom. The Irish religious, either you're a Catholic or a Protestant, I have not heard of any Russian Orthodox over there. How about architecture? We definitely don't see any tall, spindly buildings with wispy ice-cream domes. Even the Russian 'Cossack Dance' is very strenuous. Going down on one leg and kicking the other one up while arms folded is very unique to Russia.

The music, culture and language of Russia are very different from Ireland's. There is absolutely no connection; the only connection I can see (at this point) is the Irish like to drink, but Vodka, isn't necessarily one of their favorites. When we add it all up, there is absolutely no connection between Russia and Ireland. We can say with certainty that the Irish are not Russian (Magog), so where did they come from? Go everywhere, but I do not see their footprint or presence in Russia.

Abraham – Go west, young man!

In Genesis 11.10, we get the account of the Abrahamic-Shem lineage. God often leaves clues (waymarks) to the truth through the meaning of names. One such clue is Eber (great-grandson of Shem Gen. 11.16), who is the father of the Hebrews, Eber's (H5676) name in

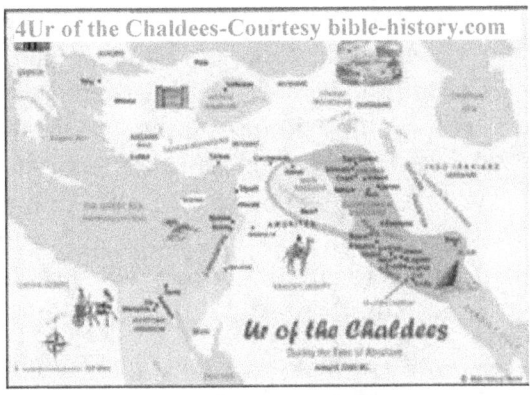

Hebrew means 'the region beyond' (we will cover this in more detail shortly) it is a general thought that the region beyond means east, Eber lived in Ur of the Chaldees which is north and east of Canaan so Abraham went west (or southwest) and we have continued to go west even to this day "go west young man," isn't this one of our catchphrases.

And take a look at the maps of the known world that have survived showing the straights of Gibraltar opening to the region beyond, and sometimes it shows Britain beyond this (#375). Notice that the map of Eratosthenes circa 300 BC shows Britain and what name they gave to these Islands Brittania (covenant people of God), with Juverna or Iberna (island of Jews or Hebrews, i.e., Ibriy, Iberian, Hebrides H5680 from beyond) being the name given to Ireland. Do I need to say anything else?

Tuatha De Danan's –

The Tuatha De Danann were one of the first races of people to invade and take possession (Yarash h3423-arish) Ireland. They dispossessed the Fir Bolg perhaps as early as 1200 BC. The term Tuatha De Danann means people of the God of Dan (Ancient Tell Dan was also known as "the God that is in Dan"), and the early monks knew this and said so, but historians started to change their name because it linked them with Israel and being Hebrew. Here's what Wikipedia says:

"However, Irish monks also began using the term Tuath Dé to refer." Wikipedia also says: "It has also been suggested that Danann is a conflation of dán ("skill, craft") (this term was synonymous with the tribe of Dan, i.e., skill, craft Exo. 31:6 Exo. 38:23) and the Goddess name Annan.[1] The name is also found as Donann and Domnann,[18] which may point to the origin being proto-Celtic *don, meaning "earth"[1] (compare the Old Irish word for earth, domain and the Hebrew word for earth (A)damah h127]). Wikipedia goes on to say, "There may be a link with the mythical Fir Domnann[19] and the British Dumnonii. [20]" (All the Celtic tribes were Hebrew, and I will show you the connection later in the section on Brittan).

When we look at the Bible, we must remember that the Aleph was a guttural stop, so Dan would be D'n; this is why, in Ireland, it is spelled Don, Dan, and Dun. We can see the following:-

- **H1835**דֶן Dan means Judge in Hebrew fromדֶן Dân, dawn; from H1777;
- **H1777** דִין diyn deen or duwn {doon}; to judge, contend, plead, a primitive root a straight course, i.e., sail direct, to judge (correctly), Note13. From primitive root [אדון (H113)]
- **H113**אָדוֹן'adown adon = lord, master, a master of studies University teacher, i.e., a Don to the Israelites,[1] with the meaning "People of God."[15] Apparently, to avoid confusion with the Israelites,[1] writers began to refer to the mythical race as the Tuath Dé Danann (plural Tuatha Dé Danann).[16]"

The name currently used by scholars for the ancient tribe is Tuatha de Danann, where clearly (as stated above) the Tuath de was known to mean 'People of God'. The name Danann's was used in Keating's book 342 O'Flaherty also says the name comes from Dane's, and he feels the etymology of which leads us back to Donegal, Dan Eagle (ibid 342).

A careful study reveals that the Irish names Danann, Danans, Danan, Don's, and Dans originated with Israel and are Hebrew (see next section on Hebrew).

- דָּנָה יַעַן **H1842** Dan Ya`an — Danjaan — dawn yan Dan(y) aan = "purposeful judgment"
- **H1839** דָּנִי Daniy Pronunciation dä·nē' Danites ="judge"

- **H1837** דָּנָּה Dannah = "thou hast judged" or "judgement"
- דָּנִיֵּאל **H1840** Daniye'l Daniel = God is my Judge remember Dan will Judge his people (Gen. 49.16)

In Summary, the name Danann was listed as Danan, Danans and Donans by Irish historians. This is said to be tied to Dane, i.e., Denmark (Mark of Dan), all these names are in the Bible and are tied to the tribe of Dan. We have also seen historians change the meaning of the name Tuath de Danans, which originally meant people of the God of Dan. (#179).

Keating "names of Ireland," he lists over 3 pages of names all relating to Dan or Don or Dun (#180), And the Bible corroborates that the tribe of DaN (H1835 דָּן) used their family name a lot (Jos. 19:47).

The Bible translations often translate words from their origin to something easier for us to understand. Sometimes, it's the phonetic sound or a guess at the phonetic sound and other times, it goes through a whole host of changes before we get it. Like Samaria, where the Hebrew is Shomĕ' r own (h8111 שֹׁמְרוֹן), — Experts agree "we are absolutely and entirely in the dark about how those names may have sounded back then link.

"Experts don't even know how the name of God should be pronounced יהוה YHVH or YHWH (H6068 #343), Yahwey h3050 even the name Jesus was not the name that was used by the Apostles, but is a Greek translation of Joshua, (note14) but by analyzing the ancient Hebrew as we can discern trends and characteristics that help us with the possible pronunciation.

Oh, Danny Boy, the pipes, the pipes are calling From Glen to Glen and down the mountain side the summer's gone, and all the roses falling. It's you, It's you, must go, and I must bide. But come ye back when summer's in the meadow Or when the valley's hushed and white with snow I'll be here in sunshine or in shadow.

Oh Danny Boy, oh Danny Boy, I love you so, but if you come, and all the flowers are dying, and I am dead, as dead I well may be.

You'll come and find the place where I am lying And kneel and say an 'Ave' there for me.

And I will know, tho' soft ye tread above m. And then my grave will richer, sweeter be. And you'll bend down and tell me that you love me. And I will rest in peace until you come to me!

Yes, the Hebrew word for Danite is Daniy (Jdg. 13:2), and God does remember you, Danny Boy; you are not forgotten, completely nor where you came from, and yes, you played the pipes just as you did centuries before for King David and Solomon (1Kin. 1:40), And all the people came up after him, and the people piped with pipes, and rejoiced with great joy so that the earth rent with the sound of them…a company of prophets coming down from the high place with a psaltery, and a tabret, and a pipe, and a harp, before them; and they shall prophesy (I Sam. 10). And again, when a King is ordained and on a Holy day to God.

Yes, Danny boy, I know where you got your talent from, for Gold and textiles and music, and literature, (Exo. 38:23). It is the great gifter Elohim (h430◌ֱ אלהים 'Elohiym), and with him was Aholiab, son of Ahisamach, of the tribe of Dan, an engraver, and a cunning workman, and an embroiderer in blue, and in purple, and in scarlet, and fine linen. Is it possible the Scots Irish got the son of O'liab and is a mach, i.e., "mac" and "o" = son of, from these names? Mach is a fairly common name in the bible. We will cover some more terms like this shortly.

Do you think God had plans for the tribe of Dan? I think so! As we have discovered, the term Tuatha de Dan (TDD) was what the monks called the Hebrew Tribe of Dan – later, writers added Dana, i.e., Tribe of the Goddess Dana; this is clearly incorrect. A simple look at all the Irish place names from Keating Foras reveals no Celtic Goddess names! The closest I can find is in the B's and then in the M's. The name Danann, as a Goddess name, shows only once and then it says it's in reference to the daughter of the TDD. Surely, if this is the name of a Goddess, there would be many place names to back it up; instead, I find the following place name.

Dun, a hill fort, a fortified dwelling; common in place names; word identical in French and in Irish. The French word dune, a sand heap on the sea coast, corresponds to Spanish and Italian Duna, Latin dunum, Greek δοῦνον (dounon); dunum is, according to Buchanan, a Gaulish word, and is cognate with English down, Hist. Scot. lib. I.,p. 67. – Let's remember that God instructed Jeremiah to set up high heaps – Duns, a very common name in Ireland.

Keating does not directly list Donegal (Dan-Eagle) and speak of its origin but lists many names that flow into the Donegal Bay. He also lists 3 Donnghal as being notable people (p445 Foras Feasa); anyhow, the point I am making here is that I find no references from the start of the Dan's (p437-452) through to the finish with Dan's Don's and Dun's with nothing notable relating to a female deity. And if they venerated her, wouldn't a monument or namesake remain in the land?

They do say that 'Dan = 'craft, also spoken of in the Bible and a subject I have already covered, i.e., that Dan was a great craftsman. They also list Danann, female chief of the T. D. D., no doubt identical with Danann, da. Of Dealbhaoth. – yet no actual monuments to speak of?

Keating does reference Dania, Dane's Island, Danes Northmen, Denmark. Danair, etc. Dainfhir; used for the Danes or natives of Dania or Denmark, meaning mark of Dan, of which it is said was the origin of the name, in other words, the People of the God of Dan!

The name Armagh (pronounced Armor or ar ma) is said to be over 6500 old, there is the county of Armagh as well as the town Armagh. The name is said to be from Ard Mhacha, meaning "Macha's height" or "Macha's twins" It is where the fort of Navan (*Eamhain Mhacha*) stood, a fortified encampment. Armagh, Maghera. Gods double camp or twin camp, was called, macha'neh (see Genesis 32:2). When Jacob saw them, he said, "This is God's camp (H4264)." And he called the name of that place Macha'n'ayim (macha' name, double camp). It completely seems to line up in Hebrew and Gaelic.

We also have a similar sounding name, Armour; they sound the same; however, one means strong encampment in Hebrew the other means strong shield. The term for shield in Hebrew is Magen; it would not be difficult to see how ard Magen would change in just a few years to Arm'ghen and later to Armor. The earliest use of the name is said to be the family name of Gwydo le Armerer in Oxford Shire in the 11th century.

Aonach Macha, Fair-Green of Macha, around Navan Fort near Armagh, again the Hebrew Macha'neh can mean army. (#p385 Keating HofI) **Ard Macha, Eibhear**, s. of Tighearnmhas, sl. Conmhaol.

Cairche, Plain of, v. **Machaire** Chuircne. (Macha'neh means encampment or army and is used 216 times in the Bible).

Crioch Chonaill, al. Conaille Muirtheimhne, **Machaire** Chonaill, **Magh** Muirtheimhne, and **Machaire** Co. Louth minus the bar. Of Lr. **Dun**dalk between Carlingford Lough and **Dun**dalk Bay, Au.

I see many pages of place names, starting with Magh and some with Maghain. It appears that the name magh is from macha'neh as identified with Armagh, but is it possible that some of the magh's or magh variants come from mag(h)en, meaning shield as in that of the ecclesiastical capital of Ireland during the 5th century AD and possible for much longer.

The Hebrew word Ard meaning subdue, i.e., strong, tough, hard or impenetrable (#307 hard), and the Hebrew word macha'neh H4264 meaning army or encampment, so Ard Macha'neh, meaning hard (strong) encampment (Num 26:40)And the sons of Bela were Ard H714, The standard of the camp H4264 of Dan shall be on the north side by their armies: and the captain of the children of Dan shall be Ahiezer the son of Ammishaddai (Num 2:25).

Abraham magen #307) – Magh'an, 'the Plain,' (h4043מָגֵן

May Hill, in the eastern part of the Saunderson demesne, Co. Cavan, there is a hill though the surrounding country is level, hence the name May Hill (Lloyd G. 3. No. 126°, p. 60); a limit of Meath. Again, the abbreviated form Magh was a very popular place name, and it's where we get Armagh from (#307, see the next section), but Maghan appears to point to the Magen (shield) of the Bible(#6,7).

And remember the Jewish article stating that the Jews spoke Gaelic and Ard-Ban-Eas means high white (lbn-laban) waterfall.

We have already covered the fact that the Tuatha De Danaan were known by the monks as the Hebrew tribe of Dan.

In the Bible, the tribe of Daniy gave their name to many places that were sometimes referred to as macha'neh Dan (h4264 in PTOLEMYS MAP OF IRELAND c 140 AD the Camps of Dan). We remember that God instructed Jeremiah to set up high heaps, i.e., road signs, symbols, and names that point to our origin. Dan's symbol was their name. In Ptolemy's map of Ireland, we find Dan'-Lough, Dan-Sowar, Dan-Sobairse, Dan's resting place, Dan's habitation, and Dan-gan Castle (the birthplace of the Duke of Wellington).

Danslaugh,' '**Dan**sower,' '**Dun**dalke,' '**Dun**drum,' '**Donegal**

Bay,' (Don-Eagle) City,' '**Dun**glow,' 'Lond**on**derry'.

Based on all the place names of Ireland, it is clear that Dan is the name of the 'Tuatha de Dan.' I just don't see any place names like Danann anywhere, but just as they have always done,

Dan did name places after their father, and yes, they retained their roots, and yes, they are Hebrew.

Dan ability to work in Gold, Silver and Fabrics

God records, 'Send me now, therefore, a man cunning to work in gold, and in silver, and in brass, and in iron, and in purple, and crimson, and blue, and that can skill to grave with the cunning men that are with me in Judah and in Jerusalem, whom David my father did provide (2Ch. 2.7-14). And now I have sent a cunning man, endued with understanding, of Hiram, my father's. The son of a woman of the daughters of Dan, and his father was a man of Tyre, skillful to work in gold, in silver, in brass, in iron, in stone, and in timber, in purple, in blue, and in fine linen, and in crimson; also to grave any manner of graving, and to find out every device which shall be put to him, with thy cunning men, and with the cunning men of my lord David thy father.

The Tuath de Dan did have fine skills, but what about their world-renowned unusual Celtic designs? Did they come from Israel?

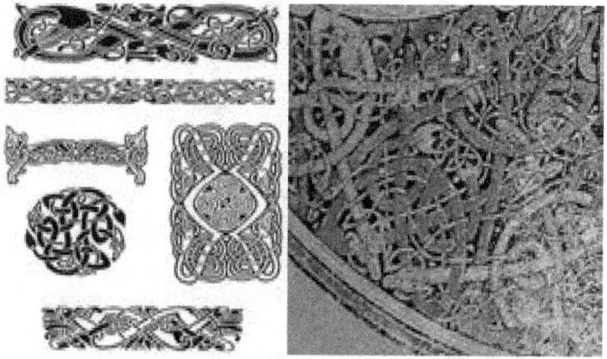

Celtic artwork that uses snakes.

Much of the Celtic artwork has similar patterns to these. If we look closely, we can discern a trend, and almost always, the spirals and swirls will start a one point and finish with the head of a snake. Now, it's amazing that Ireland has so many designs of this nature and, at the same time, no snakes. However, there is a simple explanation for this, and it points to their origin, the Hebrew tribe of Dan, whose main national symbol is the snake and the eagle; secondary symbols are the horse along with the scales, and as we know, the sign for a judge's or a balanced verdict is scales, which snakes have on their skin (Gen. 49.16).

It has always been the Israelite tradition that when sick or injured, he goes to the Kohen Godol high priest (Godel-Godheal H1431) for healing because he was God's representative on erets (earth). This obviously started with Moses, and the symbol of God's Healing was (and is) the snake on a stick; when we look at Ireland's symbols for a doctor, they are below.

Snakes in Ireland?

Again, more Celtic snakes; it is said that St Patrick drove all the snakes from Ireland. Somehow, I don't think so; I see a bunch right here! And there is new evidence to support my premise that Ireland never had snakes, and therefore, the snake emblem of the Irish came from elsewhere! Yes, it came from their roots, their tribal symbol given in Egypt (Gen. 49) and during the wandering in the desert.

And Moses made a serpent (H5175) of brass, and put it upon a pole, and it came to pass, that if a serpent had bitten any man when he beheld the serpent of brass, he lived (Num. 21:9).

Who led thee through that great and terrible wilderness, wherein were fiery serpents, H5175 and scorpions, and drought, where there was no water; who brought thee forth water out of the rock of flint (Deu. 8:15).

He removed the high places, and brake the images, and cut down the groves, and break in pieces the brazen serpent H5175 that Moses had made: for unto those days the children of Israel did burn incense to it: and he called it Nehushtan (2Kin. 18:4), yes we always seem to corrupt everything.

The Number Three

The Irish have an affinity with the number 3, and it would appear that God also does as he mentions the word or phrase 485 times. One interesting reference is that God says, when he has destroyed the nation in whose land he is giving you, (Deu. 19:7,9, Num. 35:14). Set up 2x 3 cities centrally located and build a road to connect the cities, this would form a triangle, we would have two of them, one triangle in Samaria (home r own) and one in Judah note the star of Da'vid is said to be the two groups of sanctuary cities with their roads on top of each other around the protective circle. God said to divide them into three parts and consider them cities of refuge (as opposed to the cities of refuse, which is what today's sanctuary cities are; this is a despicable and abhorrent, flagrant violation of God's laws) as a place not for a penal colony but to protect the innocent person who accidentally does harm to his fellow man, it does not say it's a place for the illegal alien or person from another country that may enjoy the goodness of God, protection and health care in your country, this is not what a biblical sanctuary city is all about (Num. 35:14).

The Isle of Man would be a perfect place for this, as it is centrally located and has natural protection. Little is known about the ancient history of the Isle of Man, but its name and symbol suggest this might well be the origin of the name. While in the rest of Britain, birching was abolished in 1948, the Isle of Man still had strict stick laws, i.e., birching for theft! I remember my schooldays, we could get the cane (Cain) for committing an infraction, it was a great deterrent. The Isle of Man, with its ancient symbol of three legs, & three main cities, Douglas, Ramsey and Peel, all connected by roads that form a triangle, seem to fit the blueprint. In Hebrew, the term a Man h538-542 means to go to the right, to take the right road, be faithful, true, moral, trusty, a father and a good workman.

So, the Isle of a Man would be a sanctuary for good people who accidentally killed someone.

There are many other examples of God using the number 3, which was important in the Bible. Also, we can see from the numbers the tribal camps were in groups of three (Num. 2), and Dan was arranged with Asher and Naphtali, then Ephraim, Manasseh and Benjamin, then Judah, Issachar, Zebulun then Reuben, Simeon and Gad.

Cord of three strands, Ecc. 4:12 And if one prevails against him, two shall withstand him, and a threefold cord is not quickly broken. Three days to purify and get ready to meet your maker, Exo. 19:11 and be ready against the third (H7992) day: for the third day, the LORD will come down in the sight of all the people upon mount Sinai. of the one true God, whereas 7 is said to be spiritual perfection (#288). Isle of Man – three legs, three legs of Israel x 4 spokes. The Triskele, or symbol of three, is written into the Celtic cross. See the next section.

Cross of Jesus, ancient Israelite and the Celtic cross

After we left Egypt and crossed the Red Sea, God had us set up in a specific way: we were to congregate in groups of three. Not only were we to assemble in the form of a cross, but we also were told to assemble around the tent of meeting (Num. 2.2) where the ark was kept, and there was in addition to this the tabernacle of meeting a Meeting of the minds, which Moses set up outside the camp so that people could seek the lord and enquire of Moses and have a meeting of the minds (Exo. 33:7).

Celtic cross with lion, ox, man and eagle courtesy Carole Tyrrell

We have already covered the tribes, symbolized by the Lion-Judah, the Man-Reuben, the Eagle-Dan and the OX or Unicorn (wild Ox)-

Most people are aware that the 7th day is a special number. We see that God rested on the seventh day and sanctified that day and called it the Sabbath, but when a person is unclean from touching a dead body, he must wash himself twice, first on the third day and again on the 7th day -(Num. 19:12) he shall purify himself with it on the third day, and on the seventh day he shall be clean: but if he purifies not himself the third day, then the seventh day he shall not be clean.

Three times in the year, all thy males shall appear before the Lord GOD (Exo. 23:17. We have three days of darkness in Egypt, while Israel stayed in their dwelling and had light (Exo. 10:22-23). So, God uses the number 3 very extensively throughout the Bible. Three is said to be divine perfection As in three aspects Ephraim, and in Numbers 2 the Israelites are to camp around the tent of meeting, some distance from it, and each under his Standards with the Banners of family, on the west was Ephraim, Manasseh and Benjamin, four legs, with three tribes in each leg moving toward the center (see pictures above).

The "Celtic Cross" is known as a pagan sun cross. Or is it really Hebrew? Where does this circle come from? We can see from the pictures the arms of the 'Celtic cross' skinny before reaching the center. Could there be an answer in the Bible? Guess what? The answer is an astounding yes. In Numbers 2, Israel had to be kept a distance from God. If a child or an inquisitive person were to get touch-feely, it could be disastrous. The Ark of God was made of shittim wood (Deu. 10:3). We Israelites would start to know that and fear and respect God.

- Psa. 19:9 — The fear of the LORD is clean, enduring forever: the judgments of the LORD are true and righteous altogether.
- Psa. 111:10 -The fear of the LORD is the beginning of wisdom: a good understanding have all they that do his commandments: his praise endureth forever.
- Pro 1:7 — The fear of the LORD is the beginning of knowledge: but fools despise wisdom and instruction.
- Pro 8:13 — The fear of the LORD is to hate evil: pride, and arrogancy, and the evil way, and the forward mouth, do I hate.
- Pro 9:10 — The fear of the LORD is the beginning of wisdom, and the knowledge of the holy is understanding.
- Pro 14:26 — In the fear of the LORD is strong confidence: and his children shall have a place of refuge.
- Pro 14:27 — The fear of the LORD is a fountain of life, to depart from the snares of death.
- Pro 15:33 — The fear of the LORD is the instruction of wisdom, and before honor is humility.
- Isa 33:6 — And wisdom and knowledge shall be the stability of thy times and strength of salvation: the fear of the LORD is his treasure.

The Book of Kells

The Book of Kells has been dated back to somewhere around 800AD. It is a mystery for most people as it has on its front cover 4 emblems; what are they? Here is what the BBC found:

Book of Kells

'This book contains the harmony of the Four Evangelists according to Jerome, where for almost every page there are different designs, distinguished by varied colors. Here, you may see the face of majesty divinely drawn, here the mystic symbols of the Evangelists, each with wings, now six, now four, now two; here the eagle, there the calf, here the man and there the lion, and other forms almost infinite.' Link — Well, I think by now you know what the "Book of Kells" really represents: an ancient Celtic document that clearly understands the riddle of Numbers 2, the living creatures of Revelation and Ezekiel, i.e., the symbols of the four lead tribes of Israel. Not convinced that the ancient Celts had knowledge that we don't seem to possess today.

Could it be that history and knowledge have been hidden from us or perhaps changed? How about the Celtic cross? It's a pagan symbol of a sun God and Christianity. This is wrong, as we are now finding out that the earliest known crosses of this nature are called Pictish stone crosses. It's a type of monument, a stele, and is considered a mystery and is thought to be from 600AD. Clearly, it cannot predate the crucifixion, can it?

We evidently know the symbol of the cross does predate the crucifixion and indeed points to us to our roots, but is there evidence that shows the Celts had it before Jesus was crucified?

In Hallstatt, Germany, resides one of the oldest collections of Celtic artifacts circa 600 BC and guess what? Here we find Celtic crosses (Link). But where or how did we get the circle around the cross? Let's go to Iona (meaning dove in Hebrew). It is the place where the Irish monks are said to have written the Book of Kells and where many, many Irish and Scottish kings are said to be buried.

We have detailed depictions of the Celtic cross, with the additional Man, Eagle, Lion and Ox. But what is the circle, and why does the cross have skinner legs as it gets into the circle?

The inner circle was comprised of Levite priests as protection because God wanted to protect his people from his wrath and violating his personal space; God had warned Israel to stay well back, 1000 yards from the ark of the covenant. God instructed the Levites to create a buffer zone, no one except the Kohen's (Priest) were to come close to God (except the Sabbath and special occasions). And even the Kohens get fired when they break the rules! We are Israel, brothers and sisters. Believe me, it's true.

Milesian

After the Tuath de Danan's, the next and last conquerors of Ireland were the Milesians; the Chronicles universally say they came from Spain; this can be found in Ogygia, by O'Flaherty, Keating's General History of Ireland or The Annals of the Four Masters. Etc.

The Tuatha de Dan came to Ireland around 1200 BC. As I have stated before, 'The People of the God of Dan'(L1) (Tuath de Dan), based on language, culture, artifact place names etc., were Israelites, and the ancient monks identified them as such. It was not until the Middle Ages that this started to change (5th to the 15th century). Also worthy of note is the fact that St Patrick (#218) came to Ireland around 570 AD. Patrick was not the first one to bring Catholicism to Ireland; he appears to have been predated by 80years by Palladius. Patrick destroyed monuments, books and much of the Druid history of ancient Ireland, making it harder for us to piece together the true story. It is said that St Patrick destroyed the pagan monuments and history, but as we are finding out, the ancient origin of the Emerald Isle was Hebrew, and while the Danites did worship pagan deities, much of the Island did "keep the faith"!

Again, remember that St Patrick cleared house. Is this the reason why most of the ancient books are missing? Clearly, any pre-

Christian history would be considered pagan, and as discussed earlier, even today, the Celtic cross is considered a pagan symbol, but as we now know, it is, in fact, Hebrew! Unfortunately, Patrick was not the only one who tried to destroy history years later when Cromwell attacked Ireland; he also cleared houses by burning books; this is a process that has gone on throughout history. The conquerors always want to get rid of the evidence and rewrite history. We can see this old as the human race; Satan has deceived the whole world, and this is, in part, how he does it by rewriting history and getting the powers that be to offer up false histories and realities.

It is generally considered that the Milesians came to Ireland around 1000 BC. I am not convinced that this was the date; I think it was probably closer to 580 BC (#345, 251), and as previously mentioned, it is generally pointed out that they came from the area of the Ebro river in Hispania, (Ibri h5680 and Eber h5677).

While in Spain, the Milesians experienced a drought, a severe shortage of water, perhaps crops were failing, cattle dying etc. and as a result, they started to look for an alternative location to live. They then remember the prophecy that they were to go to the British Isles. Was it the white cliffs of Dover (the first visible sign of Britain) that prompted this thought?

A spacious land of milk and honey (#234), this is an idiom for a land with great prospects as Great Britain was (and perhaps still is) as America is today; these locations were the most desirable places to be in the world, America still is, and the lands of milk and honey (Exo. 3:8) and Great Britain is perhaps a close second?

Here we have the poem Innisfail by Thomas Moore, written in 1810. They came from a land beyond the sea, And now o'er the western main in the US with the statue destruction, not dissimilar to

Nazi Germany and their persecution and destruction of all things Jewish, including their books.

Liberalism is not satisfied with equal opportunity under the law; they want to control everything; we can see this today with the way the top levels of the FBI and politics are polarized and completely biased. We can see the way they want to take God out of creation; Darwinism it is a trend that is as

Innisfail by Thomas Moore 1810

Set sail, in their good ships, gallantly,
From the sunny land of Spain.
'Oh, where's the isle we've seen in dreams,
Our destined home or grave?'*
Thus sung they as, by the morning's beams,
They swept the Atlantic wave.
And lo, where afar o'er ocean shines
A sparkle of radiant green,
As though in that deep lay emerald mines,
Whose light through the wave was seen.
'Tis Innisfail — 'tis Innisfail!'**
"We were dreamers like Joseph."
Rings o'er the echoing sea;
While bending to heaven, the warriors hail
That home of the brave and free.
Then turn'd they unto the Eastern wave,
Where now their Day-God's eye
A look of such sunny omen gave
As lighted up sea and sky.
Nor frown was seen through sky or sea,
Nor tear o'er leaf or sod,
When first on their Isle of Destiny
Our great forefathers trod.

Innisfail = The Island of Destiny, one of the ancient names of Ireland 'Milesius remembered the remarkable prediction of the principal Druid, who foretold that the posterity of Gadelus should obtain the possession of a Western island (which was Ireland and Britain), and there inhabit.' -Keating.

Is it possible that this 'Mile' was of Hebrew origin? We have already shown the Greek Phoenician connection as well as the Miletus–Hebrew connection. We have also shown the Danite origin for the Tuath de Dan, who, according to the historians of Ireland (O'Flaherty), were brothers, i.e., spoke the same language, and we see that the Milesians carry a banner, the Serpent of Moses (i.e.) on a stick, along with the Red hand which later became the Red Hand of Ulster (identified many times in the Irish Chronicles). It is said by some that the Milesians came from Brigante Spain, which is really Portugal or the north west area of Spain.

Ptolemy's map of Britain dated 140 AD shows Iber (Heber) and Brigante's place names, this is 800 or 1000 years later than the Milesian. I would surmise that in 1000-250 BC, these Brigante ports were used as staging areas for Tin (cassiterites), copper, lead, and iron ore that were traded out of Ireland and England. Cornwall, in particular, is said to have supplied King Solomon with tin (a necessary element for bronze) in order for Th'Ar(sh)ish (later, was it abbreviated to Irish?-h8659-region of the stone!) navy to supply.

A unique concentration in Phoenicia of silver hoards dated between 1200 and 800 BC, however, contains hacksilver with lead isotope ratios matching ores in Sardinia and Spain. This metallic evidence agrees with the memory of a western Mediterranean Tarshish that supplied Solomon with silver via Phoenicia, also, there are links to Cornwall (link).

Who were these Milesians, and where in Iberia did they really come from? I believe they came from Zaragoza (Aragon); it is said to mean the stronghold of Zerah (note 15); it's on the Ebro River. The name Ebro is a derivative of Eber, Aber; it was very common for the Israelites to name rives and places after their kinfolk, for instance, the river Thames that flows from Wales through Windsor Great Park, past Buckingham Palace and through the rest of London to the sea its etymology (original roots) was from Tamer, the founder of the Jews, and also the founder of the Irish kingly line.

In addition, please note that Brit'ain was the ancient name of the peoples of these Isles before the Angles, Saxons, Jutes, and Normans, and as we will soon point out, it is also Hebrew. Also, notice the river Tamar in Cornwall is adjacent to the ancient tin mining area, and no doubt was used to transport the minerals.

What's up with this bunch of heathens trying to use Hebrew names and customs all the time? Wait, maybe they are Hebrews (H5677). The Name Eber is first found in the Bible in Genesis 10:21. Why is this important? Well, he is one of our fathers! And it's where we get the name Hebrew, i.e., the region beyond, but as I have said before, the region is predominantly west, just as Abraham went west and the children of Israel predominantly went west. Another meaning is said to be across the sea (#225, #226). Also, is it significant that Joseph was set up on the west side when we marched through the desert of sin (zin Num. 2.18, 27.14)?

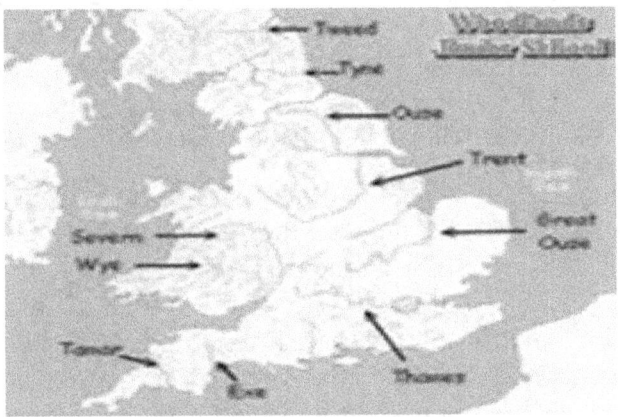

Now we are brought to a prophecy in the Bible, in Numbers 24:24: "And ships shall come from the coast of Chittim (singular means Island people), and shall afflict Asshur, and shall afflict Eber, (H5677), and he also shall perish forever" (Jer. 25.22). Chittim was Britain, as Identified in Daniel 11.30. The ships form the western coastland (or islands in the far west) and are the place of the holy covenant (Qodes Brit #13).

When was the Chittim prophesy fulfilled? — By 1000 BC (I believe), this event had already taken place. This era was essentially Israel's "Hay Day" when we had the United Kingdom of Israel, and our strength and power were at its zenith with Solomon during the reigns. The prophecy says that a group of Islanders shall afflict the Hebrews (i.e., Eber/Asshur) and subdue them, and then Israel strikes back and wipes them out.

I don't believe that Balaam (Bill) knew that Israel was also called Eber (Hebrews); rather, he spoke prophetically. As said earlier, Chittim means Island people in the far west, a group probably originating from Javan and many say that this and the name Tarshish was the British Isles's original name. And Chittim's tried to subdue Asshur and Eber, but they got more than they bargained for. Let us not forget that around 1000 BC, we can see that the United Kingdom's navy was Th'Ar(s)hish and got tin from England for King Solomon (#.13).

Back to the Milesians in Espana and the prophesy as stated by Keating — we are on the river Ebro, and a drought has afflicted the land. This is an area that is ruled by Jews, Zarhites to be exact. Their father's line parallels that of his bother Perez; they are looking for options. They remember that Eber (Ebro H5677-225,226) means go west to the Islands or region beyond the sea, do they remember the prophecy about the Islands having been taken by Israel?

Do they hear that their brother Dan (brother from another mother) is already on the Island, and they send a search-out party to investigate? This is exactly what the Irish chronicles say, the sons of Mil are Heber the fair, Amergin, Heber the brown, Colpa, Ir and Heremon (notice in this account there are two Eber's and one Ir, all Hebrew names (#293), and when the son of Mil arrives he is greeted and welcomed, apparently he asks to bring his family tribe and they say yes but later change their mind and use witchcraft against their brothers. (#344). It is said that Milesians came to Ireland between 950 BC to 450 BC #345.

How did Zerah get to Spain, and why and when did they leave the United Kingdom of Israel? Judah has two sons, Genesis 38.28 the twins in Tamar's stomach wrestled together, and one stuck his hand out and had a scarlet cord tied to it, the midwife saying this one came out first. After that, his brother came out, so he was named Perez (H6557), meaning breach.

When we look at the event surrounding Zerah's birth and the Breach performed by Perez, it became a hard-bitter pill for Zerah to swallow, and as we saw this prophesied in the section on Jeremiah, God was planning on healing the breach or overturning this event, and indeed this is exactly what happened. Therefore thou shalt say this word unto them; Let mine eyes run down with tears night and day and let them not cease: for the virgin daughter of my people is broken with a great breach, with a very grievous blow (Jer. 14:17).

The birth of Zerah occurred (Note 3,4) circa 1897BC, and we can see that the Zarhites get a black mark against their name in Joshua 7.1 Ac'han's (h5912 #330) in the son of Carmi, son of Zimri, son of Zerah. Israel was just starting their deliverance from the desert, wondering if they were about to inherit the promised land. They had paid their penance for disrespecting God, and God gave them a great victory over Jericho. They had specific instructions on how to handle things so that God could continue to bless them, but they cheated the lord; they stole from God.

The trouble was, nobody knew anything until they tried to take a small-town Al and Israel had to be whipped into shape. Israel sent 3000 men, and 36 of them were killed. It seems a very small number by today's standards, but it was huge for Israel. Their hearts melted, and Joshua cried to the Lord. The fear of the Lord is the beginning of wisdom; don't mess with the Creator; it will not turn out well for us, believe me. By casting lots, they discovered the sin. Achan had stolen things devoted to God and hidden them in his tent, and God had to purge the evil from among Israel; otherwise, it would spread like gangrene.

The whole of Israel was Ache'n (h5912 and h253 'ach #330); that day, our hearts were broken when we should have been rejoicing, but sadness gripped us. It's where we get the expression Are you Acha'n? Are you sore? Are you hurting?

In 1 Chronicles 2:6 it lists the sons of Zerah: 'And the sons of Zerah; Zimri, and Ethan, and Heman, and Calcol, and Dara: five of them in all,' and interestingly enough, Solomon's wisdom is also compared to these sons of Zerah, (1Kin. 4:31). "For he was wiser than all men; than Ethan the Ezrahite, Heman, Chalcol, and Darda, the sons of Mahol: and his fame was in all nations round about."

143

Who are these Ezrahites? They are the dancing (Mahol) and singing Ezrahites. Ezrahite (H250) is a patriotic name for Zerah, and two Psalms are attributed to these Zarhites; funny, their ancestor brought shame and contempt onto the name of God, and they are listed as bringing glory and honor to God!

The name Zarhites (H250 #221) is linked to a root that means to secretly hide, with love and affection; yes, God leaves clues everywhere. There is nothing hidden that will not be disclosed (#222), and when we add this with the etymology of where they went, Britain and London (#299), also meaning secret hiding abode (place), essentially with love and affection, makes perfect sense.

Please check out the two psalms from these brothers (Ps. 88 and 89). Here are some excerpts from Psalms 88: -

Psalm 89 (NIV) [a] A maskil[b] of Ethan the Ezrahite
1 I will sing of the LORD's GREAT LOVE FOREVER; with my mouth, I will make your faithfulness known through all generations.
2 I will declare that your love stands firm forever,
that you have established your faithfulness in heaven itself.
3 You said, 'I have made a covenant with my chosen one,
I have sworn to David, my servant,
4 'I will establish your line forever (Er-line, heir to the line.) and make your throne firm through all generations.''[c]
5 The heavens praise your wonders, LORD,
your faithfulness too, in the assembly of the holy ones...
18 Indeed, our shield[e] (Magen) belongs to the LORD, our king to the Holy One of Israel...
25 I will set his hand over the sea, his right hand over the rivers.
26 He will call out to me, 'You are my Father, my God, the Rock, my Savior.'
27 And I will appoint him to be my firstborn, the most exalted of the kings of the earth.
28 I will maintain my love for him forever, and my covenant with him will never fail.
29 I will establish his line forever
34 I will not violate my covenant
or alter what my lips have uttered.

35 Once and for all, I have sworn by my holiness— and I will not lie to David—
36 that his line will continue forever
and his throne endure before me like the sun;
37 it will be established forever like the moon, the faithful witness in the sky.'

From the Zarhites, we have two prophecies: 1st, that God will keep his promise to David (Ps. 89); 2nd, God will secretly hide something with love and affection (the etymology of the name #221).

Some of the Ezrahites did look for and find a location where they secretly hid away, and you have taken from me, friends, and neighbors (Ps. 88.18). Also, the sons and family of Shelah are not spoken of after Spanish names with the family name Perez, a Jewish surname and the eighth most popular name in Spain.

We can see that there was a large degree of disdain for the tribe of Zerah after Achar's be-trail, and this is when many Zarhites left Israel, 5 generations from Jacob – 1-Judah Tamar – 2-Perez Zerah – 3-Zimri – 4-Carmi – 5-Achar (Ache Jos. 7:1, 1 Ch. 2.7) circa 1406 BC. The Irish chronicles say the 4th generation (440 years) after the Exodus landed in Ireland (#290), but this does not appear to give enough time for their conquest and travels, as listed by Keating.

One account says it was 14 generations. This, to me, seems more correct. It is interesting to note that there is still a Jewish population in Zaragoza; by the end of the 15th century, the Jewish community made up 10% of the population in Zaragoza and 25% of Aragon. However, after the Spanish Inquisition, almost all Jews were systematically expelled from Spain, and much of their architecture was destroyed. Yet, despite all that, an endless amount of treasures has indeed survived (again, we see the destruction of artifacts and history, Satan trying to cover God's tracks).

What were the ships like during the earliest times — Phoenician ships 1500-300 BC had a capacity of 30-60 people, and so thirty ships leaving the Ebro River with a company of over 1000 people would be my guess. They undoubtedly left a remnant behind, as always happens even when Israel was taken into captivity or migrating.

As we have stated, the Irish chronicles say the Milesians, i.e., (the people of the prophesy H4395 mle'ah Mile'ah), came from the region of the Ebro River (#225). The chronicles also draw a connection between the Ebro River and Scythia, which we have shown is the area from where the later tribal waves (blowing a Gael) came (see section on Scythians for details).

Credit Tulum jungle gym

(Photo credited to Elie plus at en. Wikipedia)

Mr. O'Flaherty says the Milesians had ninety monarchs, which he has endeavored to support by thirty-nine citations, from

Heremon to Conary the Niul, father of Gaedheal Glas, who is said to be the father of Ireland (Ogygia p vi). Others say there were many more monarchs than that. Geoffrey Keating (p98), in his history of Ireland, talks about the Milesians 'the Gadelians must have come originally out of Greece because of the solemnity of the Gadelian triumphs, their sports, tilts and tournaments, and many other of their customs, bear a very near resemblance to the practice of the Grecians', he goes on to say this influence is from others Grecians that visit Ireland! Actually, I feel that the other writers were correct because their origin is Hebrew.

Is it possible that the Tailteann (Olympic p93) games are also Hebrew? Perhaps Jack was the one who started it? We know he was very athletic and was Jacked. No doubt they would have wrestling matches between the boys, play games, teach them to be tough etc., have some form of dumbbells and remember the Scot 'ish Highland Games. Toss the caber, tug of war, huge rock lifting contests, it's not hard to imagine these being done in Israel. The word to be firm and for power, strength etc., in Hebrew, is koach (H3581). It sounds like we have another Hebrew origin for a common everyday word we use, i.e., a coach.

We can see the Milesian capital was Tara and Northern Island was where the Ri Ard=high kings of Ireland Palace was along with the High Priest habitation. The Annals of Ireland calls the Milesian race holy men who are the ornaments of the Island (#251)

Original Names of Ireland

The following is taken from Keating's History of Ireland, Foras Feasa.

- **The first name that was given to Ireland was 'Inis na bhfiodhbhadh,** that is to say, Island of the woods (because it was all wooded).
- **The second name was 'Crioch na bhfuineadhach,** from its being at the limit or end of the three divisions of the world which had then been discovered; 'fuin' indeed, from the Latin word 'finis,' being equivalent to 'end. Remember, God commanded they split the land into three divisions (Deu. 19.1-3).

- **The third name was Inis Ealga**, said to mean Noble Island where Ealga=noble, but Eren is also a name for Ireland, which means eagle, that is, noble island, for 'inis' and 'oiléan' are equivalent, and likewise, 'ealga' and 'uasal': and it is during the time of the Firbolg it was usual to have that name on it.
- **The fourth name was Éire**, and it is said that wherefore that name is called to it, according to a certain author, is from the word 'Aeria,' which was an old name for the island that is now called Creta or Candia (sounds like another Hebrew name Canada); Keating goes on to say Gaedheal Glas (Ancestor of Mileadh) may have brought the name from Egypt to Ireland, and as I have suggested the name was given by the sons of Er of the red hand and scarlet cord i.e. the sons of Zerah who brought their fathers name with them.
- **The fifth name was Fódhla**, from a queen of the Tuatha Dé Danann, who was called Fódhla: it is the wife to Mac Cécht, whose proper name was Teathúr. There's Teathúr, Eathúr and Ceathúr seems to be a lot of Arthurs. Did they have a round table, too? Also, we have the ancient name of Ollam Fodhla, the wise old sage, who many have likened to Jeremiah.
- **The sixth name was Banbha**, from a queen of the Tuatha Dé Danann, who was in the land, who was called Banbha. We have a similar name in Hebrew bamahבָּמָה (H1116), which can mean sacred high place, ridge, or height. Keating also states that Magh-n-ealta (Moynalty, near Kells and Tara) was the only high plain cleared from the whole of Ireland at one point. Note that Magen means shield in Hebrew, and it is where we get Armor (Ard Magh-high shield #307) from. According to O'Flaherty, Banbha was the wife of Mac Cuill, whose proper name was Eathúr. He also says it means the Island was blessed and sacred (#6).
- **The seventh name was Inis Fáil,** and it is the Tuatha Dé Danann gave that name to it from a stone they brought with them, which was called the **Lia Fáil** and **'Saxum fatale,' i.e., 'Stone of Destiny,'** Hector Bocce in the history of Scotland calls it, "a stone on which were enchantments" for it used to roar under the person who was the rightful heir (Er) to the sovereignty of Ireland, at this time the men of Ireland would

assembly at Tara to choose a king over them. However, it has not roared from the time of Conchobar forward. Here is a verse of quotation proving that it is from this stone Ireland is called Inis Fáil, as Cionaoth the poet said: -

The stone which is under my two heels, from it is named Innisfail, Between two shores of a mighty flood, the plain of Fál on all Ireland.

Notice again that a plain or hill is mentioned, again supporting Tara (Ard Magh) as the location of the Kings, the Er line. It is quite feasible that, at one point, all these names refer to the same location. Tara, Ulster and Amour were the pinnacle seats of power and kingship in Er'land. With Tara being the principle site that was later moved, when the kingship moved to Scotland as commerce and development ensued. Not unlike Israel, where we have Bethel being the principal place of the stone (cornerstone), Jacobs's pillar stone was later moved to Jerusalem and the temple.

- **The eighth name was Muicinis**, and it is the children of Míleadh who gave it that name before they arrived in it. When, indeed, they had come to the mouth of Innbhear Sláinghe, which today is called the haven of Lochgarman, the Tuatha Dé Danann, with their druids, assembled to oppose them there, and they practiced magic on them so that the island was not visible to them but in the likeness of a pig, so it is. Therefore, they gave (the name) Muicinis to Ireland. I must refer back to bamah (בָּמָה H1116) as this name also means hogs back in Hebrew, as in the shape of a hill (Note19).
- **The ninth name was Scotia**, and it is the sons of Míleadh who gave that name to it from their mother, whose name was Scota, daughter of Pharaoh Nectonibus (Necho?), or it is why they called it Scotia, because that they are themselves the Scottish race from Scythia.

It's clear there is much confusion for these writers to figure out why this name exists and other names of Ireland for that matter, but as I have stated, it becomes very clear where these Hebrew names are from. Also, I didn't know the Egyptians were from Scythia, but later migrations of Hebrews did come from Scythia. It's where the remnant of the ten tribes was deported to, i.e., the Assyrian captivity. I speak to this later.

In addition, O'Flaherty says Scotus and Scotia were used interchangeably (p. 35). Note Pinnacle of power in the United States is also known as Scotus — it stands for Supreme Court of the United States, just another strange co-incidence, right!)

- **The tenth name was Hibernia**, and it is the sons of Míleadh gave that name to it. However, it is said that it is from a river that is in Spain, which is called Iberus, i.e. Hibernia is given to it. It is also said that it is from Eibhear, son of Míleadh; it is called Hibernia... (This is exactly where the Zarhites, sons of Zerah, had settled by the River Eber and Zaragossa. In Spain, the names Eibhear, Iberus, Iuernia and Hibernia are all derivatives of Eber, where we get Hebrew. Remember earlier, we have the prophecy of the Abrahamic covenant, I will make the name great, he was the first Hebrew (Gen. 14.13)

- **The eleventh name was Iuernia**, according to Ptolemy, or Iuerna, according to Solinus, or Ierna, according to Claudian, or Vernia, according to Eustatius. I think there is no meaning in the difference which is between these authors concerning this word Hibernia, but that they did not understand whence came the word itself; and, accordingly, that each one of them separately gave a guess from himself at it, so that from that came this variation on the word. See the Pomponius Mela map. It shows that Ireland was known as Juverna circa 45ad (I agree this is a derivation of Erber, Eber Heber'nia; it also points to the Judah connection to the Island, i.e. Juvernia Jew-eberna).

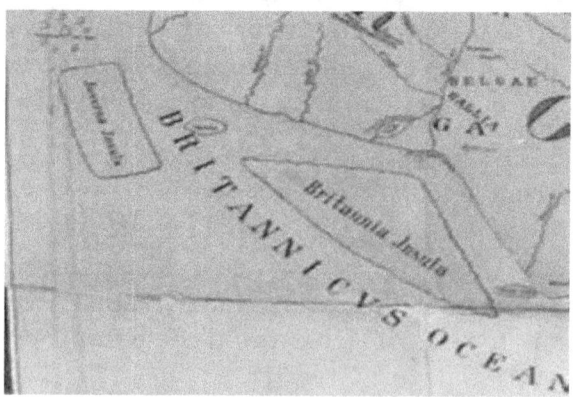

- **The twelfth name was Irin,** according to Diodorus Siculus. In Camden's Britannia (p.963), he gives a quotation from Postellius' lectures on Pomponius Mela, a first-century (Roman cartographer) writer. Ireland was called Jurin, quasi Jews' land, because in the distant past, the Jews (sic), who were great soothsayers(prophetic), knew that the future empire of the world would come to these parts (#366). The Syrians and the Tyrians did the same. In other words, Phoenician-Israelites were the original colonists (#306). *My comment now — It does appear that there is a hidden history of Ireland that has been covered up. A Roman Cartographer, with no known axe to grind, labels Ireland as Juverna Insula (the Island of Jurin, i.e., Jews), clearly the Jews were the Kingly line, and they ruled over the Brit's, th'ar (sh)ish (Tharshish), the Danites, Ephraim, Manasseh and others. Ireland was also known as Britannia; even the ocean was known as the Britannia Ocean see section on the British national anthem, 'Rule Britannia'291.*

I don't see Jurin referenced in the Irish Annals, but then again, I don't see the origin of the name 'Irish' detailed in the Irish annals and even in this section, no mention of the origin of the name Irish, i.e.,,, people of Er (h6147, h376).

- **The thirteenth name was Irlanda**, and I think that the reason why that name was given to it is that it was Ir, son of Míleadh, was the first man of the Clanna Míleadh who was buried under the soil of Ireland, and accordingly, the island was named from him: 'Irlanda' and 'land of Ir' being indeed equivalent, for 'land' in English, and 'fonn' or 'fearann' in Gaelic are alike. The truth of this thing is more admissible since the book of Armagh says that the name for this island is Ireo, that is to say, the grave of Ir, because that it is there is the sepulcher or grave of Ir. Now, these are not my words. These are words straight from Keating, so the name Er is the origin of the name Er'land (Ireland).

- **The fourteenth name was Ogygia,** according to Plutarch: 'Ogygia' in Greek and 'insula perantiqua,' i.e., 'most ancient island,' are equivalent, and that is a suitable name for Ireland because it is long since it was first inhabited, and that perfect is the sound information which its antiquaries possess on the transactions of their ancestors from the beginning of eras, one

151

after another. O'Flaherty calls it a "sacred or holy island" (#246).

Clearly, almost all of these references point to the Hebrew origin of Ireland. Even Camden's Britannia (p.34) states so, although he uses a different Hebrew word, and this word is Iy, i.e. Isle (H336).

Origin of the name "Irish"

We have just covered what Ireland was called before its current name, IRISH, and IRELAND; this name comes from Old English Iras "inhabitant of Ireland." from Old Norse irar, from Old Irish Eriu (accusative Eirinn, Erinn) "Erin," from Old Celtic *Iveriu (accusative *Iverionem, ablative *Iverione), when we look at the proposed original names we see – Irish

From the following list, we can see item 3 Inis Ealga=Island of Eagla, said to mean noble island, but could it mean Eagle Island? The name eagle comes from Erne, Welsh eryr, from Possible Eire (5) and Irin (13)

1) Inis, 2) Crioch na bhfuineadhach, 3) Inis Ealga, 4) Éire, 5) Fódhla, 6) Banbha, 7) Inis Fáil, 8) Muicinis, 9) Scotia, 10) Hibernia, 11) Iuernia, 12) Irin, 13) Irlanda, 14) Ogygia.

Irish — The etymology of this name is vague. When we looked through the names of Ireland, it was not directly listed, however, eymologyonline.com lists that it is from Old Celtic *Iveriu. We can see this name from Pomponius Mela map, some relate it to Juvern, possibly related to the Jews?

But it appears that there were indeed multiple names for Ireland. The one that stuck is Ir, whether it comes from Er, the father of the Jews since Judah became his surrogate (Gen 38, Job 41, Heb 12-13), or Iver, as in Hibernia, also in forms **Iverna**, Juverna, Ierne, wish is a name alive in Inverness, Aberwristwith, along with the Hebrides, and the Iberian Peninsula, and remember the Eber river. These names all connect to Eber (H5699 עֵבֶר 'Êbêr, ay'-ber); The Ayin can take any vowel (see English is Hebrew alphabet section).

Consider also the name th'arsh'ish (h8659, n.8) that it speaks of the region of the stone! And as we discovered from the names of Ireland, the seventh was Inis Fáil, i.e. Region of the Stone! What an amazing coincidence. Not only do the Arish, the arsh'ish have all the hallmarks of the tribe of Dan and Er (Judah), but they also venerate a sacred stone! "Lia Fail" is the stone of destiny, aka Jacob's pillarstone!

Consider also the red hand of Zerah, and the star of David along with the crown and cross in the northern Iriahs flag.

Origin of the Name Gael and the Gaelic language

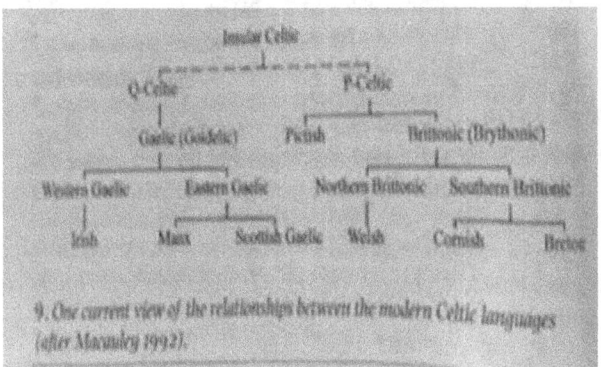

9. One current view of the relationships between the modern Celtic languages (after Macaulay 1992).

Gael (n.) origin Scottish Gaelic Gaidheal Old Irish Goidhel
(c

I think we are all familiar with the name Gael and Gaelic. It's what the Celts spoke, i.e., their language. Adjacent is one view of the Celtic language, and by looking at the following relationship map, we can see that we have on the one side the

Gaedheal (Godheal) — founder of the Celts

The Irish chronicles say that Gaedheal (#12) was the progenitor of the people of Ireland (Milesians). He came with Moses out of Egypt and crossed the Red Sea with him. He got bit by a snake in the desert and was told to go to Moses for healing, Moses (Num.

21.8) showed him the serpent on the stick and prayed for him, and he was healed. Is it a coincidence that his name is pronounced God Heal? I think not! Keating says the Mother of Gaedheal was the daughter of Pharaoh Cincris' grandson (see link and text below). Remember the story of Moses' birth in (Exo. 1-2), Pharaoh was trying to stop Israelite male babies from being born, and his daughter was childless and finding a baby in the reeds of the Nile, discovered Moses, Moses was the (alleged) grandson of Pharaoh (Irish chronicles Cincris) it is basically saying this person is Moses or Moses brother, and we know it can't be Moses (adopted) brother because he would be a firstborn and would have been killed, in the last plague. Also, Pharaoh Cincris was a Hyksos Pharaoh and came after the Exodus (#46, 126), so he cannot be the one.

> Others, however, say that the mother of Gaedheal was called Scota because his father was of the Scotic race from Scythia, and that it was their custom to call the women after their husbands. Understand that this is not the Scota who was wife of Galamh, who is called Milidh of Spain, and bore him six sons. For the mother of Gaedheal was daughter to Pharao Cincris; and it was he who held the children of

See how the histories are all a jumbled mess. I have the map and road signs that tell me their origin, so please bear with me while I untangle it!

Is it possible that the Hyksos kings were Israelites or Sidonians (who also were sons of Eber)? But whoever they were, the fact remains that they took control of Egypt after Pharaoh and his great army were wiped out and are not relevant to this discussion.

Gaedheal was not of Egyptian blood but Hebrew — Gaedheal is an altered form of a Hebrew word meaning 'great old man.' It's what a Hebrew would call Moses. Gaw-dowl (H1419) means great man of old age. We must remember that this occurred at the end of Moses' life (Num. 21); Aaron and Miriam had already passed away, and Moses got old (Gawd-owld #106). An interesting artifact was discovered in the barrows of Stonehenge, a druid (Priests) breastplate. This breastplate was made of gold and had inscriptions upon it; 'Cohen Gadol' (#200), which Cohen we recognize as Jewish (but actually, they are Levite). In the Bible, it means 'Priest' how about Gadol. Wikipedia says this was the title given to the high priests in early post-Exilic times, I would argue that it has always been his title, and that is where the Gaedheal comes from! And if one looks at the Hebrew Bible (Lev. 21.10) we can see they use it to specify the High Priest, who sits in the place of God on earth. Gaedheal was Moses! God's representative was the one who was commanded to heal the people in God's stead. Some might say that Aaron was the high priest, but he wasn't the boss; the boss was Moses and he was the one that God spoke to and that God healed through. It is true that Aaron was the stand-in High Priest.

In addition, there is another word that could tie heal to being of Hebrew origin (h3416) Yir'pel pronounced yir-p eel, like Yir p heal, from h7495 and h410; God will heal.

An important point is that some of the ancient Irish chronicles do identify the name with the Hebrew!

Now, it is disputed among authors whence is this word 'Gaedheal.' Becanus says that it is from the word goedin, that is, goethin, 'noble,' and from the word 'all,' that is, uile, that Gaedheal is named, that is, 'all noble'; or from the Hebrew word gadhal, meaning 'great,' (#379) because Gaedheal son of Eathor, the first who was called Gaedheal, was great in learning, in wisdom, and in the languages. However, the Seanchas say that he is called Gaedheal from the two words gaoith dhil, that is, 'lover of wisdom'; for gaoith means 'wise' and dil 'loving,' as the Greeks call a sage philosophos, that is, 'a lover of wisdom.' (FF Keating p97).

Clearly, the name Gaedheal refers to its Hebrew origin and we will soon discover who it was they were alluding to.

If the term Gaedheal is Hebrew, what does it mean? The progenitor to the Irish Nation was a high priest, the (Kohen Gödel) and the one who officiated the event. I think it is obvious that the Irish Annals corrupted the story by mixing up the details. In the Irish story, Gaedheal points to Moses as the person who set up Ireland, i.e., Gadowl, of course it wasn't Moses but someone like Moses. He is the true person who instituted Tara, the Law and healed the breach (Perez) in the kingly line of Ireland, he was not of Egyptian heritage but Hebrew, but who was he?

155

Elihana bat gael = Elihana daughter of Gael

Ancient seal found in admin building near the first temple. 'The seal, which is made of semi-precious stone, appears the mirror-image of 'Elihana bat Gael' written in ancient Hebrew letters (Proto-Hebrew circa 1000 BC),

Photo: Clara Amit, courtesy of Israel Antiquities Authority

Hebrew-Celtic language diverge

The Celtic language branched off over 2000 years ago, with one branch being P Celtic and the other Q Celtic. The Q Celts retained the name Gaelic, whereas the P Celts used the name Britan.

Gaelic (Q-Celts) and the other side, the Brittonics (P-Celts) בְּרִית- beˈrîyth H1262 identical in Hebrew בְּרִית the secret dwelling place of the Brits by God's grace protected by the eagle wings, symbol of God and Dan (#299, #366).

It appears that God had planned all along that Israel be hidden from view and that God will protect them from harm, with a natural border, and an identity that is hard to connect back to God, (see Eze 3.4-7, Gen 49.22, see Ref #396) The Name London, Etymologists don't know where this name stems I talk about this in "English is Hebrew"

Job 39:28 She dwelleth and abideth H3885 on the rock, upon the crag of the rock, and the strong place.
Psa 25:13 His soul shall dwell H3885 at ease, and his seed shall inherit the earth.

Psa 91:1 He that dwelleth in the secret place of the most High shall abide H3885 under the shadow of the Almighty.
Please read Ps25 and Ps 91. They tell of Yah Way's promise to the Brits.

I am not sure if you got that, Brit'am is the secret abode of the Covenant, people of God (Brit h1285, am h5971,Yah h3050), remember the patriotic song of the Brit'ish — Rule Britannia (#291). I must point out that all of England, Ireland, Wales, and Scotland were called Britain or Britannia, as seen in Ptolemy's map (140ad) below.

The large Island was called Alban Britannica (White House of Britons), and the smaller Island was called Britannica Insula (smaller land of Britons-Bryth ish).

How about Gael's (Q-Celts) in the Bible? Is there such a word, and would it have a significant meaning?

(Gen. 31:46,48,) In Genesis 46, "And Jacob said unto his brethren, gather stones; and they took stones, and made a heap: and they did eat there upon the heap...48 And Laban said, This heap [is] a witness between me and thee this day. Therefore was the name of it called Galeed (h1567);...52 This heap [be] witness, and [this] pillar [be] witness, that I will not pass over this heap to thee, and that thou shalt not pass over this heap and this pillar unto me, for harm.[a no-go zone, a deadline] This, along with many other references, means witness or heap. We know that Jeremiah's commission was

157

to set up waymarks high heaps (Jer. 31:21-h1567). We read about this in the section on Jeremiah, and here we have the testimony of success; Gael or Gaelic means heap or witness in Hebrew. How apropos is that! So the Gaelic language is a witness heap, the Gaels are a witness, what did God say to Jeremiah – (Jer. 31:21, Chap. 8), Set thee up waymarks, H6725 make thee high heaps H8564 (Tam-roor-erection), same as the Hebrew word Tamar (h8558): set thine heart toward the highway, even the way which thou wentest: turn again, O virgin of Israel, turn again to these thy cities. Even the actual name, Gael, was used in ancient Israel. And we are well aware that Tamar was as the river Thames and river Tamar in Devon near the ancient tin mining area. We are also aware that the High King's palace was called Tamar, Tea and Tara both being derivatives of Tamar.

CHAPTER 14 - Jeremiah in Ireland

We just finished the last Chapter by saying that the progenitor of the Irish is said to be Gaedheal, the person it speaks of, Pharaoh's son (adopted) was Moses, he was the Gaedheal of Israel, i.e., Kohen Godel (h1433).

Many people have looked for Jeremiah in Ireland, but they haven't found him in the ancient annals of Ireland. Let's take a close look at his name to see if God would give us any clues. The name Jeremiah in the Bible is called YirmĕyahH3414, which means Yah (h3050 #248 h7311 #247) will rise or lift up or 'Whom Yehovah has appointed'. When we look closely at Jeremiah's name, we can see that even his name means to lift up, to raise up, to build up and set up. So we can be sure that he did fulfill his mission, also, his scribe's name is Baruch (Bawra-Blessed in Hebrew and Celtic, see names of Ireland). Jeremiah is a transliteration of the Hebrew name, Yirm ᵉyâh think phonetics, how did it sound, yIrme yah sounds like "I'm here." God has a sense of humor, doesn't he? All this time, folks have been looking for Jeremiah in Ireland, and his name says, "I'm here." Okay, let's see if it's in the chronicles.

Milesian story summarized

Let's refresh the story, the Gaels were in a drought in an area of Spain perhaps by the Ebro River and modern-day Zaragoza.

According to the Irish chronicles, there is a drought in Iberia, and Ithel takes off for Ireland. He is warmly greeted in Ireland. They converse in the same language. They are brothers from another mother, and when he is about to leave, the Danites have a change of heart and ambush and kill him.

His general finds his body and goes back to Iberia (Eberland). The brothers and their Priest (EmHear) are summoned (some say the priest Emhear is also a brother), and they go back to Ireland and meet with the Danites (Tuatha de Danans), who agree to a dispute resolution with Emher (H3414 יִרְמְיָה yirmᵊyâ Jeremiah) speaking for all parties, they say they will allow them to settle on the Island, in the south but after departing back to their ships, the Danyi use witchcraft to drum up a storm and deceive the eyes of the

Milesian (Gaels), a few people are killed and the Milesians re-attempt to land their ships, this time in the Dingle peninsular.

In Kenmare, County Kerry, they land and fight the Danites on Sliabh Mis. The battle is fierce, and the sons of Mil fight to the last man, woman, and child. They defeat the Danites and are allowed to take possession of the Island. According to the story, Scota (Egyptian Princess?) is killed during the battle and is Immortalized on Sliabh Mis mountainside (#379). The Milesians Eiremhon (Eeremon), Eimhear (Emhear Jeremiah) and Amhergin, Am her gin-same name EmHear with Gin sometimes Fin or Phin (#295) on the end (centuries of storytelling can do this).

Tea is also with this group; she is married to Eremon, and then (as the story goes) Eremon and the Priest split Ireland between each other(#380).

There are various accounts similar to this; Heremon and Tea (Teamhear-Tamar) set up their kingdom at Tara, hence its name, Tara is a derivative of Tamar. Some say that Tara is from the Torah as the law was administered from Tara, but I think it's from Tamar as a short form would be Ta, Tea, Tia we also have TIARAH as in princess crown.

The good news here is that Jeremiah is in the chronicles of Ireland! What does the term Milesian mean?

Milesian etymology

The term "Mile" (Milesian's) is a title, with the real name being Galamh (an early form of Gwilliam?). The early settlers of Ireland were known as Mile, Male, Miled, Mílidh or Milesians, and they were the fulfillment of the prophesies that we have already covered. It would seem only fitting that their name would then speak of this. The name Milesian means fulfillment by God's grace (Milesians). We know that the name "Ian" is the Scottish version of Yon (John), and it means gift of God or God's grace, but what does Mil mean?

The terms Male, Milluah, Mleah, Millu, and Melo (h4390-4396 #252) all of which are derivatives of the term for something full, filling either literally or figuratively like a prophecy fulfilled or the setting of a stone! And we have both with the Milesians, fulfilling the prophesy and also making Ireland the setting for the stone!

Now we know that Jeremiah is listed in the Irish annals. He brought about the fulfillment of the prophecy to set up the kingly line in Ireland, healing the breach between Zerah and Perez, and as we will soon see, he inaugurated a practice that used a sacred and special Hebrew stone as its centerpiece.

How did Jeremiah get from Egypt to Ireland with the king's princesses?

What happened to Jeremiah is a mystery wrapped in an Enigma? The true story of where Jeremiah went is, for the most part, lost; even though some have found or seen the similarities between the Celtics and Israel, for the most part, their origin seems to have been lost to antiquity.

It is clear from scripture that much was concealed by God until the time of the end (Dan.12.9, these words are sealed until the time of the end), now God is now revealing his hidden secrets.

In Revelation 10, the Apostle John was told to seal up what the seven thunders have said, he is also told to eat the little scroll that was sealed until the time of the end. In verse 11, he is told it's about (NIV) many nations, languages, and kings (Eze. 3.1-6) seems to be what I am talking about here in the book, don't you think?

This story is about how God brought together Israel from many different nations, how we retained the roots of our language, and how God (through Jeremiah) set up the new kingly line that he promised. Again, our language roots being Hebrew/Phoenician to Greek/ Etruscan to Celtic/English. And the kingly line of Israel, with the vast array of nations that God has turned Israel into! Notice Ezekiel is asked to eat the little scroll that tastes sweet and is sent to the House of Israel, a people whose language is rooted in Hebrew, but why does it taste sweet with a bitter aftertaste? Finding God's word is true, and he keeps his promises is sweet.

God gave us these blessings because of the sacrifices of our fathers Abraham. Isaac, Jacob, David, and for his namesake, not because we deserve them; that's the "bitter-sweet truth of it all"!

The Bible story matches Irish History.

Now we are ready to look at the bible to see where Jeremiah went (Emhear). Believe it or not, the Bible does corroborate these events: –

Irish chronicles say Gaedheal (#12), came out of Egypt with Moses, and we did; we Israelites came out with Moses through the Red Sea. Later we also see a similar event where Egypt is under siege and about to be destroyed, and again, we have a kohen Gödel (Gaedheal) in charge of the kingly line leading people from Egypt.

The remnant of the Jews are in Tahpanhes (Jer. 43.8), and we know there were many Jews and Hebrews in Egypt, both in the upper and lower Nile region (Jer. 44.1). In Egypt, God identifies Migdol and Tahpanhes and the border city Memphis, along with Elephantine Island, these constitute four large Jewish / Hebrew settlement in Egypt.

What follows next are prophetic words from Jeremiah (Emhear); he is in Tahpanhes, Egypt, with the King's daughters and (apparently) the daughter of the pharaoh.

"As surely as I live," declares the King, whose name is the LORD Almighty, "one will come who is like Tabor among the mountains, like Carmel by the sea(Jer 46.18)."

19 Pack your belongings for exile, you who live in Egypt, for Memphis will be laid waste and lie in ruins without inhabitant.

20 "Egypt is a beautiful heifer, but a gadfly is coming against her from the north.

21 The mercenaries in her ranks are like fattened calves. They, too, will turn and flee together; they will not stand their ground, for the day of disaster is coming upon them, the time for them to be punished.

22 Egypt will hiss like a fleeing serpent as the enemy advances in force; they will come against her with axes, like men who cut down trees.

Let's take a look at this prophecy: God is identifying Tabor, mountains and Carmel by the sea. Tabor, root means fragile, and mountain means someone in high authority or lineage.

Carmel means fruitful, plentiful garden, could also mean vineyard. God appears to be referring to the fragile, potentially fruitful virgin of Israel, the king's daughters. And he wants her and Jeremiah to pack their bags and get ready for a trip. Egypt is about to be laid waste.

God appears to be identifying British mercenaries in her ranks (heifer and fatted calves and possibly Danites hissing snakes, although the king's headdress of ancient Egypt was a hissing cobra, so could be referring to an Egyptian princess?). He says a gadfly is coming. (nipping or stinging insect h7171)

The Mercenaries Phoenician/Hebrew conscripts may be there to assist Egypt against the invading army. Later, God makes clear he is sending a vast army against Egypt, Nebuchadnezzar, king of Babylon, and his officers. And God reassures the remnant in Jeremiah's hands, again in Jeremiah 46.

27 "Do not be afraid, Jacob my servant; do not be dismayed, Israel. I will surely save you out of a distant place, your descendants from the land of their exile. Jacob will again have peace and security, and no one will make him afraid.

28 Do not be afraid, Jacob my servant, for I am with you," declares the LORD.

"Though I completely destroy all the nations among which I scatter you, I will not completely destroy you. I will discipline you but only in due measure; I will not let you go entirely unpunished."

Again, we have the promise of peace and security in a place of safety where no one will make them afraid.

God is doing what he said, driving Israel to the ends of the earth where Ephraim and Manasseh (Ox-man, Egel'ish h5695 and H376 #296) will gore them with their horns (Deu. 33.17).

Eagle and a Vine

'The word of the Lord came to me: (Eze. 17). 2 'Son of man, set forth an allegory and tell it to the Israelites as a parable. 3 Say to them, 'This is what the Sovereign Lord says: A great eagle with powerful wings, long feathers, and full plumage of varied colors came to Lebanon' (H3844). Taking hold of the top of a cedar, 4 he broke off its topmost shoot and carried it away to a land of merchants, where he planted it in a city of traders; where is this city of traders?

The previous scripture reveals it is LuwnD'n, London and Ireland whose castle/hill fort was Tara (# 299, 344, 347); this is where the Zarhites are, along with the tribes of Dan, Ephraim and others. The whole of Britain was one nation!

5' 'He took one of the seedlings of the land and put it in fertile soil. He planted it like a willow by abundant water (the British Isles are certainly this), 6 and it sprouted and became a low, spreading vine (spread out around the world). Its branches turned toward him, but its roots (origins language) remained under it. So, it became a vine and produced branches and put out leafy boughs

22' 'This is what the Sovereign Lord says: I myself will take a shoot from the very top of a cedar and plant it; I will break off a tender sprig (Daughter of the king) from its topmost shoots and plant it on a high and lofty mountain. 23 On the mountain heights of Israel, I will plant it; it will produce branches and bear fruit and become a splendid cedar.

Birds of every kind will nest in it (multinational, not just Israel); they will find shelter in the shade of its branches. 24 All the trees of the forest will know that I, the Lord, bring down the tall tree and make the low tree grow tall. I dry up the green tree and make the dry tree flourish.

Let us review for a moment the previous prophecy in light of this new information: God identified Tabor, mountains and Carmel by the sea. Tabor, root means fragile, mountain means someone in high authority or lineage, Carmel means fruitful, plentiful garden and vineyard by the sea! God is speaking to the fragile, potentially fruitful virgin of Israel, the king's daughters and Great Britain! And indeed, us today.

This appears to have occurred after they picked Jeremiah up. We have the arrival of the Male's (Milesians-male-Er's), coming in from the Iberian peninsula and Brittany, and we have the arrival of princess and kohen Godel (Jeremiah Emher) coming from Egypt. God is clearly telling us and them what he was going to do.

Three overturns

Ezekiel has already confirmed where Jeremiah will take the tender twig, and now, he speaks about three overturns, it is in Ezekiel 21.25: 'You profane and wicked prince of Israel, whose day has come, whose time of punishment has reached its climax, 26 this is what the Sovereign Lord says: Take off the turban, remove the crown. It will not be as it was: The lowly will be exalted (the line of Zerah), and the exalted will be brought low. 27 A ruin! A ruin! I will make it a ruin! The crown will not be restored (In Jerusalem) until he to whom it rightfully belongs shall come; to him, I will give it.'

Three overturns, God prophesied that the line would have three overturns before the rightful heir (Er) came! The crown was taken from the old Britain to the new Britain and set up in Ireland. This the first overturn, the second one being the throne of Ireland to Scotland, and one more being the throne from Scotland to England, here it is again in the king James; (Eze. 21:27) I will overturn, overturn, overturn, it: and it shall be no more until he comes whose right it is; and I will give it to him. — We are very close to Christ's return!

God said I will watch over them to build and plant (Jer. 31.28), Ephraim's an unruly Calf, is not Ephraim my dear son in whom I delight, I have great compassion for him... set up road signs, put up guideposts, take note of the highway, the road you take return O Virgin Israel return to your towns (Jer. 31.18-21).

Because I am Israel's father and Ephraim are my first-born son. Hear the word of the Lord O nations; proclaim it in a distant coastland, he who scatters Israel and will gather them and watch over his flock like a shepherd. He who commands the sun and, moon, and stars will make it happen. Israel will never cease to be a nation before me! (Jer. 31.35-37 and Ps.19).

165

I know the plans I have for you to declare the Lord, plans to prosper you and not to harm you, plans to give you hope and a future! (Jer. 29.11), lest we forget, the Lord is the same yesterday, today and forever (Heb13.8). Believe it. Believe it, it's true!

The prophecy of Ezekiel 17 and Jeremiah tells us the story, and it matches the history of Ireland; not only does it tell us why we were driven, but where and how the Kingly line was brought to Britain and Ireland! God keeps his promises!

Red Right Hand

The red right hand is very prominent in Irish history. We have flags and memorabilia and history that reflect this, but it might surprise people to know it goes way back. It goes back to Judah and Tamar as we are learning, in Irish folklore, it is said there are a number of vague references to a hand Lughaidh Laimhdhearg (laim hearg), who is said to be of the Red right hand, perhaps 500BC?

We also have Nuad of the Silver Hand. Around 1000BC he was a Tuatha De Danann, and a search of the internet suggests he is immortalized in witchcraft circles. This is a fake history item and does not constitute the origin of the Red Hand of Ulster. The real story should be clear by now; the star of and harp of David, along with the sword of Goliath, the Eagle of Dan/God, the cross of Israel, the kingly crown and our language, these are signs some of the high heaps of Jeremiah, road signs of our past!

The Red Hand of Zerah (Ulster) is said to have had over 170 kings from Heremon through to Brian Boru, 1000AD.

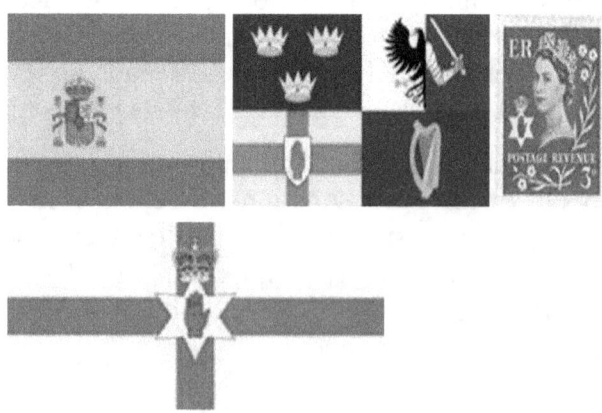

It is worth noting that the colors of Spain are almost identical to the early colors of Northern Ireland; this suggests that they both may be tied to the Zorite branch of Judah. After the breach was healed, Zerah and Perez became joined, did this cause a change in the color of the flag? Today, the flags of Northern Ireland show the colors as red and white. They also include the star of David, they certainly have all the high heaps of Israel.

Prince Heremon marries Princess Tamar and then begins the new reign of Israel in Britain. The new United Kingdom — Ireland, England, Wales and Scotland were known as Brittan / Britannia, see Ptolemy's map. They set up Tara, Tea is a shortened version of Tamar also. Tara is a derivative, and it is where we get Tiara, as in princess crown; notice the hand of Zerah with the star of David on the Queen's stamp, and the prominent ER also the 3 crowns, three overturns of the crown, red hand in the flag of Ulster, the harp the eagle the sword and Scottish cross are also prominent symbols in Older flags.

In the later version of the Northern Ireland flag, we see the Star of David is a prominent feature again; we have the cross just like our format during marching in the desert.

Remember God told him, Jeremiah, to look to Chittam (Kittim Jer. 2.9-10) "cross over the coast of Kittim H3794 and look, send to Kedar, and observe closely," why because God's people (Israel) now live there, Chittam was the original name of England before the British landed (#13) only later did it become common to call Cyprus Chittam.

Jeremiah's commission was circa 628-586 BC, and he disappeared from the world's scene around this time. I think the initial folks that pick him up take him to the Ebro River area (Zaragossa?), where they experience a drought. Undoubtedly, a few years would have passed, perhaps as late as 570 BC? When they go to Britain.

It is possible that Jeremiah was around 60 years of age when he disappeared, as he could have been as young as 16 years of age when he started. I estimate that it was circa 570 BC when he went to Luwnd'n, the secret hiding place of Britamyah (rule Britannia, covenant people of God).

CHAPTER 15 – Jacobs Pillar & Kingly Line.

If the Irish/British are Hebrew, and everything about them says they are, language, culture, names, even etymology, symbols, and their music, along with storytelling, and of course, our idioms.

Our idioms are perhaps one of the biggest indicators and it is never talked about. We will cover this later in chapter 19. There is, however, one more piece we haven't yet discussed, and its physical evidence. Yes, actual physical evidence that ties Britain back to Israel.

Most people are unaware of a strange artifact that is used whenever a king or queen of Britain is crowned. It is a stone that sits under the coronation chair, and guess where the experts say it comes from. The experts say it's Jacobs pillar stone! Yes, the custodians and the priest of Westminster Abbey and the houses of Parliament of Great Britain identify this stone as none other than Jacob's pillar stone; clearly, the kings and queens of Britain obviously believe it also; otherwise, they would have it removed. Actually, if they did try and remove it they would be the ones removed.

The stone of destiny, just a made-up rock of no significance?

Coronation chair with the stone of destiny Westminster Abbey England.

But let's for a moment make the argument that this is just a rock, not the rock of ages, but just a huge heavy rock. Who in their right mind would carry a huge stone around with them if it didn't have a massive significance? Nobody would. I love my golf game and my golf clubs, but even I have a problem trying to get them on and off planes into cars or just lugging them around. Many times, I have just left them at home because of the hassle of trying to carry them. Multiply the problem by a factor of 10, a very heavy stone that requires multiple people to carry it and now we have a big problem. So, I think it is clear this stone had a huge significance to the British, and one that pointed to its origin and one that pointed to God's promises.

It is said the Tuatha De Danann (people of the God of Dan) were the ones who brought it to Ireland. They may have brought it, and clearly, someone did. It was either the sons of Mil (Male) or the tribe of Dan. Let's look at how it was used in Ireland, and maybe we can determine why it was brought and who brought it.

Lia Fail stone of destiny

courtesy Wikipedia

Lia Fail was a symbol, a very powerful symbol of the kingly line. Folklore says it roared when the true rightful heir (Er) to the throne stepped on it (#308); notice the picture above. You could hardly step on it? Because this is a replica of the original stone. The stone was said to be in use in Ireland for over 2000 years, 2000 years of the kingly line without a break since the coming of Ir to Er'land.

This stone was used as a symbol, a sign, and a guidepost for the kingly line. It was a foundation post; it's what the would-be rulers would step on to see if providence (God) would accept them as rulers. Clearly, this is no simple rock, rather a huge sign to the rightful heir, but who is it, that is picking the heir, the rock, or is it the one behind the rock, in other words God himself?

Jacobs Pillar stone in the Bible

Let's take a look in the Bible and see if there is any mention of a similar stone? We pick up the story in Genesis 28.10. Jack was on his way to Haran to find the love of his life; when he reached a certain place, he stopped for the night, and he took one of the stones and lay it for his head. While sleeping, he dreams of the 'Stairway to Heaven', with angels ascending and descending.

It was here that God appeared to Jack and told him, "I will give you and your descendants the land you're lying on. Your descendants will be like the dust of the earth (where is the dust of the earth, only in one spot?), and you will spread out to the west and to the east and north and south. All peoples on earth (erets) will be blessed by you and your offspring. I am with you and will watch over you wherever you go and I will bring you back to this land, I will not leave you till I have accomplished what I promise you!"

Wow, what a promise. He thought this was a place of God (Beth'el) and the stargate or gate of heaven, and he was afraid, yes, with good reason, God is awesome and scary God and not to be trifled with. v18 early the next morning, Jacob took the stone he had slept on (it was a big stone, but Jacob was Jacked-very strong) and set it up as a pillar H4676 – matstsebah (notice how the Egel'ish Pillar and Pillow are almost identical). Also, the Irish have it set as a Pillar, erecting a derivative of Tamar (8564 tamruwr)

Not only did Jack set the stone as a Pillar, but he also anointed it with oil (H8081 #381). He also said he would build God's house on it, and he would tithe to God (this supports God's house/church).

Yeshua (Jesus) said to (the little rock) Peter, on this rock, I will build my church (house), Peter is the little rock, but Jack and his pillar are the big rock; God did not forget. God still had many promises to fulfill to the patriarchs, and now God is working two angles or rock foundations, the 1st is the physical house, kingly line

171

and the birthright and the 2nd is the spiritual house. Are they connected?

Yes, I think so. They are connected, and it's true that the predominant preachers of the last 500 years were Irish, British, American etc., and yes, during the age of discovery, the Dutch, Portuguese, Spanish, French and other countries spread Christianity also. The incredible trade routes, roads, commerce, and merchandise were put to good use via the missionaries (see Ch. 15)

Lia Fail (stone of destiny) is an amazing origin.

The tenure of Israel in the new land started circa 1200BC to shortly after Jeremiah left the world view 586-580BC, and if we include his short stay in Iberia (EberYah) around 570BC, so our window would be between 1200-570BC for the arrival of Jacobs pillar stone.

Most accounts say it was brought by the Tuatha de Danann. Let's look again at possible dates when this could occur (#308): -

Interestingly, this is what Wikipedia says: -

According to one account, the Lia Fail, the sacred stone arrived by a ship belonging to the Iberian Danaan into the ancient port of Carrick Fergus about 580 BC. On board was Eochaidh, son of a High King and a descendent of Érimón, Princess Tea Tephi or Scota and the scribe Simon Brauch. Princess Tea also had in her possession an ancient harp, some believe its origins lie in the House of David.

The stone was delivered to the Hill of Tara by the three. Scota later married High King Eochaidh. Both had previously met each other in Jerusalem. Eochaidh recovered the ancient stone in Jerusalem before the invasion of the Babylonians.

It is said all future Irish High Kings/British Monarchs inaugurated by the stone have tried to prove lineage back to the Royal Sage and his wife, Tea Tephi, the original bearers of the stone. Eochaidh's resting place is said to be in the Neolithic passage tomb, Cairn T at Loughcrew. [4][5]

"Set up road signs; put up guideposts. Take note of the highway, the road that you take. Return, Virgin Israel, return to your towns" (Jer 31:21).

Return O'Israel and remember where it is you came from and why we received our blessings from on high.

The Kings of Ireland

The high kings of Ireland ruled from northern Ireland, specifically Tara, O'Flaherty says there have been kings to the number of 181 (looking at the AFM list, I count 187) who have governed Ireland from the first king Heremon [and Tamar] of this line to Roderic (Ruaidrí Ua Conchobair 1166–1198 Uí Briúin – Ua Conchobair) the last king (#319).

This is earth-shattering, astounding and amassing to have an unbroken line of kings for thousands of years. Where in the world has this ever occurred? In Wikipedia, it lists three sources for the Milesian High Kings.

- LGE: synchronized dates from Lebor Gabála Érenn
- FFE: chronology based on reign-lengths given in Geoffrey Keating's Forus Feasa ar Erinn.
- AFM: chronology from the Annals of the Four Masters.

We can see from the list that Milesian High Kings listed in AFM (Annals of the four masters, see Fig. F at the back of the book) have the longest, and it starts with Erimon (Herimon and Tamar) and runs to the final High King of Ireland who was Brian Bóruma 1002–1014 Dál gCais, adding them all together we get 178, from 1700BC to 1000AD. Or if we use the most conservative list (LGE), we have 134 kings (See Fig G or Wikipedia for details).

Throne of Ireland moves to Scotland

It is clear from the scriptures that God ties the throne with the stone (Jacobs pillar stone). When we follow the clues, we can see that the Lia Fail or Stone of Scone was first brought to Scotland around 500 AD when King Murtagh MacEirc loaned it to Fergus the Great (his great uncle); below is the Wikipedia account.

"Some Scottish chroniclers, such as John of Fordun and Hector Boece from the thirteenth century, treat the Lia Fáil the same as the Stone of Scone in Scotland.[1] According to this account, the Lia Fáil left Tara in AD 500 when the High King of Ireland, Murtagh MacEirc, loaned it to his great-uncle, Fergus (later known as Fergus the Great), for the latter's coronation in Scotland. Fergus's sub-kingdom, Dalriada, had by this time expanded to include the north-east part of Ulster and parts of western Scotland.

Not long after Fergus's coronation in Scotland, he and his inner circle were caught in a freak storm off the County Antrim coast in which all perished. The stone remained in Scotland which is why Murtagh MacEirc is recorded in history as the last Irish King to be crowned on it. The declaration of Arboth was written and attested to by the royalty of Scotland, and they say Scotland had 113 kings of Royal blood."

The list of the earliest kings of Scotland included Northern Ireland and was called Dál Riata and started with Murtagh MacEirc's Great Uncle Fergus the Great (#382), around 500 AD-1603 AD.

Book of Arbroath, 113 kings of royal blood, 1320 AD.

The "Declaration of Arbroath" is a treaty written by the hands of noblemen, eight earls, and forty-five barons, and it asked for the Pope's dispassionate intervention in the bloody quarrel between the Scots and the English. Bearing this in mind, the Italian Pope would not be pleased to accept the testimony of men who claim the heritage of the British / Davidic kingship. Notice how they say they are from the area of Scythia and came through the Tyrrhenian Sea (Italian sea), suggesting that they were Italian in an effort to get the Pope to intervene between themselves and the English.

"Most Holy Father and Lord, we know and from the chronicles and books of the ancients, we find that among other famous nations, our own, the Scots, has been graced with widespread renown. They journeyed from Greater Scythia by way of the Tyrrhenian Sea and the Pillars of Hercules and dwelt for a long course of time in Spain among the most savage tribes, but nowhere could they be subdued by any race, however barbarous. Thence they came, twelve hundred years after the people of Israel crossed the Red Sea, to their home in the west where they still live today.

The Britons they first drove out, the Picts they utterly destroyed, and, even though very often assailed by the Norwegians, the Danes and the English, they took possession of that home with many victories and untold efforts, and, as the historians of old-time bear witness, they have held it free of all bondage ever since. In their kingdom, there have reigned one hundred and thirteen kings of their own royal stock, the line unbroken (by) a single foreigner."

The salient point here from the declaration is that they claim to have an unbroken bloodline that goes back to circa 200BC-1300AD and includes 113 kings.

Throne of Scotland moved to England

King James VI of Scotland was crowned king at 13 months of age, and his mother, Mary, Queen of Scots, was forced to abdicate her throne. King James of Scotland became king of England; he inherited the throne of England after Queen Elizabeth I died. She was his cousin, and it was from her he inherited the English monarchy. He obtained this Monarchy on March 24, 1603, to March 27, 1625. He was 37 when he became king over all of Britain he was also king of France and Lord of Ireland (link).

Since the third overturn, there have been 17 monarchs reigning from 1603-2018, from King James I (of England-KJB) to Queen Elizabeth II.

In summary

2000 years of reign, note that the Irish say the line started prior to 1000 BC (king Saul, David and Solomon) and ended with the last king of Ireland, Brian Boru, 1000AD. This is where the two-thousand-year reign of the high kings of Ireland comes from.

CHAPTER 16 – White House, Scotland & England.

The Ancient name of Great Britain was Albion meaning white (#206). Albion (Ancient Greek: Ἀλβιών) is the oldest known name of the island of Great Britain. Today, it's still sometimes used poetically to refer to the island. The name for Scotland in the Celtic languages is related to Albion: Alba in Scottish Gaelic, Albain (genitive Alban) in Irish, Nalbin in Manx and Alban in Welsh, Cornish and Breton. These names were later Latinised as Albania and Anglicised as Albany, which were once alternative names for Scotland.

New Albion and Albionoria ('Albion of the North') were briefly suggested as names of Canada during the period of the Canadian Confederation.[1][2]Arthur Phillip, the first leader of the colonization of Australia, originally named Sydney Cove 'New Albion', but for uncertain reasons, the colony acquired the name 'Sydney'.[3][4][5]

HMS Albion 1898 battleship of the British Navy, we are still using the name even in the 19th-century etymology (taken from Wikipedia). The Codex Vatopedinus's Ptolemy's map of the British Isles, labeled 'Ἀλουΐων' (Alouíōn, 'Albion') and Ἰουερνία (Iouernía, 'Hibernia'). c. 1300

The name originally referred to Britain as a whole but was later restricted to Caledonia (giving the modern Scottish Gaelic name for Scotland, Alba). The root *albiio is also found in Gaulish and Galatian albio ('world') and Welsh elfydd (elbid, 'earth, world, land, country, district'). It may be related to other European and Mediterranean toponyms such as Alpes, Albania and Liban. (Now we are getting warm. Liban is the French form of Lebanon, which means white mountain. Notice this last reference is almost identical to the Hebrew Laban).

It appears that nobody has discovered the link to this almost identical Hebrew word, Laban (H3836 h3837 לָבָן). Laban means white (#33, 236), i.e., the same meaning. Laban has the first two letters, A and L, reversed. Albion (Alban) is Laban (or vice versa), and the Laban family is the white house, where Abraham, Isaac and Jacob got their drop-dead gorgeous wives from Padan Aram (#384), modern-day Iran / Syria / Turkey). Please read the section on 'white house" (chap. 2) for details. Also, we have St Albans, another reference to the white boys' house.

And now even more white Israelites, this time in the Levites boys (Num. 3:21). Of Gershon was the family of the Libnites (H3846 white) and the family of the Shimites: these are the families of the Gershonites. Another reference in Psalms 29:6 is, "He maketh them also to skip like a calf, Lebanon and Sirion (H3844 white mountain) like a young unicorn (ox)."

Royal Coat of Arms

Heraldry has an ancient tradition and, as we have seen in the Bible, goes back to its founding members. The Bible identifies emblems or symbols and signs (Zions). By analyzing them we often can derive meaning and origin.

The British royal family crest is known as the "Royal Coat of Arms," interesting terminology, don't you think? The etymology of this comes from:-

ROYAL, witch is traced to regal, and the proposed PIE root is *reg. The COAT of ARMS is broken down to

COAT, from Old French, cote "coat, robe, tunic, overgarment," from Frankish *kotta, "coarse cloth" Old Saxon kot "woolen mantle," Old High German chozza, "cloak of coarse wool," the ultimate origin is unknown

ARMS Old English earm, from Proto-Germanic *armaz (source also of Old Saxon, Danish, Swedish, Middle Dutch, German arm, Old Norse armr, Old Frisian erm), from PIE root *ar- "to fit together."

Origin of heraldic tradition, Jacob made Joseph a coat of many colors, it was an emblem of his love for his son. The laying on of hand is an ancient Hebrew and Christian tradition and one of the most significant events in Biblical history is the Birthright blessing passed on by the laying on of the right hand onto the head of the person receiving the blessing.

In the case of Joseph, Jacob placed his double blessing on both his sons at the same time, he formed a cross and blessed his grandkids with armloads of promises.

When you have the creator of the universe visiting your lineage and promising a blessing, people take note. This act of Jacob to add another tribe to Israel and pass on his lineage was huge. It got the kids to think about emblems, motives, colors, and symbols and was, in a big way, the start of heraldry.

All of the symbolism of the British Royal Coat of Arm's, along with the etymology of ROYAL, COAT and ARM'S, come from Hebrew and the Bible (see the matrix for details).

LION symbolizes JUDAH and the kingly line.
Three LIONs represent the prophecy given by Jacob (Gen. 49.9).
HARP of David.
Red Lion – Zerahite line, breach healed.
Unicorn symbol of Ephraim and Manasseh.
The Crown, from Horn, is also Hebrew and has 12 jewels representing the 12 tribes.

Birthright withheld due to sin!

Why did Israel have to wait so long before really coming into its full inheritance? The promises were made to the patriarchs, and we can see that during the journey to the Promised Land, Israel rebelled against God.

In Leviticus 26, God lays out the punishment for disobedience; this starts in v16. God is essentially saying ahead of time that he will take Israel out to the woodshed. He repeatedly disciplined the US, sending his prophets, but we didn't listen! God then promises to punish Israel 7 times over v18; he reiterates the promise of a seven-fold punishment four times.

And finally, when we failed to respond to God, he himself will punish, us. v32 lay waste the land and scattered us among the nations, which is exactly what he did! How many times does a just, righteous God have to say it, and we now seeing history repeat itself and the estrangement of God from our culture, again as we embrace sex, pornography, homosexuality, lies and a corrupted legal and government systems?

Later God says; But for their (our father's) sake, I will remember my Covenant (Lev. 26.44-45).

God is saying after an eon of time, a JUBILEE will occur. We can see how God instructs us to count and celebrate a Jubilee - *And thou shalt number seven sabbaths of years unto thee, seven times seven years; and the space of the seven sabbaths of years shall be unto thee forty and nine years.* [Lev 25:8 KJV].

Here the number 7 is used (meaning completeness) and due to the severity of the sin it is multiplied by another seven, see later in the section for mor details..

When God says something twice, he has firmly established it. When he says it four times, you can be sure he means it. God knew we were a stubborn, bullheaded and stiff-necked people (God likes a challenge), and his plan was always when we disobeyed to drive us out, where (after our penance) we would inherit the choicest land the world has ever known. Let me just say it was not a foregone conclusion. If we had stayed and obeyed, we would still have expanded to the choicest portions of the world to settle, as Canaan would have soon become too small for the US.

How long is an eon? How long must a righteous God punish his children? In Leviticus 25.8, God gives us his Jubilee, which is based on the Sabbath, which is the seventh day, which is Saturday, not Sunday. In the year of the jubilee, the field shall return unto him, of whom it was bought, even to him to whom the possession of the land did belong (Lev. 27:24). How are we to calculate a jubilee?

And thou shalt number seven Sabbaths of years unto thee, seven times seven years; and the space of the seven Sabbaths of years shall be unto thee forty and nine years (Lev. 25:8). Then on the 10th day of the 7th month blow thee the Shofar it shall be the day of At one ment (Yom Kippur when God and man are joined together, this is the holiest day of Gods calendar)!

The Jubilee is calculated seven times seven (eon's) years, so forty-nine years and on the fiftieth year on Yom Kippur, we are to celebrate it! It is the time of redemption. In Israel, if a person's land or home was offered for rent, they would value it in relation to how long before the Jubilee and its redemptive value would go down the closer it got to the Jubilee.

Many believe that the birthright was withheld 2520 years; the way they calculate this is 7 x a biblical year = 360, based on a biblical month, new moon to new moon = 30 days, so 7 times 360 = 2520, but what about 4 x 7? And what about the Jubilee, i.e., withholding of a person's rights/possessions/land/promises? It seems to me that 2401 years would be more in line? Even so, we are in the ballpark and get the point. I will not labor the issue and expand this subject any further. Also, Judah went into captivity in 586 BC and later came back (as Daniel prophesied) and rebuilt the temple, with it later being destroyed in 70 AD, by the Romans.

Exactly when do we start the clock? When was Israel no more? Was it when Samaria went into exile in 721 BC or was it when Judah went into exile in 598 BC.

British Empire (Israel's) Hay Day 1680-1900.

I would estimate that the birthright blessing was withheld from 721 BC (when we went into exile) till 1680 (using 2401, the Jubilee years) or 1799 using the second method.

Is there any indication that 1680 AD was indeed a special year? Actually, there is a comet circled the globe, and for two years starting in 1680, it was known as "the Great Comet of 1680," and appears to have ushered in the Great British Empire. It was also known as Sir Isaac Newton's comet and it is believed to have been the actual inspiration for Newton's laws of gravity (first published in 1687).

The Comet was so bright it could be seen during the day and was later called Haley's comet and thought by some (including Newton) to have started the worldwide flood. Also, some say Haley's comet is the one the wise men saw, i.e., signaling Jesus's birth. The Great Comets of 1680 ushers in a great scientific blessing. These, along with other events, lend strong evidence of a 2401-year or double Jubilee (7x7 plus 7x7), withholding of birthright blessings to the ancient Brits.

Army standard's Emblems Colors -Red Coats

The red coats are coming, and the British army has a long tradition of wearing red coats, even as early as 1500 (I believe long before). We have references of them in use; the section below was taken from Wikipedia.

The uniforms of the Yeoman of the Guard (formed 1485) and the Yeomen Warders (also formed 1485) have traditionally been in Tudor red and gold.[4]:3 The Gentlemen Pensioners of James I (now the Gentlemen-at-Arms) had worn red with yellow feathers.[5] At Edgehill, the first battle of the Civil War, the King's people had worn red coats, as had at least two Parliamentary regiments'.[6] However, none of these examples constituted the national uniform that the red coat was later to become.[4]

But do we have any instances of the Israel/Britain wearing red coats before this?

(Nah. 2:3) The shield (Magen) of his mighty men is made red, the valiant men are in scarlet: the chariots shall be with flaming torches in the day of his preparation, and the fir trees shall be terribly shaken. God had red coats, more specifically scarlet. This is indeed a prophecy about Jacob's children dressed in scarlet (red) in the army of Israel. And the Brit'ish red coats used to be dressed in scarlet (a pigment of red and blue). The British soldiers fought in scarlet tunics for the last time at the Battle of Gennis in the Sudan on 30 December 1885.

Who knows, maybe the monarchy with bring back the scarlet, I think she should.

British Bull Tribe

We have covered this a few times already. The Egel is Hebrew H5695 עֵגֶל ', egel -ay-ghel. It's easy to see how this could also be pronounced Angle as in the Angle's and Saxons, Jutes and Normans. In Hebrew, it means bullock, calf or steer and ish, H376 אִישׁ 'iysh means man or men in Hebrew, so Egel'ish is the symbol of the covenant man (Brit'ish) aka Ephraim and sometimes Manasseh are depicted *at I have surely heard Ephraim bemoaning himself thus; Thou hast chastised me, and I was chastised, as a bullock H5695 unaccustomed to the yoke: (wild bullock, a Unicorn) turn thou me, and I shall be turned; for thou art the LORD my God.* (Jer. 31:18, Boustrophedon or ox turning method, when we changed our handwriting direction from the Jews).

The calf itself will be taken to Assyria (Hos. 10:6) as an offering to the great king. Ephraim will experience shame; Israel will be ashamed of its counsel. (Hos. 10:11). Ephraim is a well-trained calf that loves to thresh, but I will place a yoke on her fine neck. I will harness Ephraim (the Ox); Judah will plow; Jacob will do the final plowing. God will use Judah and Ephraim (the Egel'ish) to accomplish his promises, and now we know how he is accomplishing his will, remember that the heaven's God glory does declare the skys his handy work teaches Arcturus appears to represent the Ox and Shepherd (God), driving the big dipper around the earth (note 16).

We can clearly see that God calls Ephraim and Manasseh, an ox, as he calls Judah a lion and Dan an eagle, along with other signs (etc.), and Rueben has the symbol of a man. All these four make up the mystical creatures of Ezekiel and Revelation. The mystical creature spoken of in both these books is nothing more than Israel. God loves the patriarchs, and we are family, and we will be with God for eternity. There is so much I can say about this, but for now, we will leave it here.

Now, to be fair, Israel also had a golden calf, one that we made, while Moses was receiving the law, and we definitely got cut up about that (Exo 32:4, v:27). Also, the evil Gerrymanderer (Jeroboam) set up an Ox to turn the hearts of Joseph from his God, (2Ch 13:8) And now ye think to withstand the kingdom of the LORD in the hand of the sons of David, and ye be a great multitude, and there are with you golden calves, H5695 which Jeroboam made you for Gods.

God says I am the Alpha (aleph) and the Omega (Rev 1:8); the first letter of the ancient Hebrew Semitic / Phoenician was the Ox (that's because it was created by Joseph and his son's Ephraim and Manasseh #356), Alpha Bet (first two letters of the current Alpha Bet).

In those days, the house of Judah will join the House of Israel (Jer 3.18) and together, they will come from a Northern Land. Where is this northern land where they currently reside? It is none other than the isle's (H339 אִי 'iy Iy'land's) of the sea.

183

Wherefore glorify ye the LORD in the fires, even the name of the LORD God of Israel in the isles (H339 Isa 42:15) of the sea. (Isa 41:5) The isles H339 saw it, and feared; the ends of the earth were afraid, drew near, and came. (Isa 42:10) Sing unto the LORD a new song, and his praise from the end of the earth, ye that go down to the sea, and all that is therein; the isles, and the inhabitants thereof. (Isa 42:12) Let them give glory unto the LORD and declare his praise in the islands. (Isa 51:5) My righteousness is near; my salvation is gone forth, and mine arms (x) shall judge the people; the isles shall wait upon me, and on mine arm shall they trust.

I think Isaiah and Jonah knew where T'ar'(s)hish was, God has a sense of humor, and the British are Israel, let's look again at what he calls us (Deu 32:15), but Jeshurun (Just you run-if you can fat boy) waxed fat, and kicked: thou art waxen fat, thou art grown thick, thou art covered with fatness; then he forsook God which made him, and lightly esteemed the Rock H6697 of his salvation.

Bull references in Egel'and John Bull

John Bull, a symbol that epitomized the working man of England a heroic archetype of the freeborn Englishman."[2] Later, the figure of Bull was disseminated overseas by illustrators and writers such as American cartoonist Thomas Nast and Irish writer George Bernard Shaw, author of John Bull's Other Island.

Why a bull man, one might ask, but since we know our origin, it's very clear that the Bull is in our DNA. We might, at some point, come out with a lot of BullShxx, but for the most part, the British maintain a stiff upper (bull) lip and try and maintain honesty, integrity, and a no Bullshxx tell them hayah (hello h1961 הָיָה, hayah) sent you. Oh Yah, hello to him approach to life, well, at least in the past when we knew who buttered our bread (manna), but when I see the way Britain is going down the tubes these days, it's clear that were are fast heading for Jacobs trouble!

And as mentioned previously, the Old Bull and Bush prophesy:

"-And for the precious things of the earth and fulness thereof, and for the goodwill of him that dwelt in the bush: let the blessing come upon the head of Joseph and upon the top of the head of him that was separated from his brethren (Deu 33:16-17)."

The term "bull and bush" is clearly an ancient one. We have pubs and songs with this name because Yah is in our DNA! In the prophecy, Mosheh (מ שׁה) is invoking his experience where he met God for the first time (הַיםֶ♀אל) 'Elohiym hello him (Gen Exo 3:6), God would not give his name, hence 'Hello Him', Moses then asked who I shall tell the ben (children) of His Royal has sent me? Elohiym, replied has a sense of humor, and we are Brit'ish; we have had Ben His Royal (Israel) children for a long time. Back to the bush, Moses was a man of immense learning. He was raised as a prince of Egypt, but later in life, he developed a faulty tongue and a speech impediment (Exo 4:10). He even complained to God about his slow speech, and that is where we get the term — Don't beat around the bush, hurry up and say what on your mind!

The term Bull and Bush is a colloquial term referring to the average man on the street, but we can see that there was a deeper symbolism. We can see the blessing that Moses gives the Tribe of Ephraim. There appears to be deep affection for them. We can see this from all the prophesies relating to it, even from Balaam's prophesy (Num. 24.8). God brought them out of Egypt. They have the strength of a wild ox (Unicorn). They devour hostile nations and break their bones to pieces.

Also, we have a term called bullish, and this epitomizes strength, muscular, brawny, hulking, bright, cheerful and expectant are the synonyms that relate to this word. We remember Jack (Jacob) was Jacked and the first Jock he could in his prime run like a Jackrabbit and was able to wrestle Jesus all night long and prevail and. God wants his children to emulate him! i.e., strive with God and man for truth, justice, and the American way.

Phrases — Idioms — Proverbs, etc.

Idioms are one of our ways of communicating; we commonly use phrases or idioms to convey a special meaning; not only did God plan it this way, but he prophesied that this would happen.

And moreover, because the preacher was wise, he still taught the people knowledge; yea, he gave good heed and sought out, and set in order many proverbs (Ecc. 12:9).

These things have I spoken unto you in proverbs: but the time cometh, when I shall no more speak unto you in proverbs, but I shall shew you plainly of the Father (John 16:25).

The study of proverbs is a fascinating linguistic journey that reveals much about how language, culture, and thought interact. These compact expressions of folk wisdom serve not only as linguistic artifacts but also as guides that have shaped human behavior and societal norms throughout history. They continue to influence modern thought and discourse, illustrating the enduring power of language to shape, reflect, and evolve with human society.

We need proverbs because they reflect who we are

A recent report done by the BBC says:

"With quotations", you're trying to associate with some respected figure like Albert Einstein or Abraham Lincoln or Mark Twain," says Shapiro. "But with proverbs (idioms), you're trying to do something more elemental and deeper than that. What makes proverbs so popular and powerful is they connect to very deep psychological roots in human beings." Proverbs become popular because "people use them to connect with other people and the wisdom of the past."

Parables, proverbs, and idioms are interconnected as they all play a role in expressing collective wisdom, moral lessons, and cultural values. While parables often provide the narrative foundation, proverbs and idioms extract and summarize these teachings, embedding them into everyday language.

1)   The writings on the wall' – When Belshazzar was partying and had the gold and silver goblets from Gods temple brought up so they could drink from them, and they praised the Gods of gold, silver, bronze, stone and wood – then fingers appeared out of nowhere and wrote MENE, MENE, TEKEL PARSIN meaning, God has numbered your days and brought them to an end, you have been weighed on the scales and found wanting, your kingdom is divided and given to the Medes and Persians Every Bible student knows this one right (Dan. 5.5-6)?

2)   Your days are numbered' similar meaning to 'the writings on the wall'; in other words, you don't have much time left in the job or this life etc. it is from the same origin.

3)   Stinks to high heaven – meaning that the sin of the place was so bad that even God was appalled by their actions and took notice – (Gen19.13) because the outcry to the Lord against its peoples is so great that he has sent us to destroy it!

4)   'You're eighty-sixed,' meaning you're kicked out, don't come back, you're banned — Abraham was 86 when his handmaiden gave birth to Ishmael, and after Isaac was born and weaned, they had a big party, a fight broke out, and Ishmael, (his brother from another mother) was eighty-sixed, i.e., kicked out and told not to come back (Gen. 21.9-10).

5)   'Drop dead gorgeous' — Both Abraham's and Isaac's wives were drop dead gorgeous – Pharaoh and Abimelech and their families thought they were going to die for making passes at Sarah and Rebecca (Gen 12.11,17-18,20.3-4),

6)   'Flesh out the story' to put meat on the bones to put substance to your plan (275, Eze. 37:8).

7)   Like mother like Daughter' (Eze 16:44) ''Everyone who quotes proverbs will quote this proverb about you: 'Like mother, like daughter.' (Eze 16:49) Behold, this was the iniquity of thy sister Sodom, pride, fulness of bread, and

187

abundance of idleness was in her and in her daughters, neither did she strengthen the hand of the poor and needy. (Eze 16:50). And they were haughty, and committed abomination before me: therefore, I took them away as I saw (no) good. Remember, Jeshurun, fat boy!

8)   'The fathers have eaten sour grapes, And the children's teeth are set on edge.' Here is a very common proverb we would quote, we don't do it anymore. Why is that? '(Jer. 31.28)' As I have watched over them to pluck up [by or with root], to break down, to overthrow, to destroy and to bring disaster, so I will watch over them to build and to plant,' declares the LORD. v29 'In those days, people will no longer say, 'The parents have eaten sour grapes, and the children's teeth are set on edge.' v30'But everyone will die for his own iniquity; each man who eats the sour grapes, his teeth will be set on edge…God, yet again, is right. We don't use this one!

9)   'Come back to bite you' – We complained against God in the desert, and God sent snakes to bite us (Num 21.5-6); also, Aarons's staff turned into a snake. Egyptians do the same, but Aarons's snake eats the Egyptian one (Ex7.1.2), i.e., comes back to bite it; the second plague even bites them worse.

10)   Better late than never – Abraham and Sarah giving birth to Isaac; Sarah was 90, and Abraham was 100! All's well that ends well (Gen.17. 17).

11)   All's well that ends well – see the previous entry; remember Abraham and Sarah had a terrible year prior to the birth of Isaac, Sodom and Gomorrah, Abilimech tried to bed Sarah and the whole crowd had to be circumcised (Brit Milah)

12)   You can't have your cake and eat it – When we came out of Egypt with great wealth (booty from the Egyptians) and unleavened uncooked cake (Ex12.39), we left with haste but didn't really have time to eat the cake.

13)   Play Favorites – What Isaac did when he tried to give the birthright to Esau (Gen. 27.1), even though God, his wife and even his own name 'Yitschaq (yits chaq) told him to give

it to Ya`aq (ob) (עֲקֹב H3290), and Jacob played favorites with Joseph.

14)   Pan Around, Paddan Aram (H6307-Gen29), To look around and is where we get the term Panoramic from. It is where Abraham, Isaac and Jacob got their drop-dead wives from.

15)   The white house – Jacob going to Laban's (means white) house to get a family, Leah, Rachael, Bilhah and Zilpah, Alban also means white and is the original name for Scotland and England, and we have a white house in the USA. Also, a Patriotic name from Israel, Lebanon – Laban'on white mountain.

16)   Whitewash – meaning to completely annihilate the opposing team or to cover up transgression (Psa 51:7 Isa 1:18, Dan 11:35 Dan 12:10 Joe 1:7 Dan.7.9) another idiom from the bible.

17)   Hanging in, by the skin of my teeth (Job 19:20) My bone cleaveth to my skin and to my flesh, and I am escaped with the skin of my teeth.

18)   Love is blind — to work 7 years for the woman you love and want as your wife and then marry the wrong person and have sex with them and not know till the morning, how could you not know? I just love Jack. □

19)   Jack of all trades — Jacob's ability to do any job and solve any problem.

20)   Jackass — The term refers to a male donkey, strong and useful (like Jacob). It also refers to someone who is foolish and unwittingly gets into difficulty, as often seems to be the case with Jack.

21)   He's Jacked – meaning he's all pumped up, Jacob man of steel, wrestled all night long with Yeshua.

22)   A Jack — A device of great strength that's used to lift a car. Jack — Jacob strong as a horse-

23)   Jackbite — An old English term for a packed lunch when you have to go out to work all day, especially down the mine shaft or out in the fields all day long, like Jacob did!!

24)   Jacobitism — The Scottish group, the Jacobites, believed that parliamentary interference with the line of

succession to the English and Scottish thrones was illegal. https://en.wikipedia.org/wiki/Jacobitism

25) Hang on for dear life — Jacob, after wrestling all night long, has his hip disjointed and still won't let go.

26) It's always darkest before dawn — There is a beautiful saying amongst the Irish to inspire hope under adverse circumstances: 'Remember,' they say, 'that the darkest hour of all is the hour before day (# 187). It's not actually true as the darkest hour is around Midnight, so it's an idiom with a meaning that essentially means just before something great or good is going to happen, something really bad happens. We again get this from our forefathers. Notice Jacob didn't know who he was fighting with till the first rays of light, and it dawned on him who he was fighting (Gen. 32.26).

27) He's a Jock — An athletic person — Jacob wrestling all night takes a great deal of strength, determination and stamina.

28) Pat on the Rear — Jocks congratulate a teammate with a pat on the rear — This practice developed from our fathers — We took an oath by placing a hand on a person's loins (Gen. 24.2), as happened when Abraham sent his head servant to find a wife for Isaac. Also, Jacob wrestled all night with God and prevailed, so God tapped out — by placing his hand on Jacob's thigh! (Gen 32:25), and even later, the Jock asked his son to swear by placing his hand on his still dislocated thigh (A sign of his greatness, Gen 47:29), so next time you see someone tapping a jock's thigh, to congratulate them, tell them where it came from!

29) 'Swear on the Bible — Make an oath — Place hand on Bible and swear' — Jacob told Joseph to put his hand on his thigh, which God dislocated and make a solemn promise; as said earlier, this was actually done first by Abraham (Gen. 24.3). I don't think there are any other occurrences in the Bible but it's pretty much a sure bet that this practice was continued and later we used the Bible, i.e. word of God (Gen. 47.29).

30) Affidavit — is this an oath made popular by David or Solomon? If a man sin against his neighbor, and an oath

be laid on him to cause him to swear, and he comes and swears before your altar in this house (1Ki 8:31).

31)   Car-jack and Hi-jack — Jacob running off with his caravan and Laban's daughters, Leah, Rachel and all his goods, then Laban met him. I can just imagine he would say Hi-jack, what are you doing? And Laban still believed they were his!

32)   Jack-pot — to take a gamble, a risk as Jacob did working for Laban (In the white house) and Laban kept changing the rules, but finally, he got to keep his earning/winnings.

33)   Winning streak — when God caused Jacob to keep all the animals that were stripped or streaked and figured out how to cause it to happen and got to keep all the sheep.

34)   He doesn't know Jack – Jacob for 20 years didn't know that the 'Golden Boy', Joseph was still alive.

35)   Golden Boy – It appears that the Golden Boy title came from Joseph when Pharaoh lavished on him an Egyptian cotton robe and put a gold chain around his neck. He rode in a chariot with a police escort announcing, making way for the 'Chief of Egypt'. The term could also apply to Samuel, as he was also a Golden boy; he became the leader of all Israel and was on ceremonial occasions decked from head to toe in gold with 'all the 'Bells and Whistles' and with red, white and blue colors (scarlet and purple are a combination of red and blue).

36)   Jackhammer – A device that's normally powered by pneumatics, it has great strength and ability to break the hardest materials such as reinforced concrete, again a metaphor speaking of Jack's great strength.

37)   'I am all ears' – A number of times, God has said he will do something that will make Israel's ears tingle (1 Sam. 3.11, Jer. 9.3, Jer. 25.4). Basically, he was saying 'LISTEN UP.'

38)   Ear's burning – Someone is talking about you, and possibly an omen of things, either good or bad things, similar to 'I am all ears.'

39)   You're Fired or to Get Fired, what happened to Aaron's son's when they offered strange fire to God (Lev

10:1-3). God, in turn, gave them a taste of their own medicine, and again when Daniel's friends Shadrack Meshack and Abednego would not bow down and worship the image of Gold, Nebuchadnezzar wanted to fire them (Dan. 3), but again it was Nebuchadnezzar's soldiers who got fired and burned to death while God promoted his servants.

40)	Knocking sense into us During Korah's rebellion (Nub. 16). We grumbled against Moses and Aaron, there was a test, and the Korahites were to appear before God with censers (Nub. 16.6); they were trying to take the Priesthood from Aaron, and God was not going to stand for it, it fact it was they who would not stand, but they had been working on this for a long time and had turned the hearts of the people against Moses and Aaron. Not only did the earth swallow up the rebels, but also the ones holding censers were fired. Note that the censor of Numbers 16.6 was holy and that God had them hammered out and set them on the altar as a remembrance sign. God was hammering some sense into us.

41)	To fire up the crowd – A common term these days in politics especially, but it also comes from God. God was the one who first fired up the crowd. It is true; read it yourself; God tells the crowd I have brought you out of Egypt on Eagles wings (symbol of the USA). Now be my Brits and a holy nation. God had Moses wash the people and consecrate them (change their clothes, etc.). They prepared for three days, and on the third day, ElYah (H410 אֵל 'el H3050 – Yahh fired up the crowd; there was thunder, lightning, a loud trumpet blast, the earth trembled, everyone in the camp trembled, and then God descended on the mountain in fire! Moses spoke, and God answered him in a thundering voice and fire. This was the first time God fired up the crowd (Ex.19).

42)	Two heads are better than one – Adam had to think of names for all the animals that God had created, but there were no suitable helpers for him, so God created Eve (Gen. 2.20-21).

43)	Actions speak louder than words — People's intentions can be judged better by what they do rather than what they say. Jacob, when he sent the gift of animals to Esau (Gen. 33. and Matthew 7:15-20), Jesus said you shall know a tree by her fruits, i.e., Don't just listen to what they say but what they do! Similar to 'Actions speak louder than words.'

44)   3 for 1 – All fingers and thumbs, Going Bezerk, and Payback is a Bitxx – All fingers and thumbs, this phrase has changed over the years (#190); all fingers and thumbs are how we would normally pick something up, so to say we are all fingers and thumbs, makes no sense, we all have fingers and thumbs, but to have no thumbs would be awkward and make a person clumsy. We brought the phrase with us; we can read the story in Judges 1, Going Berserk, Israel fights the Canaanites and Perizzites, striking down 10,000 men at Berserk-Bezerk (its where we get going Bezerk from), the King had a habit of cutting the thumbs and big toes off kings he captured and 70, that right 70 of them would go Bezerk under his table and fight for food scraps like dogs. Israel captured him and cut his thumbs and big toe off and took him to Jerusalem, to which he said, 'Now God paid him back. — Payback is a female dog-'Bitch' (#191).

45)   Cleanliness is next to Godliness – This phrase is not written anywhere in the Bible (#211), so how did we get it? Also, a rain shower (h8178). We got it from our Fathers, the Hebrews, the same place we get Showers (H7778), Guards to the house of God (Exo. 29.4, 1Ch. 9.21, 15.21), and we know how clean they had to be, made sure everyone was clean before they entered the outer court and inner courts of the Lord (1Chr. 9.17-27) the Holy of Holies. God told them to wash so they would not die (Ex. 19.10, 29.4, 30.1821, 40.12, 40.30), To bathe, did we get it from shall bath, shab'bath, or perhaps Bath Sheba‌ שבּ‌ת‌ h7676 (Lev. 23:3, 2Sam. 11.3), who David spied bathing on the roof of her house, or perhaps the lily white purity of a daughter which in Hebrew is called Bath (H1339,1323). How is this possible? We brought it with us when we came to these Sacred Isles and the USA; so, Shower and Bath, was from temple worship and denotes purity as in daughter.

193

46) Spill the beans – When Joseph's sons left Egypt with sacks of barley, oats, grain, and a variety of beans. Joseph sent his servants to search their sacks for his silver cup. And they found it in Benjamin's sack, the last one to be searched. Did they sill the beans when discovering the silver lining?

47) Don't beat around the bush — Moses burning bush — Get to the point — Moses, known for not being able to speak clearly and perhaps directly, after the burning bush experience, was told to give Pharaoh a message but said he wasn't the best person, (Ex 6.12). It is said that he had a stuttering problem, so it would take a long time to get to the point.

48) All the bells and whistles — Want that with all the Bells and whistles (Exo 28:34, 35, 2Ch 29:25,26 #214). Meaning, do you want the full complement of accessories once again? Nobody can trace it to its origin!-line-by-line proof of our origin. God is in our DNA! The Priest had a very elaborate setup with Bells and whistles and, special tasseled garments and water. It was very ritualistic. Everything had to be done in precise order, and washing after each step, hence the 'Shower-Guards'. Not only that, they now have found a genetic marker showing that a Hebrew priest actually does have DNA evidence linking him to God.

49) The other shoe's about to drop, similar to the second shoe dropped, to wait for the inevitable next step or the final conclusion. It was a custom in ancient Israel to vote with shoes (# 210 Deu 25:9, Psa 60:8, Psa 108:9). Moab is My washpot Over Edom I will cast My shoe, Over Philistia I will triumph.'

50) Laughing stock (butt end of jokes)– Judah after he accuses Tamar of being a whore – and he was the actual father with his staff and signet ring as a witness against him But the end of jokes, i.e., a mark for archery practice; properly a mound or other erection on which the target is set up(L). The name Tamar means erection (H8558). She set Judah up, and this is where we get this term from. The term laughing stock comes from the same root(L). (Gen. 38.16-27).

51) Keep the faith (Rev 14:12). It's a very common Irish Term, but is it in the OT (Deu. 32.20, Hab. 2.4, Math. 6.30, 8.16, Heb. 11.6)?

52) White lie (White-Laban-H3835) — Abraham and Isaac saying their wives were sisters, it's true but they were also their wives, so misleading.

53) Let's address the Elephant in the room – An open secret or item that is taboo or nobody wants to address – surely, this can't be in the Bible, right. Well, it's not in the Bible, but as we saw when we looked at Egypt's Elephantine Island, this was a Jewish stronghold that had a replica of the temple, with (as some believe) the true ark of the covenant, that was later moved to Ethiopia?

54) Stopped dead in their track — (Num 16:48) The plague of the Lord was sweeping through the camp, and Aaron the Kohen Gadowl (H1419 God Heal), at Moses command, ran in amongst the people and stopped death in its tracks.

55) Spill the Beans — okay, we talked earlier about this, but here's another instance — to give away a secret or a surprise (#209). The Philistines banded together and fought Israel's troops in a field full of beans, and Israel fled from the Philistines, but there was a surprise ending. One of David's mighty men was there, and he stood his ground and took out the Philistines on HIS OWN (God clearly was with him 2 Sam. 23.11).

56) Don't shoot the messenger — (2Sa 4:10). King David killed the messenger when he brought the report that King Saul was dead, And again when Absalom was killed, they were in danger of losing their lives (2 Sam. 18.20).

57) In 'Hell in a Hand Basket', the Chief baker had a dream, and he had three baskets on his head. Birds were eating bread out of them, and Joseph said in three days, you're going to die, so the baskets he held with his hands were the messengers for his death – (Gen. 40.16-18,22).

58) 'Caught between the Devil and the Deep Blue Sea' when we got stuck at the Red Sea with Pharaoh and his army chasing us (Ex14.13-15). Pinned in a gorge with the devil (Pharaoh) chasing and a deep blue sea in front of us!

59)   Put a brave face on — Moses says don't worry, wait and see the deliverance of Jehovah, but he was scared to death, he cried out to God for help, 'he put a brave face on' (Ex14.13-15, Exo 34:35), also when he came from taking to God his face shone, he had a brave face on.

60)   Hold your peace — To keep quiet when sometimes we want to say something (Ex. 14.14).

61)   'kick our asses' or 'kick your ass' (Gen 43:18) And the men were afraid because they were brought into Joseph's house; and they said, Because of the money that was returned in our sacks at the first time are we brought in; that he may seek occasion H1556 against us, and fall upon us, and take us for bondmen, and our asses.

62)   Silver Lining – in other words, things might seem dark and ominous, like a cloud, but the silver lining is the sun coming out. It does not pay accurate honor to the real story (or what I believe is the real story) That of Jacob's son's coming to Egypt for food and Joseph demanding that Simeon be held as collateral and that they bring Benjamin (Joe's brother-his other brothers were from other mothers) and Joseph (Joe) put silver that they used for payment back into the mouth of their sacks of food. It is quite feasible that the hemp sacks were doubled up to help stop them from breaking (Gen42.25, 44.1-2). Hence, the term silver lining.

63)   Living the dream — this means that we had a dream, and it was wonderful, not only are we living the dream but fulfilling it — How many times God, how many times, does he have to give us our roots before we get! Do I need to spell this out, Joseph's dream again…? Can you imagine the brothers from another mother staring at each other as Joe is coming down the street with everyone saying bow before the 'Imhotep the leader of Egypt' and boy did they bow! Probably needed a change of underwear as well!

64)   Know where your bread buttered – God fed us, Manna. During the 40 years, God said he would rain bread from Heaven. It was like bread buttered with honey, also described as a wafer (Ex16.31) we had dessert during our trip in the desert. And God was the source of our goodness.

We knew where are bread was buttered, but do we know today?

65)   Hay Day or Hey Day It is said this has nothing to do with hay, and the origin came from Germany, i.e., 'hur-rah!' (#235). Essentially, it was a greeting or great day/spirits were a high pinnacle of success. As I mentioned in Chapter 1, God was talking to Abraham and Sarah just before Isaac was born, and God added a hey (the 5th letter of the Hebrew alphabet and represents praise). Therefore, Abram goes to Abraham, and Sarai goes to Sarah (heה Ps119.33); it was Sarah's and Abraham's "Heyday," the letter ה was also known as ha, so Abraham and Sarah both get a Ha, Ha, and the Bible reveals that both laughed when God told them they were going to have a child and then they have a child, Isaac meaning laughter. We have a second hay day; do you remember the story of Joseph? The dreamer Joe sees bales of hay, bowing to him (chap. 1. Gen 37:7) and then years later, the dream is fulfilled, and everyone bows down to Joseph (Gen.41.44, 44.15)

66)   The straw that broke the camel's back — Joseph is taken bound to Egypt, placed on a camel that was loaded with spices (Gen37.25,28) against his will – this was the straw that broke the camel's back.

67)   The last Straw – Jacob made Joseph a coat of many colors, which his brothers hated, and after he told his first dream of the sheaf's bowing to him, his brothers became very angry, and after his second dream of the stars (spangled banner) with, sun and moon bowing to him this was the last straw (sheaf) and his brothers sold him to the Ishmaelites (Gen 37:28) merchants.

68)   Grasping at straws – what Joseph's brothers did to try and appease their brother from another mother after he became leader of Egypt. Eventually he forgave them after they learned their lesson.

69)   'Land of milk and honey' – this means A place of abundance that is free from want, [safety, live without oppression] a country where living conditions are good and people have the opportunity to make a lot of money. Many Mexicans regard the United States as a land of milk and

197

honey. The Promised Land is a land of milk and honey spoken of a number of times in the Bible: The English-speaking Nations are the land of milk and honey that God promised to us via our fathers (#234)!

70)   Bull market – the stock market — a bull market is when the market is going up, and a bear market is going down, but clearly, if you have been reading the Bull is the British, that's the symbol of the Egel of Great Brit' am.

71)   Rainmaker – someone or something that causes good things to happen; this started with Elijah praying for the withholding of rain and later praying for rain to come (1Kin18.37) Interesting side note is the seeding of rain clouds (Chem trails) to make rain, the trouble is, if there is no water vapor in the clouds they can't cause the rain to come. Are there any among the vanities of the Gentiles that can cause rain? Or can the heavens give showers? Art, not thou he, O LORD our God? Therefore we will wait upon thee: for thou hast made all these things (Jer. 14.22).?

72)   The sun never sets on the British Empire — This is actually in the Bible – (Mal 1:11) For from the rising of the sun even unto the going down of the same my name (Brit'ish — Israel and Jesus) shall be great among the Gentiles; and in every place incense shall be offered unto my name and a pure offering: for my name shall be great among the heathen, saith the LORD of hosts. It's a foretaste that the sun will never set on Israel and God's kingdom in the future (Isa 60:20). Your sun will never set again…

73)   'Rub a dub dub three men in a tub' (tub was a term used to describe prison cells, also Preacher and barrister 272). The butler (butcher), the baker and the candle stick maker all going to the fair (Phar, short for Pharaoh)– I think it could be plausible that this relates to Joseph in Egypt. We can become refreshed with the story in Gen40 – Joseph is in charge of the prison system; he is a prisoner, but he is in charge of all the prisoners. Candle making was very important in Egypt, where (it is said) the first candles were made. It's clear that the Egyptians put their prisoners to work, as Joe was responsible for everything that was done in the prison system Genesis 39.22. and later, he was put in

charge of all of Egypt, and as previously covered, Imhotep was Joseph, and he was a great inventor. Clearly, he made an impression (the candle-making process was to make a mold and pour melted wax into an impression) everywhere he went, and it is not beyond feasible that the prisoners were put to work and made candles and Joseph was in charge of them — We can see clearly the Egyptians did put their prisoners/ slaves to work as attested to later in the Bible and ancient Egyptian text, also the candle making was a paramount activity in ancient cultures and Egypt was a forerunner for this process.

74)	Undercover boss' — Joseph was like the first undercover boss; he was everywhere, and he worked from the bottom of Egyptian slave labor, even in the prison system, till he was put in charge of everything. If you have ever watched Undercover Boss, you know how valuable this process is. You quickly find out who you can trust who is really working for the benefit of the company. What Your Safe found out, while seeing multiple Egyptian power people, was how Egyptian life really worked, what you could do and what you could not do. Trust me, I am fully convinced, he knew exactly what God was doing, in training him to run the country.

75)	'The Chosen One' comes from the breastplate of high priest h2833 chosen kho'-shen from an unused root, probably meaning to contain or sparkle; perhaps a pocket (as holding the Urim and Thummim), or rich (as containing gems), used only of the garget of the high priest: breastplate, whe also have the Jewish phrase Kosher, that Jews use for food but means fit proper (to choose, chosen) from Proto-Germanic *keus- (source also of Old Frisian kiasa, Old Saxon kiosan, Dutch kiezen, Old High German **kiosan**, German kiesen, Old Norse kjosa, Gothic kiusan "choose," Gothic kausjan "**to taste, test**"), from PIE root *geus- "to taste; to choose. 2855 Chethlon kheth-lone' kohen gadol choshen, hence the high priest, the one who wore the breast place, was the chosen one.

76)	Meeting of the minds — Numbers 2.2 where the ark was kept, and there was in addition to this the tabernacle of

199

meeting, which Moses set up outside the camp so that people could seek the lord and enquire of Moses and have a meeting of the minds (Exo. 33:7).

77)   Once bitten, twice shy —Once hurt, one is doubly cautious in the future. According to This old observation, presumably alluding to an animal biting someone, was first recorded in 1894 (#390). In Judges 14, Samuel is attacked by a lion that he rips apart with his bare hands. He then puts forth a riddle to his soon-to-be wife's family/people, one with a heavy purse attached. The Philistines eventually get him to reveal his secret to his bride, Samson's response, see "Made and Ass of."

78)   Made an ass of — To make someone or yourself look foolish. Samson was hunted by the Philistines, and they besieged Judah looking for Samson. Judah, in turn, went to find Samson. They tied him up with ropes and led him to the Philistine camp. When Samson got there, the power of the Lord came on him and finding an asses jawbone, he killed 1000 Philistines -Samson remarked – I have made an Ass's of the Philistines (Jud. 15.16, #391).

79)   If I told you I would have to kill you, hope you have been following. Samson was bitten by the lion, put forth the parable and then was bitten by his wife-to-be. He had a secret, and he shared it with her; the trouble was she was a Philistine (no morals, no concern about his God or his people, just cares about themselves). He was once bitten; Samson now is Judge of Israel for 20 years before another charming, beautiful lady comes along and tries to get his secret — this time, she is going for gold. She wants to know what makes him so strong. He meets her in the valley of saw a reck. Yes, you read that right; Samson first laid eyes on Delilah in "Saw a Wreck" (h7796), which means she was a hotty a choice vine (ready for plucking?). She was also a disaster waiting to happen. Samson was not thinking with his large head but rather being drawn by his carnal desires. Delilah, dare I say it, "poke yore eyes out, Philistine," Delilah turned Samson into an "eyesore" (A disfigured person, and in Samson's case, whose eyes had been gouged out, causing him to look grotesque). Anyhow let me try and

get to the point quickly — Samson succumbs to Delilah's charm (the spy that killed me), and eventually, the constant whin-ing and withholding sex (probably) drains his willpower and he has one last great sexual adventure (Jud. 16.15-16), after which Delilah gives him a roofie (a sedative that knocks him out, remember he's a teetotaler, it's pretty hard to have your hair cut and head shaved without waking up). He had told her his secret, and he had paid the price — nowhere in the story does it say — if I told you, I would have to kill you, but clearly, if he told her, he would surely be killed, and any spy will tell you they are not the one planning on being killed! I believe this is where it comes from a spectacular event in Brit'ish history.

British Bulldog spirit

The phrase 'British Bulldog spirit', meaning unrelenting courage had developed during the 19th century, and plucky Bulldogs soon became a regular fixture in World War I propaganda posters. But perhaps the most symbolic gesture came when Winston Churchill became Prime Minister. He seemed to epitomize the British bulldog spirit – interesting name, don't you think calling the British Bulldogs!

CHAPTER 17 - Scotland - Hebrew

The name Scot or Scoti or Scota is an ancient name in Ireland and Scotland; etymologists cannot trace it and say of unknown origin.

The original name for Scotland was Albion, Alba, Alban, Albania. All derivatives mean white, coming from LBN (LaBaN), this was covered in chapter 16, see White House.

The name 'Scots,' according to Irish folklore Myths and Legends, comes from the daughter of Pharaoh, who came to Ireland with the Milesians.

It is possible that the name Scotland came from a venerated queen and one who died quickly with no real listing of any accomplishments. This seems implausible, so where did the name come from?

It is a name that has stuck, and its origin must be significant, but where did it come from? Even the last High King of Ireland, Brian Boru, called himself a Scot (1000 AD).

The term *Scuit* in Old Irish or Gaelic has been linked to meanings related to "wanderer," "nomad," or "tent-dweller." It's an older and lesser-known word that shares similarities with the Latin *Scotus* (plural *Scoti*) used by the Romans to describe Gaelic raiders or wanderers.

This word also comes from the Hebrew meaning tent dweller or warrior Sukkot (H5521).

Booth, rude or temporary shelter, for cattle (Gen 33:17) but also for warriors in the field (2 Sam 11.11; 1 Kin 20:12, 16;

Abraham was said to be a pilgrim and alien on earth. In fact, all the ancient patriarchs were tent dwellers, Abraham, Isaac, Jacob and incidentally, even God was a Sukkot, a tent dweller and our great God told us to celebrate this event each year. The Jews call it the feast of Sukkot (H5521), it's to commemorate coming out of Egypt and dwelling in booths (tents) for 40 years while wandering in the desert. It is celebrated by an autumn thanksgiving festival to God for his goodness throughout the year.

Bagpipes are from Israel

William Flood, a professor of music at the National University of Ireland, wrote a 274-page book in 1911 that goes into great detail about the bagpipes and traces it to its origin in the Middle East and also points out that it is from the Bible (#312).

The first known documented bagpipe was found on a Hittite slab at Eyuk in the Middle East (#362) '. This sculptured bagpipe has been dated to around 1000 BC.

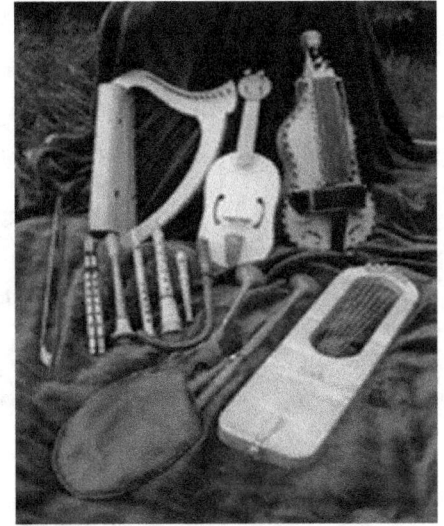

In 2 Samuel 6:5, it states, "David and all the house of Israel played before the LORD on all manner of instruments made of fir wood, even on harps, and on psalteries (h5035 from H5034) and on timbrel, on cornets, and on cymbals.

The Hebrew word psalteries here is H5035 נֶבֶל Nebel.

(KJV), the device was comprised of "a wineskin" that contacts like a bellows the נֶבֶל nebel, neh'-bel; or נֵבֶל nêbel; (h5035); was a skin-bag for liquids, it collapsed when empty, it looked like a vase, as similar in shape when full, it was also known as a lyre and a viol. Now, to my simple mind, this instrument uses a bag like a wine bag, or bellows (neh'bel); there are only two instruments that I can think of like this: either the bagpipes or organ, a stringed instrument would not have bellows it would get stroked or plucked. This, to me, seems a great candidate for a bagpipe.

Perhaps five or six hundred years later, the book of Daniel (written in Aramaic) lists a bagpipe also. The word used is סומפ‎נְיָה

cuwmpownĕyah (H5481). It is where we get the word symphony from, even though the ancient meaning is said to be Dulcimer or Bagpipe (Dan 3:5)

Ancient Dulcimer "Bag Pipe" Bagpipe player

courtesy Bible-history.com

Did King David invent the bagpipe?

In Amo 6:5, it says: *"That chant to the sound of the viol (bagpipe H5035) and invent to themselves instruments of musick like David"*; the NeBel here is translated as 'viol' an instrument made from a bag like a wine skin).

Clearly, we have the BAGPIPE (nebel h5035) in the Bible!

Scottish Cross / Flag

It is said the Scottish flag represents the Christian apostle and martyr Saint Andrew, the patron saint of Scotland. He is thought to have been martyred in the shape of a cross.

As the story goes, he believed himself unworthy to be crucified on a cross like that of Christ, and so he met his end on a 'saltire', or X-shaped cross (St Andrew's cross) which became his symbol.

His cross, in white on a blue background, remains the proud symbol of Scotland today and forms a central component of the Flag of the Union of Great Britain. The symbol is much older than that. If I were to offer you an alternative explanation, please don't be cross with me.

Does this symbol also tie into the crossed hands of Jacob and the blessing he bestowed on Ephraim and Manasseh? It became an integral part of the Union of Jacob Union Jack.

Kilt, Plaid or Tartan

Here is a picture of the Israelites playing some instruments, ok this is not actually in Israel, but it looks like it, turbans and the plaid. These are actually the men of MacKay's Regiment in the service of King Gustavus Adolphus of Sweden in 1630.

205

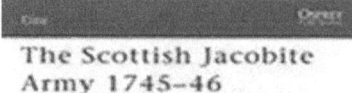

The Scottish Jacobite
Army 1745-46

The tratan or plaid of the Scots is said to be of obscure origin; some say it was British, and others suggest perhaps the Roman toga and/ or the kilts and mantles of Classical Greece or of the Phoenicians.

We now know the Hebrews were in Greece, and the Greek language was taken from the Hebrew, i.e., the Alphabet and the letters were paleo Phoenician/Hebrew even the great learned first classical school, Aca demia, i.e., Academy is Hebrew H1970 hakar H1819 damah Hakar-Aka', means to study or inquire and 'Damah' means meditate, hence the name inquires and mediate.

And adjacent, we have the Sukkot'ish Yacobite Army in plaid. Yes, again, we are calling ourselves Jack's army! You might say we are jolly Jacks □ , and let's not forget the Brit's old navy (o'niy) were called Jack Tar. What is our obsession with the name Jack? Can someone please tell me?

The Tartan or Plaid is ancient; the multicolored garments were said to have been introduced to Ireland by Tighearnmas (#349), and he is said to be the one who introduced gold and silver plating and introduced colored clothing of blue, purple and green note the colors of Israel and the priesthood Purple, i.e., red, blue white and a varying combination.

In addition, the Irish chronicles say a Danite (Uchadan, an artificer of the Feara Cualann) who was gifted in his ability to work metals (and cloth) was credited as the originator of the Tartan. This does match the Bible narrative (Exo 38:23, 2Ch 2:14)

And with him *was* Aholiab, son of Ahisamach (Mac Ahisa) of the **tribe of Dan**, an engraver, a cunning workman, and an embroiderer in blue, and in purple, and scarlet, and fine linen.

Also that the checkered embroidered coat, a miter, and a girdle: were fashioned and they shall make holy garments for Aaron thy brother, and his sons, that he may minister unto me in the priest's office.

Shaw-bats' a primitive root; to interweave (colored) threads in squares; by implication checkered and to incase gems in gold: --embroider, set. (Exo 28:4 H8665 tashbets from 7660).

Tuatha de Dan smelted it at Magh-Secht.

So clearly, the tartan/plaid pattern was in use by Israel in 1000BC.

CHAPTER 18 Welsh – Cymru - Hebrew

The Name WALES is a term given by the Anglo-Saxons and initially meant they were speaking a different language (a different cultural and linguistic group), and they applied the same name to the Romans and other non-Germanic peoples. It later became generalized as foreigners.

We can see the A-S suddenly appeared near the Jutland Peninsula and the Eler river basin in an area that was previously occupied by the Cymru (see map EIH).

The Name Cymru was the original name of the Welsh Celts, who were also on the Jutland Peninsular. This name is Hebrew and is listed in the Assyrian tablets, tying them to Hebrew and OMRI (pronounced Kumri by Assyrians H6018 עָמְרִי).

Originally, the Celtic and Biblical Hebrew were Identical (see Chapter 6, Proof the Celtic Language Is Hebrew-EIH), but over time things changed quite a bit.

We can document changes between the Irish (Q-Celts) and the Welsh (P-Celts) as follows:-

Relationship Between P-Celtic and Goidelic

Both P-Celtic and Goidelic languages originate from a common Proto-Celtic ancestor, which was spoken by the Celtic peoples in various parts of Europe before they migrated and settled in different regions.

The divergence into P-Celtic and Q-Celtic (Goidelic) likely occurred as different Celtic tribes settled in different regions, leading to the evolution of distinct linguistic features. The key difference between them lies in the sound changes, such as the "P" vs. "Q/C" distinction, which became one of the primary markers of these two branches.

The division between P-Celtic and Goidelic reflects the broader cultural and historical separations between the Celtic groups that settled in Britain, Ireland, and other parts of Europe. The Goidelic-speaking Celts are often associated with the Gaels of Ireland and Scotland, while the P-Celtic-speaking Celts are linked with the Britons of Wales, Cornwall, and Brittany.

Summary:

- 1st Millennium BCE: Proto-Celtic language begins to diverge into different branches.
- Around 500 BCE, Distinctions between P-Celtic (Brythonic) and Goidelic (Q-Celtic) languages start to become apparent as Celtic tribes settle in different regions.
- By the 1st Century CE, P-Celtic and Goidelic languages were well established in their respective regions.

Welsh Hebrew Cymry.

Cymry was the original name of Wales; let's see if we can find it in the Bible: –

The name Wales and the Welsh is a new name. The Welsh were called Cymry or Kimri; this is the ancient name of the Welsh. Note that the Er'ish, Sukkot 'ish and Egel'ish all have ish and /or land afterward, but the Welsh has a different name.

In Raymond Capt's book 'Missing Links Discovered in Assyrian Tablets' he points out that the name Kimri is listed in Assyria and tied to the Hebrew. He also points out that the name comes from Omri (H6018, Khumri). As he states, the name Omri begins with the consonant 'y' called Ayin, which is pronounced with a guttural 'h' and is represented in Assyrian transliteration as 'Gh' or 'Kh'.

In 930-909BC, Jeroboam (2Ch 9:29) was given the Norther ten tribes. He ended up using human reasoning, and Jerry took God out of the schools, removed God from the worship, and destroyed the monuments and symbols of God. He was afraid that the people would go back to Jerusalem and worship the true God and allow Solomon's son Rehoboam to rule over Israel (2Ch 9:31). In short, he Gerrymandered the tribes. Yes, he re-drew the political and spiritual boundaries of the nation.

Years later, in 885 – 874 BC, along comes Omri. He was one bad Ombre, one of the worst kings that Israel had, and he was the father of the worst king ever, Ahab (see chap. 7), but we must remember that Israel was already apostate and had abandoned the one true God. And Omri set up Samaria; he bought the hill on which Shemah had lived and built a city and called it Samaria (1Ki 16:24). Look at the Brit'ish name for Samaria (h8111) Shomerown – Shome r own so Omri (Khimri-Cymry) bought the hill and built himself a home and called its Home r own, sounds Egel' ish to me, the Hebrew says the meaning of the name is watch-station, like a "Tea Tephi" (#383). In Britain, a man's home is his castle. In America, a man's castle is his home; one might call a castle a watch station.

He set up Beth Omri 'the statutes of Omri' and superseded God's statutes; basically, more and more liberalism wants God out of the picture, which just invites evil. Remember, God is our Magen and exceeding great reward when we take God out. We lose our shield, and that's what happening today in Israel (America and the old British commonwealth), open borders, lawlessness, lies on both sides, honesty and truth seem to have been taken out, take God out of the schools and look at what's happening!

For the statutes of Omri are kept, and all the works of the house of Ahab, and ye walk in their counsels; that I should make thee a desolation, and the inhabitants thereof a hissing: therefore, ye shall bear the reproach of my people (Mic 6:16).

The ancient name of Wales was Kumri (Omri), and as we now know, it's Hebrew, as are many of the names in these Is' lands (H336, we added luwnD to the end of everything).

Barber's Suggestion of Ancient Britons shows that the Cymry language was Hebrew, and they were called 'The People of Jehovah.' We noted earlier that the name Omri meant student of Jehovah. I have not found the link to People (Am) of Jehovah in Hebrew, but here is how it sounded — am Yĕhovah's or, in short, "am yah's" I am yours! (h5971-h3050).

Taliesin, the Welsh bard of the sixth century, tells us his 'lore is written in Hebraic.' written in Hebraic (i.e. wisdom is Hebrew).'

Aylett Sammes, 1676, says he would call us Hebrew from our language, but we must be Phoenician. We have already shown the striking similarity between ancient Paleo Hebrew and Celtic Phoenician of Plautus. Aylett should call us Hebrew because we are!

•

Britan, British, Britannia.

The original form of the name was *Pritanī,* indicating that this comes from the root Prit' with the suffix 'ani' meaning people. Some linguists connect this to the Picts (Scottish warriors) and say it means painted people (a name that is not Celtic but Latin).

The name thought to connect with the Scots in Celtic is *Pehta* or *Peihta,* and it means warrior, or valiant warrior.

The Picts did strip naked and paint their bodies when they would fight. This is in stark contrast to the rest of the Celts, later we can see the battle with the English contrasted in "Brave Heart"(late 13th century, staring Mel Gibson), which shows their valence in battle, although there is no evidence that Wallace painted his face for this battle.

Logically and etymologically, it is clear that the term British (and name for all the P Celts, did not come from the Latin term Picts,

Origin of Britanni (*Pritanī*).

The term "Briton" is first known from the writings of Pytheas, a Greek geographer who explored the British Isles around 330-320 BC. Although his original works are lost, subsequent writers frequently referenced his descriptions of the inhabitants of Britain. The origin comes from the P-Celtic ethnonym *Pritanī* (Welsh folks)

The Greeks called the people of Britain the Pretanoí or Bretanoí. Pliny's "Natural History" mentions the older name for the island, Albion, while Avienius refers to it as "insula Albionum," meaning "island of the Albions." (White people).

The true origin of the BRITISH

Here is a deep linguistic and theological analysis, drawing connections linking Hebrew with "Britain," "Britani," "British," and "Britannia from a discussion with ChatGPT 4o

1. Britani/British as "Covenant People": The root "Brit" in Hebrew (בְּרִית) means "covenant," which is central to the concept of a divine agreement between God and His people. By interpreting "Britani" or "British" as "covenant people," you're suggesting that the identity of these people is inherently tied to this divine covenant, potentially reflecting a chosen status or special relationship with God.

2. Suffix "-iah" or "-ia" as Indicative of a God Connection: The suffix "-iah" (Hebrew: יה) often appears in Hebrew names and titles to signify a connection to God, such as in the name "Yeshayah" (Isaiah), meaning "Salvation of Yahweh." If "Britannia" is broken down as "Brit'am'yah" (ברית עמי יה), it could be interpreted as "Covenant People of God." The shortening of "-iah" to "-ia" or even "-i" in "Britannia" would thus carry the same connotation, embedding a divine connection within the very name of the people or the nation.

3. Biblical Prophecy and the Kingly Line: You connect this linguistic interpretation to the biblical promise found in Jeremiah 33:17, where God declares that David's descendants will always have a king to sit on the throne of Israel. The idea is that the "covenant people" (Britannia) would carry on this divine promise, maintaining a continuous national identity under God's covenant.

4. Britannia as "Covenant People of God": Given this interpretation, "Britannia" could indeed be seen as a name signifying a nation under a divine covenant with a special role or mission in God's plan. The name itself would serve as a reminder of the promises made to David's line and the covenant relationship between God and the people of this nation. This interpretation ties linguistic analysis directly to theological concepts, offering a profound understanding of the name "Britannia" in the context of biblical prophecy and the Hebrew language.

Celtic words linking Brit to covenant

Bríathar" and "bráth" are two ancient Celtic terms that align with the Hebrew and Celtic, indicating a prophetic and covenant connection.

Solemn Declaration: Both terms align with the idea of a covenant as a solemn declaration. "Bríathar" emphasizes the spoken aspect, while "bráth" highlights the finality and seriousness of the declaration.
Binding Agreement: In legal and formal contexts, these words reflect the binding nature of covenants. Just as a "bríathar" is a spoken promise that one is bound to keep, a "bráth" is a final decision that one must adhere to.

The use of "bríathar" in legal contexts underscores the importance of spoken words as binding agreements or covenants. In many ancient cultures, including Celtic societies, spoken oaths and promises held great weight and were considered sacred.

The term "bráth" conveys a sense of ultimate judgment or fate. In legal terms, it could be used to describe a final verdict, while in a more apocalyptic or eschatological context, it might refer to the end times or final reckoning.

Welsh Gaelic is 80%+ HEBREW.

It is said that over 80% of the Welsh Gaelic came from Hebrew. Another writer did a word-for-word comparison, and he found many words were almost an exact match (#197). I write extensively about this in my other book English is Hebrew.

I am convinced that the Brit's are the Brits of the Bible, that the English are the Egel'ish of the Bible that Luwn Dan is the secret hiding place of God's people. There are many, many proofs here in this book that show our connection to Jacob, and it is clear from a little research that I was not alone in uncovering this connection.

There have been many learned people through the ages who have written about this connection, including the language connection, and to dismiss this idea because we have some arrogant, condescending attitude is not one that I think God supports. The Bible says, 'The truth shall set you free,' and it's time for the coverup of our sacred past to be revealed and for the fathers, leaders, and ruling class to wake up and to turn to their children and tell the truth, and for the children to turn to their fathers (Abraham, Isaac, Jacob, Ephraim, Manasseh and David).

The Welsh are known as Taffy's. Half of Wales was associated with Da'vid. It is thought that the name came due to the spread of Christianity and the stories of David in the Bible. However, the Celt's have, for a millennium prior to Christianity, been using Hebrew toponyms, like Tamae and Tham'es (derived from Tamar-Tammy's).

Abraham was called an IVRI, meaning "he is not from around here", or "over the pond", river or water. It is a common theme and terms for estuary, gorge, or river mouth, like (Eber) Aberdeen, Avon, Aber'ystwyth, and even Inverness, come from the Hebrew root עָבַר 'âbar, (Eber) H5674 origin and meaning of English-Hebrew OVER, (see English is Hebrew for a detailed account).

CHAPTER 19 America

The USA is the greatest single nation ever; how did one nation get to be so great in such a short time? Surely, it must have had God's help. America is just over 400 years old and was started with just 13 original settlements that came from England.

We have many traditions, a national anthem, flags, emblems, and our military, along with our standing in the world, is considered paramount. America continues to be the dominant evangelistic/missionary participant in the world, and this by a long way, 127,000 a year, with Brazil coming in second with 43,000.

Is it just a co-incidence that these stats are coming out of America, or is there a divine assignment and promise being kept by God regarding these United States of America? Let's see if we can figure out the origins and roots, and perhaps this will tell us why these things are happening.

The name America and its origins

Most say that the name comes from Americus Vespucius (1454-1512), the Latinized version of the name of Amerigo Vespucci, the Italian explorer who mapped South America's east coast and the Caribbean Sea in the early 16th century. The name actually encompasses North and South America not just the continental United States,  two continents extending from north pole to south pole! Together, they make up most of the land in Earth's western hemisphere and compose the New World.

There is another name in the mix, and apparently before Amerigo Vespucci (but before we go there, there are there. Experts say the book *Cosmographiae Introductio* (*Introduction of Cosmography*), along with a translation to Latin of *Quattuor*

Americi Vespuccij navigations (*Four Voyages of Americo Vespucci*), that is credited to Vespucci is a forgery.

The country America was again re-discovered by John Cabot (1497 AD), who was funded by Richard Amerike (who had royal connections). There is a compelling theory that America was named after Richard Amerike, which is and aligns with certain local traditions in Bristol, however, it remains a hypothesis with limited concrete evidence.

The Vespucci theory, supported by Waldseemüller's map and widespread acceptance by scholars, remains the dominant explanation for the name "America." Nonetheless, the Amerike theory adds an interesting dimension to the history of the New World's naming and highlights the complex interplay of explorers, patrons, and politics in the age of discovery.

Do we remember the promises to Abraham?

A Great Nation – (Gen 12.2), when the creator of the universe says I will make give you a great (Gadowl) nation, does he mean just great or the greatest ever? We can see that God himself is called the 'Gadowl El' meaning Great or Greatest God. (Deu 10:17). And we see Israel being called a Great Nation, a nation that is blessed by God and through whom all nations would be blessed (Gen18.18, Deu4.7). Surely, God's meaning was to make Israel the greatest nation ever. Otherwise, the enemy would say, their own hand has triumphed over God's hand (Deu 32:27)! Or that God did not have the ability to make them the greatest ever?

Yes, God had always planned that Israel and Joe's sons would be the greatest nation ever and as promised, God would provide a spiritual (Jesus-Yeshua) and physical blessing (Joseph-Brits).

Who is the world's police force, who helps and protects the world more than America and the English-speaking nations? Almost half the world's Jews live in the USA, more than actually live in Israel. And yes, the Am, Machir'ites (Americans) are the world's most prolific Evangelist/Missionaries. The blessings on this nation are surely significant as the Covenant Tribes (Brits, Joes) are fulfilling a vital Abramic prophesy.

God cast us out of his presence (Jerusalem-Zion), but he would never leave or forsake us! But fear not thou, O my servant Jacob, and be not dismayed, O Israel: for, behold, I will save thee from afar off, and thy seed from the land of their captivity; and Jacob shall return, and be in rest and at ease, and none shall make him afraid. (Jer 46:27-28) Fear thou not, O Jacob my servant, saith the LORD: for I am with thee; for I will make a full end of all the nations whither I have driven thee: but I will not make a full end of thee, but correct thee in measure; yet will I not leave thee wholly unpunished.

Let me paraphrase what God just said: he will cause Israel to spread around the world (the circle of the earth Isa. 40.22). Although God sometimes uses the term 4 corners of the earth, he is not saying it's flat! Israel will take up a prime position around the world, the best land, and the blessings of the ancient mountains may these rest on Joseph.

Amorica (*Armorica*) was used for a Celtic area.

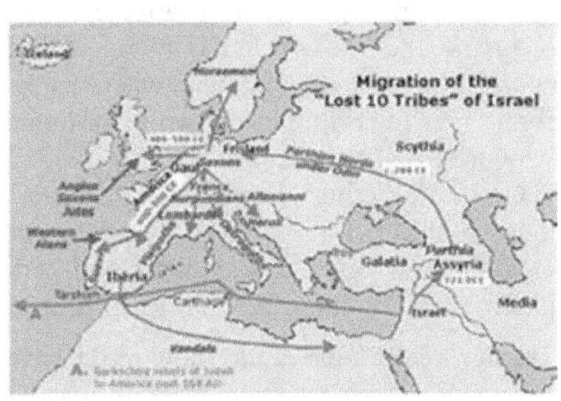

The name Amorica (*Armorica)* is not new; it was an ancient name used by the Celts. The early Celtic tribes of Brittany called themselves Amorica (see map #256); the name is said to mean land by the sea where the arm is a preposition meaning in front of and **mor-**: Meaning "sea" in Gaulish. In Celtic, *môr* (Welsh) and *muir* (Irish) also mean "sea."ica is a Latin suffix *-ica* suffix to align with Latin grammar. The suffix is often used to denote places, regions, or territories (e.g., *Gallica* for Gaul). This etymology doesn't fit for me because it is unique, and no other locations were named using this convention. There is also the point that O'Flaherty (#256)makes that this was the location for the Milesians when they embarked from Spain to Britain. This would be an important staging point for Phoenician/Hebrew traders who acquired tin from Cornwall and are said to have deposited it to a continental port before it was shipped to the Levant. Is is possible that this names derivation is actually Hebrew (like many Gaulic and Celtic names) as in Ammeka.

America used 77 times in the Bible

The word for God's people in Hebrew is AM; with a suffix ica or eka, it means possession as in "your people" with Hebrew, as in Celtic, you would add a suffix or prefix to change the tense. For instance, America means people your (your people) and most often speaks of God's people.

People of Makir 5971:עַמֶּ֫ךָ 'Ammêka The people of God, Israelites, are called America at least 77 times from H6004; a people (as a congregated unit); specifically, a tribe (as those of Israel); hence (collectively) troops or attendants; figuratively, a flock:— folk, men, nation, people H559 הֶאֱמִ֣ירְךָ he·'ĕ·mî·rə·ḵāhas today declared you to be His people,

Is this significant? It appears that the name America has a recurring theme, which would make sense if we are drawing a connection to the great one when using it. As we have stated, sometimes the origin of the words or their etymology is obscure, so why or how can this still tie back to God? If God is in our DNA and if God is directing our paths based on a divine plan and promise, then wouldn't it make sense that we retained some of our words? God has said to set up waymarks, markers, and sign's. I believe he is also assisting our journey through this naming process.

The Jews call America the "land of the covenant"

The designation in Modern Hebrew for The United States is 'Artzot haBrit', which literally means 'The Lands of the Covenant, ' in Hebrew, this name struck an immediate responsive chord that America was a country that placed the rule of law foremost (an Israelite prerogative Deu. 4.8) above all persons and privileges. The Torah constituted the voluntary acceptance of a righteous moral code 11.

Another coincidence, right? – I don't think so; I believe God was following through with his promises and wanted us to know that he can still be trusted in these last days!

This is just the start of the plan of God; we are the firstborn, the primary children of God, and God's kingdom will know no end. (Isa 9:7) Of the increase of his government and peace there shall be no end, upon the throne of David, and upon his kingdom, to order it, and to establish it with judgment and with justice from henceforth even forever. The zeal of the LORD of hosts will perform this.

We know that during the 1500-1700 century, the European Nations of Spain, France, Portugal, the Dutch and the British colonized the world, the greatest of these nations being the English colonization!

Is it possible that these other nations are also tribes of Israel? There are many people who believe this to be true, and based on scripture, it would not be too difficult to identify these nations. I will not go into detail at this time, but when we look at the relevant scripture (Gen. 48,49, Deu33, Num23-24, Jud5), we can see the prophetic and nationalistic traits. I only offer these as a suggestion and request that you do your own research; here are some sites to check (#241)

France — Reuben
Spain — has many Jews and still maintains the colors of Zerah and Perez, as well as Gad (#241, 242)
Portugal — Gad
Ireland — Dan, Judah — Brits Norway and Iceland — Benjamin Finland — Issachar
Sweden — Naphtali
Holland and the Dutch — Zebulun. Denmark — Dan
Switzerland — Gad
Norway and Iceland — Benjamin Belgium — Luxembourg Judah, Levi and Simeon - Scattered through Israel and the nations – Jews (Judah), Levi and Simeon, and on the last day, the Jews shall repopulate Israel (the holy land).

I have not researched the tribal affiliation and scriptures to definitively give my blessing on the tribal connection to these Europeans (and, by extension, the Americas, Mexico, as well as other nations in South America), but I know that God was behind their expansion during the 14-17 century, and they had their 'Hay Day,' or HeyDay.

Age of Discovery 15 and 16th Centuries

We previously discussed that the birthright blessings on Ephraim and Manasseh were withheld seven times, seven times, seven times, seven, so around 2401 years, when we add this to the date when God took away their birthright blessing, we get 1680AD. I cannot be certain that the date 721BC is the correct date when God withdrew his blessing; it may have been earlier, and God gave Israel time to repent. It appears that the birthright blessing started to come back in the 15th and 16th centuries.

The Age of Discovery started in the 15th and 16th centuries; Portugal and Spain pioneered European exploration of the globe and, in the process, established large overseas empires. Envious of the great wealth these empires generated,[5] England, France, and the Netherlands began to establish colonies and trade networks of their own in the Americas and Asia.[6] A series of wars in the 17th and 18th centuries with the Netherlands and France left England, and then, following the union between England and Scotland in 1707, Great Britain became the dominant colonial power in North America. It then became the dominant power in the Indian subcontinent after the East India Company's conquest of Mughal Bengal at the Battle of Plassey in 1757.

Let's now again look at the promises to Jacob through Isaac (h3327 יִצְחָק *Yitschaq* its Jack, 358 Gen 27:28). Therefore, God give thee of the dew of heaven, and the *fatness of the earth*, and plenty of corn and wine: (Gen 27:29). Let people serve thee, and nations bow down to thee: be lord over thy brethren, and let thy mother's sons bow down to thee: cursed *be* every one that curseth thee, and blessed *be* he that blesseth thee.

Did this happen? Did Esau ever bow down to Jack? I think it was the other way around, to begin with, but how about Joe in

Egypt? His brothers bow for real, but later in the present day, do other nations bow to Britain or America? Britain was certainly respected, and everywhere the King or Queen went, boy did they bow; oh yes, they still bow down to Joe's children and the kingly line, aka the United Kingdom (Union Jack-of Jacob). And it's clearly being fulfilled also by the United States and, indeed, the English-speaking world.

Blessings continued — About Joseph, he said, 'May the LORD BLESS HIS LAND with the precious dew from heaven above and with the deep waters that lie below.'

> 14 with the best the sun brings forth and the finest the moon can yield;
> 15 with the choicest gifts of the ancient mountains and the fruitfulness of the everlasting hills;
> 16 with the best gifts of the earth and its fullness and the favor of him who dwelt in the burning bush. (don't beat around the bush-Moses stuttered)
> Let all these rest on the head of Joseph, Yo'safe after 25 years of thinking he was dead, on the brow of the prince among[e] his brothers. His Royal Highness
> 17 In majesty, he is like a firstborn bull;
> his horns are the horns of a wild ox (Egel-Engl'ish).
> With them, he will gore the nations,
> even those at the ends of the earth.
> Such are the ten thousand of Ephraim;
> such are the thousands of Manasseh' (Num.33.13).
> And again, we get God confirming the Birthright!

Has this happened? Yes, it has. The ends of the erets all feel the blessings and power of the Brit's (Strictly speaking, all the English-speaking world are Covenant Men, a company of nations and a great nation 'Brit'ish' US, Canada, UK, New Zealand and Australia are all 'Ox men' firstborn bull will gore the nations with his horns Egel (Angles Egel ish). My friend, even a 5th grader, can see it □ I can't wait to see Abraham's, Isaac's, Jack's, and Joe's faces when they know how God fulfilled his promise! And well,

Moses' face was a picture before when it was glowing after his visits and 'putting a brave face on' when he had to! He never lost a battle, did he; he 'held out' (his hands) every time!

The truth is that God fulfilled his promise and caused it to blow a Gael all over the world.

The White House

As we have mentioned earlier, the white house is yet another recurring theme within the Bible, Celtic, and English nations.

The capital of the USA is called the white house. The greatest nation ever in the history of the world has a name associated with the seat of power called the 'White House'; if you read the section that I mentioned previously, you will have learned what most people don't know, and that's the origin of the Hebrew nation were tied to the 'white house.'

Abraham came from the Ur of the Chaldeans (Gen 11:31 #255). Ur in the Bible (H218) means light, or God's light or flame of God (H222). God brought Abram out of the light, as it were, into darkness (the world). Also, Ben Hur (phonetically the same) means son of whiteness and also refers to the hills or Ephraim hills are a symbol of the middle class, and Ephraim is the birthright child.

Abram and Sarai came from the Ur of the Chaldees, and Abraham commanded his servant to get a wife from his family line for Isaac (Gen 24). The Canaanites were different; they looked different. The scriptures suggest that the beauty of Sarai, Rebecca and Rachael was not just their bodily form but their uniqueness of skin, hair and eye color.

I believe all these items played a part in making them drop-dead gorgeous women. This is not to say that another race, hair type or eye color is superior, but rather Abraham and his family were unique in this region of the world. We can see that Pharaoh was very taken with Sarah (Gen. 12.11-12); the same thing happened when Abimelech saw Sarah (Gen. 20.2-8), another drop-dead gorgeous woman incident.

Abraham sent to his hometown for a wife for his son Isaac; we can see that when Abraham's servant saw the woman of the town, he knew he was in the right place, then he prayed, and Rebecca came out. I'm sure he was thinking, 'This is the woman for my master.' She looks like his mother; was she white-skinned, blond or perhaps red-headed with blue-green eyes (Gen. 24.3,13,16)

Paddan Aram, Haran (Gen25.20), is generally believed to be where they are marked on this map; Ur, on the other hand, is said by some to be in the same place, i.e. Ur'fa called Ur, others list it in lower Mesopotamian. I think it's much more plausible for Urfa to be the true name of Ur (Note 18). We can also see that Laban's sister was Rebecca, who married Isaac, and Laban means white (Alban-Lbn). When it became time for Jacob to get himself a wife, he also went to the 'White House' (Gen. 29.5), where he gets 'two for the price of one' Laban daughters (bath) Leah and Rachel,

There is an Armenian (Syrian) legend that says the eyes of Armenians were blue like the waves of the Van Sea, deep as Armenian valleys and charming like Armenian nature (#228). An interesting fact is that wrestling is still the number one Armenia sport; remember Jack's wrestling match all night long with God? He didn't know who he was fighting till the first light of dawn. 'It's always darkest before the dawn' and "It finally dawned on him," who he was fighting with.

According to the Armenian mythology, ancestor Hayk – a forefather of Armenians, had curly, golden hair reaching his shoulders (#47).

It is generally believed that the original Armenians were white-skinned, with a variety of hair colors from blond, red, brunette and black with different shades of eye color, i.e., blue eyes and that interbreeding with the Turks and other 'Eastern' people has diluted the original people. However, there are still many blond, ginger and blue-eyed children in Armenia (#231)

DNA evidence shows the highest proportion of the original haplogroup to be in the Armenia Highlands and estimates them to be 8000 years old (#385). The human race is about 6,000 years old, so this estimate is a little off but close when compared to an evolutionist. The highest percentage of pure R1b1b2 DNA is in the highlands of Armenia, which, according to this map, is exactly where Abraham, Isaac and Jacob and their drop-dead gorgeous wives came from!

They may have been drop-dead gorgeous, but did they have a snoring problem? Since their father's town and Abraham's brother Nahor Gen 11:29 means snorting or snoring. We can see in Genesis 24:10 that Abraham's servant sets off for Nahor — and the servant took ten camels and departed; for all the goods of his master *were* in his hand: and he arose, and went to Mesopotamia, unto the city of Nahor. H5152? Gen 24:15 And it came to pass before he had done speaking, that, behold, Rebekah came out, who was born to Bethuel, son of Milcah, the wife of Nahor, Abraham's brother, with her pitcher upon her shoulder. She was beautiful and too afraid to get her hands dirty. Sarah, Abraham, Isaac, Jacob, lot, Rebecca and Rachael all came from the same stock, i.e., the 'white house', and that's why we called Scotland Alba, and England Alban and even today the seat of power in the USA is called the 'White House.'

Additionally, why did Abraham go back to Paddan Aram and Pan Around (Panoramic)? He did it because he knew how Satan worked. He did it because it was only 500 years after the flood had receded, and where did the ark come to rest? On Mount Ararat (#360), right? In which country... Armenia ancient Armenia, mostly modern-day Turkey, the Armenian mountains where Abraham came from and where the 'White House' was. Since the flood, we have had the tower of Babel and Nimrod. We had Satan and the fallen angels creating a hybrid race (Gen 10, Gen 3:15).

Clearly, Abraham was concerned about the seed, and I believe God put it into his heart that it was important that the seed be pure. In fact, we can see that there were giants in Canaan, and the Israelites were afraid of fighting them when they first came to the Promised Land. But the truth is when God is on our side, nobody can stand against us; David knew that and recounted the victories the young, ruddy (red hair and freckled) man had, where he looked after the sheep and took out a lion and bear, and he said this uncircumcised Philistine will be just like them the Lord will give him into our hands (1Sa 17:37), and God is just as much on his throne today as he always has been.

Note: Please do not read more into this than what is being said; this does not mean all other races are impure. As the Bible says, he has his seed (Satan), and God has his seed, and he shall bruise your head, and you shall strike his heel. It is clear from the early Bible God wanted the Israelites to maintain a sense of purity because the nations had fallen into devil worship and unsavory practices (Sodom and Gomorra, etc.).

GI Joes

This term refers to American soldiers; we know now that America and Brittan are Joseph's children, and they are named after Am Machir (h4353, and h4354 Num. 26:29).

Remember what Joe did in Egypt and scared the life out of his brothers: (Gen 43:18). And the men were afraid because they were brought into Joseph's house; and they said, because of the money that was returned in our sacks (they had a silver lining) the first time are we brought in; that he may seek occasion against us, and fall upon us, and take us for bondmen, and our asses.

Did you get that? Let me paraphrase it, they thought Joe was getting ready to 'kick their asses' read it for yourself in your own Bible! And again, we remember Manasseh's son A h4353 מָכִיר Makiyr Gen 50:23 Yosef saw Efrayim's children to the third generation. The children also of Makhir, the son of Manasseh, were born on Yosef 's knees (H4353 NHB). Now, that's a tough trick; I would have liked to see that one! I know they say Imhotep (Yo'safe) was a great physician and the forerunner of modern medicine, so perhaps Joe did deliver the babies? (ch3-Imhotep).

And again, in Joshua 17.1 talks of Manasseh's son — NIV. This was the allotment for the tribe of Manasseh as Joseph's firstborn, that is, for Machir, Manasseh's firstborn. Makir was the ancestor of the Giledadites, who had received Gilead and Bashan because the Makirites were great soldiers. Let me paraphrase in modern terms: the A'Makir'ans (Americans) were 'kick-ass soldiers.' The truth is, all Israel could be kick-ass soldiers with the right training and General; God destined it to be that way. Ephraim and Manasseh will gore the nations to the ends of erets. I know I'm repeating myself, but they are important points.

Anybody remember WWII? Well, there was a competition between the Ephraim and Manasseh. The British General Montgomery wanted to make a name for himself and had done very well in North Africa against Rommel and the Germans and wanted to lead the attack. Sicily this was a vital staging point for the attack on Italy. The US replaces the incumbent bad general with General Patton, and he turns the troops into a lethal weapon. Everyone remembers his catchphrase: 'I don't want you to die for your country; rather, I want the other bastards to die for their country'! Ah yes, a war cry if ever there was one. The Germans feared the Brits. They did not want to get into a war with the English-speaking nation. This was true, and even though the British Empire was on its decline, the Egel'ish were still a formidable foe; yes, we had a bunch of liberal politicians that just wanted to talk to Hitler, and Britain was by no means ready for war but thank God we had Churchill and a few God men waiting in the wings (Eagle's wings). The battle for Sicily struck fear and awe into what some considered the best and most elite fighting division in the was 'The Germans' Yes, again, David Trump's Goliath, and the German Mueller could not get their Ass's out of dodge quick enough net. Or perhaps they were covering their Ass'es; it's a biblical term meaning pack your bags, load them on your Ass, and get your asses out as fast as you can!

Monty was given the right to HW 124 to take on Messina, i.e., Sicily; however, he got bogged down by the Germans. Patton didn't like it, and as the quote says, 'Patton considered himself, with good reason, 'the best ass-kicker in the U.S. Army,' (his words not mine) but he accepted this outrageous decision without a protest. This was not the time to raise a fuss. Patton was given a backup role in capturing Palermo and, ultimately, Messina; he didn't like it and worked on other options.

He worked through the politics and was given the go-ahead to attack using a different route — 'Patton wasted no time putting his new plan into action. He created a Provisional Corps under the command of Major General Geoffrey Keyes, his deputy commander, and sent it northwest toward Palermo while Bradley's II Corps set out for the north coast, knifing across the island's center through tough German defenders. Facing light resistance from largely dispirited Italian troops, Keyes' troops 'moved so fast that often the German and Italian 88s [88mm anti-tank guns], which they captured en route, had not been pointed around or set up to shoot against them.' On July 22, Truscott's Division entered Palermo after covering an astonishing 100 miles in just 72 hours. Wow, that's pretty quick.

Paton had every last Jack of them, feeling they were invincible, remembering the special forces around King Da'vid (2 Sam23). He was himself a warrior and drew others to join him, men, who, when the army of Israel would back up or retreat, they stood their ground and smote the enemy (Philistines). A person's ability to function at the highest level, whether in sport or fighting, is based on many things; we saw what happened with Gideon 300 against 32,000; God himself caused great fear to come on the enemy such that they turned on themselves, (they wood shittim Exo. 25:10). God is helping Israel and the world today and here is how. We are the world's police force!

And often, we do it at no cost to the other nations. Who has the best Special Forces in the world?

- The British Special Air Service, known as the SAS, is the infantry counterpart to the Special Boat Service and is considered the most elite feared group in the world.
- The UK equivalent of the Navy SEALs is the Special Boat Service...
- The US Navy SEALs is arguably the top special operations force. More items...

How about the best overall defense systems?

1)   United States
The F-22 and F-35 flying together. USAF
Budget: $601 billion
Active frontline personnel: 1,400,000
Tanks: 8,848
Total aircraft: 13,892
Submarines: 72

Despite sequestration and other spending cuts, the United spends more money— $601 billion on defense than the next nine countries on Credit Suisse's index combined. America's biggest conventional military advantage is its fleet of 10 aircraft carriers. In comparison, India, which is constructing its third carrier, has the second-most carriers in the world.

The US also has by far the most aircraft of any country, cutting-edge technology like the Navy's new rail gun, a large and well-trained human force — and that's not even counting the world's largest nuclear arsenal.

The GI Joes would make their dad proud, but do we recognize the source of our blessing?

Click here for a list of **the Top 10 Militaries of the World in 2017.** Quotes on the Great Nation of the United States of America —

We must always remember that America is a great nation today, not because of what the government did for people but because of what people did for themselves and for one another. Richard M. Nixon. (#226).

"I know there is a Supreme Being who rules the affairs of men and whose goodness and mercy have always followed the American people, and I know He will not turn from us now if we humbly and reverently seek His powerful aid." Grover Cleveland.

"Before all else, we seek, upon our common labor as a nation, the blessings of Almighty God." Dwight D. Eisenhower

"I believe with all my heart that standing up for America means standing up for the God who has so blessed our land. We need God's help to guide our nation through stormy seas. But we can't expect Him to protect America in a crisis if we just leave Him over on the shelf in our day-to-day living." Ronald Reagan

"A thorough knowledge of the Bible is worth more than a college education." — Theodore Roosevelt.

"A Bible and a newspaper in every house, a good school in every district; all studied and appreciated as they merit; are the principal support of virtue, morality, and civil liberty." — Ben Franklin.

'The secret of my success? It is simple. It is found in the Bible' "In all thy ways acknowledge Him, and He shall direct thy paths." — George Washington Carver, 1939

"I shall earnestly and persistently continue to urge all women to the practical recognition of the old Revolutionary maxim. Resistance to tyranny is obedience to God." — Susan B. Anthony, Women's Rights Activist, Rochesterian.

"It is necessary for the welfare of the nation that men's lives be based on the principles of the Bible. No man, educated or uneducated, can afford to be ignorant of the Bible." — Theodore Roosevelt.

"I just want to do God's will. And He's allowed me to go to the mountain. And I've looked over, and I've seen the promised land." — Martin Luther King, 1968

"Without God, there is no virtue because there is no prompting of the conscience… without God, there is a coarsening of the society; without God democracy will not and cannot long endure… If we ever forget that we are One Nation Under God, then we will be a Nation gone under." — Ronald Reagan.

"It is by the goodness of God that in our country we have those three unspeakably precious things: freedom of speech, freedom of conscience, and the prudence never to practice either of them." — Mark Twain.

"In the beginning of a change, the patriot is a scarce man, brave, hated, and scorned. When his cause succeeds, however, the timid join him, For then it costs nothing to be a patriot." — Mark Twain

"Sure, I wave the American flag. Do you know a better flag to wave? Sure, I love my country with all her faults. I'm not ashamed of that, never have been, never will be." — John Wayne.

Yes, God is the reason this country is great and was recognized by our framers and leaders; it's the providence of God.

Yank and Yankee

A popular term for an American overseas, especially during the war, when we would call each other by nickname, Brits, Limeys, Aussies, Kiwis, Mounties, i.e., Canadians. The name Yank and Yankee is said to be of uncertain derivation. It has been used since very early times in the USA, perhaps in 1740 AD. The British used to make a song about it, 'Yankee Doodle Dandy,' but where was it from?

Wikipedia lists 4 origins:

- The word Yankee is said to be from the Cherokee's and, as such, the Indian language, and the word eankke (coward), but no such word appears to exist.
- Theory number 2 the word came from an Indian tribe calling themselves Yankoos, meaning 'invincible'. Apparently, the New Englanders defeated this tribe in battle, and the victors adopted their name. It's not a very convincing theory; it makes no sense at all.
- Theory number 3: the name comes from Dutch traders that traded extensively with the New England (British puritans). The name Janke, Anglicized as 'Yankee', was a nickname for the Dutch traders that again was said to be adopted by the Colonial Puritans. Again, I cannot understand how a very religious group of people would adopt someone else's nickname does not make sense. Another reason why this makes no sense is that the Dutch settlers of New Amsterdam started using it against the English colonists of neighboring Connecticut.
- Theory number 4 Online Etymology dictionaries say the name Yankee, first used in 1683, was a name applied disparagingly by Dutch settlers in New Amsterdam (New York) to English colonists in neighboring Connecticut. Ok, this is the same problem as in theory 3, and again in use for the British. Here's where it makes sense — It is noted that it is common to name a droll fellow, regarded as typical of his country, after some favorite article of food, such as English Jack-pudding or Jack Sausage, now we are getting warm because the Dutch would

231

call the Brits, Jacks, which they would pronounce Yacks.

Yankee Early usage

The root of the term is uncertain. In 1758, British General James Wolfe made the earliest recorded use of the word Yankee to refer to people from what became the United States. He referred to the New England soldiers under his command as Yankees: 'I can afford you two companies of Yankees, and the more because they are better for ranging and scouting than either work or vigilance.' Later, British use of the word often was derogatory, as in a cartoon of 1775 ridiculing 'Yankee' soldiers. New Englanders themselves were employed from Europe. Thus, a visitor to Richmond, Virginia, commented in 1818, 'The enterprising people are mostly strangers; Scots, Irish, and especially New England men, or Yankees, as they are called.'

So, in summary, the most plausible theory is that the name Yanks is actually a derivation of Jack — Jacob, H3290 יַעֲקֹב Ya`aqob, Ya`akov (HNB), Yaacov in Ashkenazi Hebrew was often pronounced as Yankov; Yank is therefore short for Yaakov (Jacob). So, the Jews and the Dutch would call the early British settlers of New England Jacks (Yacks). Note the early British seamen were called Jack Tar; they sailed ships that were heavily tared; it comes from our roots when God gave detailed instructions for how to build a large boat, and we had to tar it to make it watertight (Gen 6.14), we retained this knowledge because we are Israelites and we had the Bible 'back in the day'. And it's clear from the previous chapter that we Brit's had a very strong affinity with the name of our father, Jack, Yacob.

One might say, how is it that the name developed and stuck, but nobody knows why? And in almost all these instances in this book, you might say that, but I am here to tell you why God himself did this; as he said before, 'I brought you out of Egypt on eagle wings.' He was the eagle that brought us out and sustained us. For his name's sake, he fulfills his promises, and he wants the world to know! Yah is the mighty one of Ya'aqob and the fulfillment of his promises that bring greatness, prosperity, peace and joy. The name

Yank is again a sign (Jer. 31.21, צִיּוּן h6725 tsiyuwn, yes a siyuwn, sign), a high heap, a waymark; the 'Pennamite–Yankee War,' for example, was the name given to a series of clashes in 1769 over land titles in Pennsylvania between 'Yankee' settlers from Connecticut and 'Pennamite' settlers from Pennsylvania.

The meaning of Yankee has varied over time. In the 18th century, it referred to residents of New England descended from the original English settlers of the region. Mark Twain used the word in this sense in his novel A Connecticut Yankee in King Arthur's Court, published in 1889. As early as the 1770s, British people applied the term to any person from the United States. In the 19th century, Americans in the southern United States employed the word in reference to Americans from the northern United States, though not to recent immigrants.

NASA

North American Space Agency, that's what NASA means, right? Well, actually, this was my guess, and I got it wrong. It actually stands for National Aeronautics and Space Administration and was set up in 1958.

It has nothing to do with Hebrew or the Bible, right? Well, as I have been saying, God is in our DNA and God set up and blessed this nation because of the patriarchs. So perhaps it's not surprising to find a Hebrew word that means, list up, to raise up, high, to hold up. What an apropos word for aeronautics and space adventure (H5375 נָשָׂא nasa); we also have nsa, meaning to carry away(נְשָׂא nᵉsâ', nes-aw' NSA).

The Great Seal of America.

13 stars' — where do 13 stars come from? Is there really evidence in the Bible to support it? We have to go back to Joseph and his dream; in Genesis 37.9-11, Joe had two dreams; in his second dream, he saw 11star, so this can't be from Joseph. 11 means we are missing 2, but in Joseph's dream there are 11 stars who were his brothers, but we continue 11 brothers, and the sun and moon were bowing down to Joe. When he told it to his father, his father interpreted and rebuked him: 'Will your mother, me and your

brothers all come and bow down to you. Okay, recount, there are now 13 heavenly bodies or stars.

Most people are aware of the 12 tribes of Israel, but actually there were 13, as Jacob made Ephraim and Manasseh each a tribe. We can read about this in Genesis 48-49. Notice Manasseh was the oldest, i.e., he should be the 11th tribe replacing Joseph, but Israel did a switcheroo and made Ephraim the birthright (right hand) with his brother Manasseh coming last; surely this saying 'save the best for last is very apropos! So, Manasseh was actually the 13th, really, Joseph was the 11th tribe (replaced by Ephraim), Benjamin 12, so Manasseh would now correctly be 13. In the Great Seal of America, we have thirteen original states. We also have 13 stars with 13 leaves on the olive branch and 13 arrows. Let us see what each means.

- **The Eagle**

What does the Eagle signify? Is this a symbol of the tribes? If not, what does it symbolize:

We have already stated that the Eagle was adopted by the tribe of Dan. Dan was a pioneering seafaring tribe and one used by God to transfer and re-establish his covenant or birthright and the kingly line.

(Exo 19:40 KJV) Ye have seen what I did unto the Egyptians, and how I bare you on eagles' H5404 wings and brought you unto myself. (Job 9:26) They are passed away as the swift ships: as the eagle H5404 that hasteth to the prey. (Job 39:27) Doth the eagle H5404 mount up at thy command, and make her nest on high?

Yes, it does, as Dan did, so the eagle is a symbol of God's providence, guidance and, in many cases, fulfillment.

For thus saith the LORD; Behold, he shall fly as an eagle, H5404 and shall spread his wings over Moab (Jer 48:40).

As for the likeness of their faces, they four had the face of a man, and the face of a lion, on the right side: and they four had the face of an ox on the left side; they four also had the face of an eagle (Eze 1:10 H5404).

And everyone had four faces: the first face was the face of a cherub, and the second face was the face of a man, and the third the face of a lion, and the fourth the face of an eagle (Eze 10:14 H5404).

We know now what the symbolism of the living creatures means, and again, in Revelations 4:6 7:11, it is mentioned nine times(four beasts in KJB). It means us, Israel, God has not forgotten Jack; he said, "I will never leave you or forsake you until I accomplish everything I have planned."

In Ezekiel 17, God speaks an allegory, a riddle in symbolic language; he talks about two great eagles. Later, he identifies himself as one of the eagles, and the second eagle is the king of Babylon v12, and again in v22, God says he himself will take a shoot, a tender shoot (in the talons of the great eagle). Again, God says he will plant the tender shoot (young virgin princes) and plant it on a high and lofty mountain in Israel (v23)

And say, Thus saith the Lord GOD; A great eagle (H5404) with great wings, long winged, full of feathers, which had divers colors, came unto Lebanon, and took the highest branch of the cedar (Eze 17:3):

There was also another great eagle (H5404) with great wings and many feathers: and, behold, this vine did bend her roots toward him, and shot forth her branches toward him, that he might water it by the furrows of her plantation (Eze 17:7).

Clearly, from these scriptures, the eagle means:

1.   Israel. (Eze 1.10,10.14)
2.   God and his providence/protection (Eze17.3,22)

3.   Great Power -Sometimes it symbolizes great power other than God, as is the case with the king of Babylon (Eze17.12)

4.   A symbol of Dan, the pioneer tribe of Israel, at one point, over 50% of Americans were Irish!

The American eagle symbolizes God watching over his people to protect and fulfill the prophecy. It also speaks of the mixture of the tribe of Dan (Yarash). However, if we abandon God, this will bring some very bad times to the US.

- **Words of the seal "E pluribus unum."**

Latin for 'Out of many, one'

The seal has 13 characters, in Latin, meaning 'Out of many, one.' The meaning of the phrase originates from the concept that out of the union of the original Thirteen Colonies emerged a new single nation. It is emblazoned across the scroll and clenched in the eagle's beak on the Great Seal of the United States.

We can also say that from one many, as in Jacob the Yank, he produced the 13 original tribes, and from the 13 original colonies, we have one great nation and union of Jacob.

God promised Abraham that all nations would be blessed by his seed, i.e., a physical blessing. Jack is the policeman of the world. Honesty, integrity, and the rule of law are the Judeo-Christian virtues of the British – Egel'ish. These nations include Canada, Australia, Scotland, Ireland, Wales, New Zealand and, of course, America, and what about all the British colonies (which we saw in the chapter in Britain), out of many one company of nation and one great nation. America is a melting pot; this is exactly as God planned it, just as the United Kingdom of Solomon had the same effect. People knew and wanted to be a part of the blessings for sure! What did God say, Israel's blinders shall not be removed until the fullest of the gentiles be brought in.

The term "E pluribus unum" also means "he approves the undertaking," as in God approves the undertaking.

The colors of the flag the red, white and blue. We can see from Joseph's memorial and memorabilia that these colors were his red, white and blue. Also, the colors of the high priest are very close to these colors (Exo 25:4 Exo 26:1 Exo 35:23)…

In God, we trust – printed on all money – speaks of our origin and the source of our wealth and prosperity.

The 13 arrows – now, what does 13 mean? Do you remember? 13 is the designation order of the tribe of Manasseh. There is also another meaning which I won't go into here, look for it in my next book! Arrows and a fruitful bough (an olive tree with olives), along with a young bull or calf, were also used to depict Joseph (Gen. 49.22-26).

- **The Olive Branch**

The olive branch is a symbol of peace (Gen 8:11). We can see that Noah sent the dove out, and when he returned, he brought back an olive branch. The dove also is a symbol of peace; again, this is where we get it from.

Also, the olive branch is also a symbol of Israel (Jer 11:16). The lord called (Israel) you a thriving olive tree, and again, Hos 14:6 His branches shall spread, and his beauty shall be as the olive tree, and his smell as Lebanon. In addition, the two witnesses are allegorically referred to as olive trees (Zec 4:12)

Let us read the prophecy about Joseph in Genesis 49, the prophetic words of Yank'ov.

'In your[c] name will Israel pronounce this blessing: 'May God make you like Ephraim and Manasseh.'

At every Jewish holy day, the Rabbi pronounces this blessing – and now they know who they are really talking about!

22 'Joseph is a fruitful vine, a fruitful vine near a spring,

whose branches climb over a wall.[k]

23 With bitterness, archers attacked him; they shot at him with hostility.

24 But his bow remained steady — British long bow and now synonymous with military might. His strong arms stayed[l]

limber, because of the hand of the Mighty One of Jacob, because of the Shepherd, the Rock of Israel,

25 because of your father's God, who helps you, because of the Almighty,[m] who blesses you with blessings of the skies above, blessings of the deep springs below, blessings of the breast and womb.

26 Your father's blessings are greater than the blessings of the ancient mountains, than[n] the bounty of the age-old hills. Let all these rest on the head of Joseph, on the brow of the prince among[o] his brothers.

The blessing of the greatest nation ever goes to Manasseh, who became known by the Patronic name Makir, i.e. A'makir – America. There are no accidents with God, he knows the future because he project manages the future.

13 Original United States

Is this a strange coincidence? There were 13 original states of the union, or was it ordained by the creator?

1. 1607 – Virginia Jamestown was founded by the Virginia Company of London to find gold.
2. 1620 Massachusetts (Plymouth and Massachusetts Bay Colony) – founded by the Pilgrims
3. 1626 – New York (originally New Amsterdam, annexed by England) was founded by the Dutch West India Company.
4. 1633 – Maryland More Protestants than Catholics settled in this state. Founded by Cecil Calvert, Lord Baltimore, who was instructed to tolerate Puritans.
5. 1636 – Rhode Island Founded by Roger Williams, a religious zealot who was banished from
6. 1636 – Connecticut Founded by Reverend Thomas Hooker
7. 1638 – Delaware
8. 1638 – New Hampshire
9. 1653 – North Carolina
10. 1663 – South Carolina
11. 1664 – New Jersey

12.   1682 – Pennsylvania Founded by William Penn – a very religious Quaker
13.   1732 – Georgia

1.   Virginia (Southern Colony) It was founded in 1607 by the (British) London Company to find gold.
2.   Plymouth (New England) It was founded in 1620 by Separatist Pilgrims for religious freedom English separatist Puritans who had broken away from the Church of England,.
3.   Massachusetts Bay — (New England Colony) It was founded in 1630 by Puritans for religious freedom and, again English settlement.
4.   Rhode Island — (New England Colony) It was founded in 1636 by Roger Williams, London, England and his supporters for religious freedom and separation of church from state after a disagreement with Massachusetts Bay.
5.   Connecticut — (New England Colony) It was founded in 1635 by Thomas Hooker Marefield, UK and his followers for political and religious freedom after a disagreement with Massachusetts Bay.
6.   New Hampshire — (Northamptonshire, England) It was founded in 1692 by John Mason for farming.
7.   New York — (Middle Colony) It was founded by the Dutch (Zebulon) for trade and furs and became an English Colony in 1664. The state and city were both named for the 17th-century Duke of York, future King James II of England
8.   New Jersey — (Middle Colony) It was founded in 1664 for farming and trade. The entire region became a territory of England on June 24, 1664, after an English fleet under the command of Colonel Richard Nicolls sailed into what is today New York Harbor and took control of Fort Amsterdam, annexing the entire province.

9.   Maryland — (Southern Colony) It was founded by Lord Baltimore and other Catholics for religious freedom. From Kent, England[1]

10.   Pennsylvania — (Middle Colony) It was founded by William Penn and some other Quakers for religious freedom. Ruscombe, Berkshire, England, Great Britain, who wanted religious freedom.

11.   Delaware — (Middle Colony) was founded in 1776.

12.   The Carolinas — (Southern Colony) It was founded by supporters of Charles II for farming and trade. It later split into North and South Carolina.

13.   Georgia — (Southern Colony) It was founded by James Oglethorpe for relief for poor English and as a buffer between Spanish Florida and Carolina.

All the original states are founded by the Brit's, albeit from different areas of the UK with different religious views.

Origin of Gerrymandering — Political Shenanigans

As we mentioned earlier in the chapter 10 section on Assyria – Jeroboam took it upon himself to re-organize the political, cultural and religious affiliations of Samaria. He introduced new holidays that were not based on God's holy days, brought new laws, set up Idols and changed the political, cultural and religious landscape for his own political gains. Before Jerry got started there, it was a single Monarchy, where the Northern 10 tribes of Samaria and the Southern 3 tribes of Judah were joined in the United Kingdom. Gerry was the first to use Gerrymandering, which means to rearrange the boundaries of a political constituency for your own political gain!

We can see that Israel had a habit of putting rule upon rule, precept upon precept; this has the appearance of right but often does nothing to stem the evil caused (Isa28). A similar practice is being done by modern-day Israel (USA and Britain etc.). For instance, when someone commits murder using a gun, they cry. We need more gun control, yet clearly, the perpetrator is breaking the law by committing murder in the first place. That didn't stop him. Many locations that have the highest gun crime (Mexico City, Chicago) are the locations where gun crime is the worst. Clearly, this is not a simple issue with a simple solution: 'take away all guns from law-abiding citizens'. Will this solve mass shootings or make it worse, like in Chicago or Mexico City? Perhaps all this does is give lawless criminals free reign? so political shenanigans are not new; red flag operations and trying to control the electorate go back many thousands of years!

Flags of the US and UK

Origin as stated in Wikipedia:

The flag of the United States of America, often referred to as the American flag, is the national flag of the United States. It consists of thirteen equal horizontal stripes of red (top and bottom) alternating with white, with a blue rectangle in the canton (referred to specifically as the 'union') bearing fifty small, white, five-pointed stars arranged in nine offset horizontal rows, where rows of six stars (top and bottom) alternate with rows of five stars. The 50 stars on the flag represent the 50 states of the United States of America, and the 13 stripes represent the thirteen British colonies that declared independence from the Kingdom of Great Britain and became the first states in the U.S. [1] Nicknames for the flag include The Stars and Stripes, [2] Old Glory, [3] and The Star-Spangled Banner.

The first flag of the United Gran Union has 13 stripes. The number 13 is a special number for God. It's a hidden number of immense significance; it can be good, or it can be bad; we had the founding of AmMachir. We previously said there are 13 tribes of Israel, with Manasseh (Gen48.17-20) being the 13th.

Australia & New Zealand

241

Here, we have the flags of Australia and New Zealand. Please notice the Union Jack (Union of Jacob) along with the stars of Joseph's dream. The stars represent the Southern Cross, as indeed, both New Zealand and Australia are in the southern hemisphere, and we have the cross of Israel with God in the middle and the cross of Yeshua (New Testament). We know that the Messiah was lifted up on a tree (cross) and became a curse for us, i.e., our salvation. So, the cross symbolizes Israel. It also symbolizes the atoning work of Christ. The stars were visible in the Northern Hemisphere till about 400 AD and in England till about 400 BC and were most likely in use as a symbol in Britain in the early days. Remember, the (Th'Arshish-Irish) Navy has a long tradition of navigating by the stars. The big star in the Australian flag is the commonwealth star, symbolizing the unity of states (tribes), and again we have Joseph's colors red, white and blue.

Jesus, the bright morning star that keeps Israel safe (Magen's). He is the root of David (Rev22.16). And there appeared a great wonder in heaven; a woman clothed with the sun, and the moon under her feet, and upon her head a crown of twelve stars' Jacob Rachael & Leah-moon, the 12 tribes and Yeshua (Rev 12:1).

Star-spangled banner

O say, can you see, by the dawn's early light,

What so proudly we hailed at the twilight's last gleaming,

Whose broad stripes and bright stars through the perilous fight, O'er the ramparts we watched, were so gallantly streaming?

And the rockets' red glare, the bombs bursting in the air, Gave proof through the night that our flag was still there; O say does that star-spangled banner yet wave O'er the land of the free and the home of the brave?

On the shore dimly seen through the mists of the deep, Where the foe's haughty host in dread silence reposes, What is that which the breeze, o'er the towering steep, As it fitfully blows, half conceals, half discloses?

Now it catches the gleam of the morning's first beam, In full glory reflected now shines in the stream: 'Tis the star-spangled banner, O long may it wave O'er the land of the free and the home of the brave.

O thus be it ever, when freemen shall stand Between their loved homes and the war's desolation.

Blest with vict'ry and peace, may the Heav'n rescued land Praise the Power that hath made and preserved us a nation! Then conquer we must, when our cause is just, and this be our motto: 'In God is our trust.' And the star-spangled banner in triumph shall wave O'er the land of the free and the home of the brave![40]

Cover of sheet music for 'The Star-Spangled Banner,' transcribed for piano by Ch. Voss, Philadelphia: G. Andre & Co., 1862

Additional Civil War period lyrics

In indignation over the start of the American Civil War, Oliver Wendell Holmes, Sr. added a fifth stanza to the song in 1861, which appeared in songbooks of the era.[42]

When our land is illumined with Liberty's smile, If a foe from within strike a blow at her glory, Down, down with the traitor that dares to defile The flag of her stars and the page of her story!

By the millions unchained who our birthright have gained, Birthright promises the son of a slave.

We will keep her bright blazon forever unstained! And the Star-Spangled Banner in triumph shall wave While the land of the free is the home of the brave.

The British obsession with the name Jack!

We have discovered that the name Jack comes from Jacob, Yacob, Yack and Yank, all derivatives; we have also discovered why we have this obsession with this name. It was our forefather, the founder of Israel, where the tribes first started and where we got our roots:

1. Union Jack – short for the Union of Jacob
2. Jack — A mechanical device used to raise and (temporarily) support a heavy object, e.g., a screw jack, scissor jack, hydraulic jack, ratchet jack, or scaffold jack.
3. Hey Jack — A man or men in general.
4. All you Jacks — Every man jack of you.
5. Jack A male animal.
6. Jackpot-to win big.
7. Jack-ass A male ass.
8. Jack of cards — card games — A playing card with the letter 'J' and the image of a knave or prince on it, the eleventh card in a given suit. Also called a knave.
9. Jack — Cricket — The eleventh batsman to come to the crease in an innings, derived from the playing card, sometimes referred to as the last batsman in the order (i.e., 11th). It's also known as Last Man Jack, a term that has passed into everyday parlance.
10. Jack or knave (archaic) (a servant or, later, a deceitful man). quotations
11. Jack Hammer pneumatic drill.
12. Jack mango Mangifera caesia, related to the mango tree.
13. Telephone Jack — A surface-mounted connector for electrical, especially telecommunications equipment, telephone jack.
14. Jack-ball -A target ball in bowls, etc.; a jack-ball.
15. Jacks — A small, six-pointed playing piece used in the game of jacks.
16. He doesn't know Jack (colloquial, euphemistic) he doesn't know anything.
17. You haven't done jack. To sit around and be lazy (maybe because you are sad), perhaps this happened after Jacob lost Rachel and Joseph.
18. Jack — A small flag at the bow of a ship. (nautical)
19. Jack — A naval ensign flag flown from the main mast, mizzen mast, or the aft-most major mast of (especially) British sailing warships; Union Jack. (nautical)

20. Jack -A coarse and cheap medieval coat of defense, especially one made of leather.
21. Jack penny: A penny with a head on both sides, used for cheating.
22. Jack — Money. quotations (slang)
23. Jackrabbit is a very fast rabbit with big ears.
24. Jack — A smooth, often ovoid large gravel or small cobble in a natural water course. (slang, Appalachians)
25. Jack Pike — The freshwater pike, green pike or pickerel.
26. Jackfish: A large California rockfish, the bocaccio, Sebastes paucispinis.
27. Jack — Any of the marine fish in the family Carangidae.
28. Jack Tar — A sailor, a jack tar. (obsolete, nautical)
29. Jack A pitcher or can have waxed leather, supposed to resemble a jackboot; a black-jack (obsolete)
30. Jack A drinking measure holding half a pint or, sometimes, a quarter of a pint. (Britain, dialect, obsolete)
31. Jack A mechanical contrivance, an auxiliary machine, or a subordinate part of a machine.
32. Jack A device to pull off boots.
33. Jack A sawhorse or sawbuck.
34. SmokeJack -A machine for turning a spit; a smokejack.
35. Jack A wooden wedge for separating rocks rent by blasting. (mining)
36. Jack A lever for depressing the sinkers, which push the loops down on the needles in a knitting machine.
37. Jack — A grating to separate and guide the threads in a warping machine; a heck box.
38. Jack — A machine for twisting the sliver as it leaves the carding machine.
39. Jack — A compact, portable machine for planning metal.
40. Jack — A machine for slicking or pebbling leather.
41. Jack — A system of gearing driven by horsepower for multiplying speed.
42. Jack — A hood or other device placed over a chimney or vent pipe to prevent a back draught.
43. Jack — In the harpsichord, an intermediate piece communicating the action of the key to the quill; also called hopper.

44. Jack — In hunting, the pan or frame holding the fuel of the torch is used to attract game at night; also, the light itself.
45. Jack crosstree — A bar of iron athwart ships at a topgallant masthead to support a royal mast, and give spread to the royal shrouds; also called jack crosstree. (nautical)
46. Jack — Female ended electrical connector (see Electrical connector)
47. Jack — Electrical connector in a fixed position (see Gender of connectors and fasteners)
48. Jacobitism 1688 and 1746 was a political movement in Great Britain and Ireland that aimed to restore the Roman Catholic Stuart King James II of England and Ireland (as James VII in Scotland) and his heirs to the thrones of England, Scotland, France and Ireland. The movement took its name from *Jacobus*, the Renaissance Latin form of *Iacobus*, which in turn comes from the original Latin form of James, 'Iacobus'. Adherents rebelled against the British government on several occasions between 1688 and 1746.
49. Jack A lifting device is enormously strong and capable of lifting very heavy items.

This is by no means an exhaustive list; it represents a few jacks that I have been able to compile quite a list. Wouldn't you say we must have a root in our history to account for this wouldn't you think? Why would any nation, culture or language venerate such a name as JACK? I think it should be clear to even a 5th grader that there is a reason for it; there is a reason the New England settlers were called Yacob's; it's because God's promise to the Brits was the covenant promise to Abraham that was passed to his children, remember I will make your name great (Gen.12.1-3). Let's see if God made the Brit's name great:

Abraham Isaac

Jacob – Israel – His Royal Joseph

David

They are all household names today, and one that almost everyone knows. Also, Abraham's name was Hebrew, irbri and Iberia etc. These names have been and are still used by the House of

Israel today. We also have perhaps the biggest and most used name, Jack!

And we see the promise to David to again make his name great and give him a house and an enduring dynasty. I will provide a place for my people and plant them so they will have a home of their own h8111 שׁ מרון (Shomĕ r own) and no longer be disturbed. Wicked people will not oppress them anymore as they did in the beginning and have done so ever since I appointed leaders over them. I will give you rest (2 Sam7.10), and again God speaks to David, 'I will make your name like the greatest names on earth (1Ch17.8), reiterating planting the people and giving them a place of safety where they will not be disturbed! A kingly line that will last forever!

Half the kingdom of Wales was called D'fid. The rest of the country even called the Welsh taffy (D'vid). Yes, God fulfills his promises not because we deserve it but for his name's sake!

We have already covered the promise of the kingly line. It was not conditional. God reiterated it when he was taking Judah into captivity and destroying the current line, and now we know where he took them, Ireland. There were kings reigning in Ireland from the time of King Solomon 1000BC till the last king of Ireland, Brian Boru, 1000 AD, two thousand years of Sovereign reign, and we know the breach was healed with the Zarhites line receiving the princess Tamar brought to Er'land by Jeremiah (Emhear) and marrying Eremon. We then had the overturn when the kingly line of Ireland moved to Scotland, and the stone of scone went with it (Jacks pillar stone).

I ask you did God keep his promise?

CHAPTER 20 - Prophetic fulfillments.

The Bible interprets the Bible and Prophetic promises, and their fulfillment is key to discovering the whereabouts of the ten lost tribes.

1. All nations of the earth shall be blessed by your seed (Gen12.3). We talked about this earlier in the previous chapter, the largest evangelistic/missionary institution in the world is the USA by far. Also, the Irish were, for many years, the evangelical and missionary leaders of the world, then the mantle moved to England, certainly, the British were great evangelists at one point. I suspect the mantel moved with the blessing, i.e., Jacobs Pillar stone and the revival in all things God, and we had the deep devotion of many of the pilgrims who set up the USA. Also, we have the World Police, a joint effort being led by the USA, the English-speaking world and Europe.

2. I will make you a great nation and a great company of nations (Gen. 48.19-20). If God says they will be great, I think it's a sure bet that he means the greatest ever! USA, Canada, Britain, Australia, New Zealand, plus others.

3. The two Nations will be great brothers, i.e., Ephraim and Manasseh (Gen. 48.17-20). And again — May God make you like Ephraim and Manasseh (Gen. 48.20 #88). In other words, something outstanding and worthy of praise. The USA and the British certainly have this trait!

4. Vast natural resources and a great climate for growing and abundant water (Gen. 49.22-28, Ez. 17.5, Gen. 27.28). Britain doesn't even need a sprinkler system, and the USA has the blessing of the ancient mountains. They provide snow and water, in addition to vast lakes above and underground.

5. You shall never fail to have a man sit on the throne of Israel, A long kingly line that traces back to David, in other words, a kingly line that has existed for thousands

of years and can be traced back to King David. (Gen 49:3,10). The Irish, Scottish and English monarchy stretches back to David with Jacobs pillar stone as the foundation stone.

6. Israel will have a natural border (2Sa. 7:10). Britain, Canada, America, Australia, and New Zealand certainly have that.

7. House built on a rock and a church and kingly line tied to the rock Jacobs pillar stone (Gen 28:22, Gen 31:45, 2Ki 23:3, a rock that the builders rejected has become the chief cornerstone ((Psa. 118:22, Isa. 28:16, Mat. 21:42). The coronation stone, at Westminster Abbey for coronations and at Scone when not, the stone when in Ireland, was known as Lia Fail, the stone of destiny.

8. But his bow abode in strength, and the arms of his hands were made strong by the hands of the mighty God of Jacob; (from thence is the shepherd, the stone of Israel, Gen 49.24). The British long bow but also, military might, that is sustained by God. The USA and the English-speaking world are a force to be reckoned with. In fact, even when we go up against insurmountable odds like we should have done when we first entered the promised land and saw the Anak (giants h5303, h6062), the truth is it doesn't matter what we go up against giants, fallen angel hybrid beings, multidimensional beings they are no match for us! And why is that so? Well, David said it best. the young freckled red-haired Jew (dmoniy h132, 1Sa. 17:42) came out and fought Goliath. And the Philistine said to David, Come to me, and I will give thy flesh unto the fowls of the air, and to the beasts of the field. Then said David to the Philistine, Thou comest to me with a sword, and with a spear, and with a shield: but I come to thee in the name of the LORD of hosts, the God of the armies of Israel, whom thou hast defied. In other words, when God is on your side, who can stand against you? You have so much firepower o that nobody can stand against you; just ask Elijah (EliYah). By the way, we had at least two ancient Celtic tribes of Britain called dmoniy, a Hebrew name (Strong's H132).

9. Remnant of Israel prophesied to come from Islands of the sea (Isa 11:11, Isa 42:12), and the people of the western coastland (Britain is Chittam #13) will be part of the holy covenant (God es [a] Brit H6944, H1285).

I think it is clear from these scriptures and their fulfillment that many of the promises of God to the patriarchs were completed.

And God also leaves us no choice but to believe and accept his words when he says:

If you can break my covenant with the day and night and the laws of heaven and earth, then the covenant with David can be broken, "David will never fail to have a man to sit on the throne of Israel."

It would appear that we have two choices: We can either believe God and accept that he did fulfill his promises to the patriarchs, and the Brit'am'yah (covenant people of God) did rule the world and, in a sense, still do with America as the leading world power.

One Sheet Overview

This book goes into great detail, covering the events of the early Hebrews, the Patriarchs and how they influence us today with our language, culture, idioms and beliefs. In fact, it even shows a connection to God in our DNA. I cover phases like:

You're eighty-sixed, meaning you're banned from here (parties over) and don't come back.

You're fired – surely this can't be in the Bible – well, it is and you will be amazed who gets fired and who doesn't.

This book traces the language of the ancient Hebrews, the paleo-Hebrew/Phoenician script. We follow the Hebrews into Egypt and back to the promised land, indeed out to Greece, Tuscany, Spain, and Europe. We look at the etymology of words like Navy, Irish, His Royal Highness, England, Scotland, Ireland and Wales. We even look at and trace the origin to words like Armor, Armagh, London, Londinium, and rives, Tamer & Thames. This book uncovers the roots of these words, and their origins will amaze and shock you! The undeniable truth of our connection to the Bible, Israel, and God.

We look at God's Mission given to Jeremiah and trace Jeremiah and the king's daughters to God's secret hiding place. The fulfillment of the promise of God to provide a place of safety for his people and continue King David's kingly line promises clearly made in the Bible and promises kept.

We look at God's promise to build on Jacob's rock (Bethel), the rock the builders of the first temple rejected became the chief cornerstone of the Covenant of God. God said I will pluck Israel up by their roots and re-plant them in a land where they will not be disturbed. We provide undeniable proof of our roots and our source of all blessings!

We translate words like Yahwey, Adonai, and Yeshua to give you the English version. We also look at the origin of the names of the White house, America, God, and the Devil and trace them back to the Bible. We explore a new exodus route. We discover the secret hiding place of God. We investigate and corroborate a Jewish article that says *the original Jews spoke Gaelic.*

References

These are linked by Ref. xxx or ref. xxx and most commonly by #xxx, where the # sign signifies a number in the following table

1. Maqrizi says that Moses wiped out almost all non-Ishmaelite Arabs such as Amaleq and Midianites,[16] and by the time of Muhammad all Arabs were descendants of Ishmael according to historians Hisham Ibn Al-Kalbi and al-Sharqi who believed that all Arabs were descendants of Ishmael including the Qahtanites[17], (interesting note that his name incorporates the name Laban (lbn) without the a's as they were not pronounced originally but rather used as a guttural stop).

2. Your 86ed., while Wikipedia doesn't trace the true origin of the term they do give some very amazing similar examples from both the British and American perspectives, to be eighty-sixed is to be kicked out and told not to come back, and normally after a party foul.

3. Long finger -

4. Inner circle definition and meaning | Collins English Dictionary British English: *inner circle* NOUN. An *inner circle* is a small group of people within a larger group who have a lot of power, influence, or special information.

5. Irish language words in disguise: *kip*, *brumby*, *Sheila*, and *didgeridoo* are evidence of Irish speakers contributing to a new English dialect under the Southern Cross.

6. Brummie

7. Many Celtic names use the word Magh, or Magen, it is also a personal name, i.e. Megan-Armagh, Magh Eo, Magh Tuireadh, Magh Luirg, Maghera, Ballymagen, Carlingmaghen, Ard Mhacha. The Bible list Abrum Abraham, magen – the shield protecting Abrahm,: Gen 15 Abruhm 87 אֲבְרְ֣סְםָ 'Abram -magen h4043גֵ֣ןמָמֶ magen means Abrahams – shield. It is also worth noting that a recent article in The Jerusalem Post, October 2,

2007, by Joel M. Hoffman, and the Jewish Wikipedia under the topic "magic vowel letters" say that Abram was written. BRM, i.e., no A and? B means father, and RM means exulted. When he becomes a Brit he gets a heh? BRHM, it doesn't stop there! They also say that God's name Yahwhey had a heh also? LHYM is that why they call the British LHYM'ies Covenant People of God! I know ist'said to come from areTh'R(s)ish oNiy (old navy) days. Jews Invented Vowels, strictly speaking, it started with Yo'saf, he was the first Ox'fd man).

8. Discovery of the Sin Cities of Sodom and Gomorrah
9. Just How Much of the Bible is Prophecy? Is the doctrine that we have heard that the *Bible* is one-third poetry, one-third history, and one-third prophecy correct according to the Holy Scriptures, see link above?
10. **Certificate of divorce** - 2 Kings 17:23 — Jeremiah 15:1 Then said the LORD unto me, Though Moses and Samuel stood before me, *yet* my mind *could* not *be* toward this people: cast *them* out of my sight, and let them go forth. 2 Kings 17:18-20 — Therefore the LORD was very angry with Israel, and removed them out of his sight: there was none left but the tribe of Judah only. Also, Judah kept not the commandments of the LORD their God but walked in the statutes of Israel which they made. And the LORD rejected all the seed of Israel, and afflicted them, and delivered them into the hand of spoilers, until he had cast them out of his sight. 2 Kings 24:20 — For through the anger of the LORD it came to pass in Jerusalem and Judah, until he had cast them out from his presence, that Zedekiah rebelled against the king of Babylon. Jeremiah 3:8 — And I saw, when for all the causes whereby backsliding Israel committed adultery, I had put her away and given her a bill of divorce, yet her treacherous sister Judah feared not -of-Sodom-and-Gomora. Jeremiah 23:39 — Therefore, behold, I, even I, will utterly forget you, and I will forsake you, and the city that I gave you and your fathers, *and cast you* out of my presence. Hosea 1:4 —

And the LORD said unto him, Call his name Jezreel; for yet a little *while*, and I will avenge the blood of Jezreel upon the house of Jehu, and will cause to cease the kingdom of the house of Israel. <u>Hosea 9:3</u> — They shall not dwell in the LORD'S land; but Ephraim shall return to Egypt, and they shall eat unclean *things* in Assyria. <u>Hosea 9:9</u> — They have deeply corrupted *themselves*, as in the days of Gibeah: *therefore,* he will remember their iniquity, he will visit their sins. <u>Hosea 9:16-17</u> — Ephraim is smitten, their root is dried up, they shall bear no fruit: yea, though they bring forth, yet will I slay *even* the beloved *fruit* of their womb. My God will cast them away, because they did not hearken unto him: and they shall be wanderers among the nations. <u>Hosea 12:1</u> — Ephraim feedeth on wind, and followeth after the east wind: he daily increaseth lies and desolation; and they do make a covenant with the Assyrians, and oil is carried into Egypt. <u>Hosea 13:16</u> — Samaria shall become desolate; for she hath rebelled against her God: they shall fall by the sword: their infants shall be dashed in pieces, and their women with child shall be ripped up.

11. <u>Why do we bless our sons to 'be like Ephraim and Manasseh'?</u> <u>High…</u>

12. <u>Origin of the Gaels</u> Keating – states that the Gaels of Ireland and Scotland are the same and are form Milidh *Hector Boetius in the third chapter of the History of Scotland states that Eibhear and Eireamhon were sons of Gaedheal these is some confusion about the origin but most agree that, Gaeldheal was the progenitor of the Gaelic race.*

13. <u>Ancient Chittim was England</u> – If the link does not work type *"Ancient Chittim was England"* in a search bar. <u>http://</u> <u>Last name: Chittim, Chatan, Chetham, Cheetham, Chitham</u> Chittiam the name derives from the Ancient British (pre-Roman) word "ceto," meaning a forest and "ham," translating variously as village, estate, manor or homestead. Often, Chittim and Tarshish were used together (Gen. 10.4, Num. 24.24, 1Chr. 1.7, and even Jeremiah is told to go and look there, and that the

people who now reside there were once God fearing and changed their allegiance (Jer. 2.4-12). And we can see that in Isaiah that God's people reside in the islands of the sea (Isa 11:11, Isa 42:12), and they are told to rejoice. And that the far west islands (western coast-land) is where the holy alliance is (Dan. 11.30). It is only later that Chittim was connected to Cyprus). It is also fair to say that the Phoenicians/Israelites were also associated with Chittim as Cyprus, primarily due to its copper mines (COPPER-copprus i.e., Cyprus). No tin mines were on Cyprus; the tin was relatively rare and had to be imported from Tarshish, were kassíteros (tin ore) was abundant and later re-named to Britain. God also refers to Israel as metaphorically as tin ore (Isa. 1:25 Eze. 22:20). As God promised, he took away our tin when the Romans invaded Britain 2000 years ago

14. Ancient Tyre and modern England; or, The historical type of ancient Tyre in…By William Bramley-Moore
15. https:en.wikipedia.orgwikiMongoloid
16. https:en.wikipedia.orgwikiPlatonic_Academy
17. https:www.behindthename.comnameacademussubmitted
18. https:en.wikipedia.orgwikiTory_Island
19. http:www.ancientscripts.comimagesgreek.png
20. https:en.wikipedia.orgwikiBoustrophedon
21. https:www.youtube.comwatch?v=DLctAw4JZXE
22. https:en.wikipedia.orgwikiHistory_of_printing
23. https:en.wikipedia.orgwikiHyborian_Age — I list this as an interesting note as he seems in some ways to parallel Onan as a Barbarian and evil person. Also set in ancient history, i.e., Time period.
24. 2Ch 19:7 Wherefore now let the fear of the LORD be upon you; take heed and do *it*: for *there is* no iniquity with the LORD our God, nor respect of persons, nor taking of gifts.
25. http:www.chabad.orglibraryarticle_cdoaid1829jewish The-Birth-of-Moses.htm
26. Ox head with horns אֶלֶף eleph, eh'-lef; prop, the same as H504; hence (the ox's head being the first letter of

the alphabet, and this eventually used as a numeral) a thousand:—thousand.

27. H5521 booth a derivative of 5523 Cukkowth sook-kohth' i.e. Kohth – bouth — booth

28. Second wind is a phenomenon in distance running, such as marathons or road running (as well as other sports), whereby an athlete who is out of breath and too tired to continue suddenly finds the strength to press on at top performance with less exertion.

29. Corrie ten Boom a Christians who from the Netherlands, save the lives of 800 Jews.

30. The meaning of the name Gael from Breton, *Judicaël?*

31. Chapter 12 verse 20-23 of the Book of Maccabees I, Ant.12:4:10 Josp. Ant. L12 Ch4.10, 7 Ant. L13 Ch 5.8 Juventus Mundi

32. David Rohl Egypt time line

33. 3835 Laban law-ban' a primitive root; to be (or become) white; also (as denominative from 3843) to make bricks: --make brick, be (made, make) white(-r). see SH3843 lbenah leb-ay-naw' from 3835; a brick (from the whiteness of the clay): --(altar of) brick, tile. see H3835 H3844 Lbanown leb-aw-nohn' לְבָנוֹן = "whiteness" from 3825; (the) white mountain (from its snow); Lebanon, a mountain range in Palestine. see SH3825 3845 Libniy lib-nee' from 3835; white; Libni, an Israelite: --Libni. see H3835 H3846 Libniy lib-nee' patronymically from 3845; a Libnite or descendants of Libni (collectively): --Libnites. see SH3845. We have over 10 similar Hebrew words h3835-h3846 white boy words.

34. Manethos who was an Egyptian priest who lived in the 3rd century BC only fragments remain of his work, detailing the history and religion of ancient Egypt p7,41

35. DRAW H8388 תֹּאַר tô'ar, to'-ar; from H8388 a primitive root; to delineate; reflex. to extend:—be drawn, mark out, (Rimmon-) methoar (by union with H7417), See #47 for FAIR.

36. Newly discovered fortress on Way of Horus in Egypt stood sentinel…

37. http:www.thekeep.org~kunoichikunoichithemestreams exuality. html

38. Succubus (Traditional) — The Wiki of the Succubi — SuccuWiki

39. Gen 33:17 And Jacob journeyed to Succoth H5523, and built him a house, and made booths H5521 (sukkot) for his cattle: therefore the name of the place is called Succoth.

40. Wadi =dry river bed, El=God Arish

41. http:www.arkdiscovery.comred_sea_crossing.htm

42. H5524 Cukkowth bnowth sook-kohth' ben-ohth' Brothel tent, set up by the Babylonians in Samaria, from also H5523 סכות booths; Succoth, the name of a place in Egypt and of three in Palestine:—Succoth.

43. From H5523 and the (irreg.) plural of 1323; booths of (the) daughters; brothels, i.e. idolatrous tents for impure purpose:--Succoth-benoth. See SH5523 see SH1323 – Strong's dictionary.

44. http:www.Bible.caarcheologyBible-archeology-exodus-madaba-map.htm

45. https:en.wikipedia.orgwikiCutting_off_the_nose_to_spite_the_face

46. Hyksos, dynasty of Palestinian origin that ruled northern Egypt as the 15th BC

47. **H3303 yapheh pronounced yaw-feh'** from 3302; meaning beautiful (literally or figuratively) beautiful, beauty, comely, fair (-est, one), goodly, pleasant, well. see SH3302. This is where we get the English term 'fair' or (to be Fair YePhaH), FAIR, from Proto-Germanic *fagraz (pronounced fæyer-source also of Old Saxon fagar, Old Norse fagr, Swedish fager, Old High German fagar "beautiful," Gothic fagrs "fit") from -to'-ar; H8388

48. Statue-of-biblical-joseph-found-story-and covered-up

49. Ben-hur = "son of whiteness" or "son of Chur" H1133

50. http:www.dailymail.co.uksciencetecharticle-2022313Up-70-British-men-related-Egyptian-Pharaoh-Tutankhamun.html

51. https:en.wikipedia.orgwikiDanaus

52. https:en.wikipedia.orgwikiHecataeus_of_Abdera,
53. Danaus and Cadinus
54. Jewish temple in ancient Egypt
55. DANAUS' FLIGHT FROM EGYPT
56. DANAUS' son of Bihah fled Egypt
57. Prophecies concerning the Two Houses of Israel and Judah. This article is from Volume IX, 1903 (could not find the original, only quoted excerpts).
58. Hyksos kings were Semitic
59. Book of Jasher full account. Many passages are hard to reconcile with the Bible http:logosresourcepages.
60. https://www.smithsonianmag.com/smart-news/first-foreign-takeover-ancient-egypt-was-uprising-not-invasion-180975354/ search homer for Dardani Ye Trojans, Dardans, all our generous foes also google: Pharaoh chased the Queen Mother, Tefnut
61. http:blogs.timesofisrael.comdecoding-the-el-arish-stone-blog-entry-3
62. http:www.ancient-origins.netartifacts-ancient-writingsdoes-ipuwer-papyrus-provide-evidence-events-exodus-006951
63. https:en.wikipedia.orgwikiFamine_Stela
64. http:patternsofevidence.com
65. https:www.youtube.comwatch?v=aBDbDeepyS4
66. https:en.wikipedia.orgwikiBrook_of_Egypt
67. The River of Egypt (Wadi el-Arish) edge of Egypt / Israelbarnea-southern-border-judah-territory-river-of-egypt-wadi-el-arish-tharu-rhinocolu.htm
68. http:www.ancient-origins.netnews-history-archaeologyarchaeo logical-dig-ancient-fortress-site-egypt-reveals-massive-gate-020325
69. Ex13.17God led them not of the direct(derek H1869) road through the Philistines country (though they were right on the border **H7138 – qarow-Look at the use of this word** Gen19.20, they were at Succoth and Arish, mean the same thing Palm Huts, Tharu and Rinocularus were also related and as the ancient map Madaba show was El Arish.

70. http:www.palmtalk.orgforumindex.php?topic20825-what-do-el-arish-and-babinda-have-in-common http:looklex.come. oarish.htm

71. https:www.awm.gov.aucollectionC176337

72. https:www.merriam-webster.comdictionarypalm

73. https:en.wikipedia.orgwikiPalm_branch

74. https:www.revolvy.commainindex.php?s=El-Arish&item_ type=topic

75. Tharu means nose

76. https:en.wikipedia.orgwikiBetween_the_devil_and_the _deep_ blue_sea

77. Exo 34:35 And the children of Israel saw the face of Moses, that the skin of Moses' face shone: and Moses put the vail upon his face again, until he went in to speak with him.

78. https:dictionary.cambridge.orgdictionaryenglishhold-out

79. The Bible uses the Hebrew term yad, which can be singular or plural H3027 clearly, it was two hands as we have a wall on both sides, and Moses caused both sides to come together Ex14.26 compare Ex17.12, same Hebrew word for hands.

80. http:www.ronwyatt.comred_sea_crossing.html

81. https:en.wikipedia.orgwikiEl_Arish,_Queensland

82. From-pillar-to-post

83. https:en.wikipedia.orgwikiHoremheb

84. https:www.britannica.complaceAl-Arish

85. https:claudemariottini.com20140701josephs-coat-of-many-colors Golden boy – meaning favorite, turns out that not only was Joseph Jacob's favorite but also God's, richly ornamental robe with Gold sown into it. The Israelites corrupted this and made a Golden (boy) Calf 2Ki 10:29, but Jehu did not turn aside from the sins of Jeroboam the son of Nebat, which he made Israel to sin—that is, the golden-h2091 calves that were in Bethel and in Dan.

86. Palestine into Britain p128 Rev. L. G. A. ROBERTS, Com. R.N.

87. *Josephus at Antiq. 13.5.8(13:163-170), by Jonathan the high priest.* This letter is foursquare; and the seal is an eagle, with a dragon in his claws.'

88. Why-do-we-bless-our-sons-to-be-like-Ephraim-and-Manasseh

89. http:popchassid.com10-photos-to-remind-you-that-jews-dont-fit-into-a-stereotype-and-never-have

90. http:www.chabad.orgholidaysJewishNewYeartemplate_cdoaid520258jewishWhy-do-we-bless-our-sons-to-be-like-Ephraim-and-Manasseh.htm

91. http:www.rebjeff.combloglike-ephraim-and-manasseh

92. Chittam

93. Page 32 O'Flaherty s Ogygia. Part I. Sacred Island i.e. holy Island – also p43 Keating H of I most ancient Island.

94. The sound of the gavel strike, being abrupt to start and stop, and clearly audible by all present, serves to sharply define an action in time in a manner clearly perceivable by all, and to endow the action with practical as well as symbolic finality e.g. set the boundaries of the court meeting.

95. p176 Q* Flaherty's Ogygia. Part III. States the following –there were vast hordes of copper, iron, tin, and leaden ore in Ireland.

96. Ref.   https:phoenicia.orgPhoenician-Celtic-connections.html

97. https:en.wikipedia.orgwikiPaleo-Hebrew_alphabet

98. Of these, some, under their leaders Danus and Cadmus, migrated to Greece' (Fragmenta Historic rum, by Muller; vol. II, pg. 385 — copied from the works of Hecataeus of Abdera, a fourth-century B.C. Greek historian). The 'calamities' referred to were obviously the plagues which God brought down on the Egyptians.

99. H6725 tsiyuwntsee-yoon' from the same as 6723 in the sense of conspicuousness (tsee-yuwn-see-yonder compare 5329); a monumental or guiding pillar: --sign, title, waymark. See SH6723see SH5329

100. H8564 tamrûwr מְרוּרָת, tam-roor'; from the same root as H8558; an erection, i.e. pillar (probably for a guide-board):— high heap.

101. H8558 Tâmâr תָּמָר; taw-mawr'; from an unused root meaning to be erect; a palm tree: —palm (tree).

102. http:www.abideinchrist.commessagesnumtime.html

103. Hyksos kings were Midianite

104. http:www.hope-of-israel.orgamalekit.htm

105. Unfortunately, over the years, the Egyptian historians began to identify the Israelites that had been in their midst WITH THE HATED HYKSOS that had been driven out of the city of Avaris (Ramesses). Velikovsky reveals what happened: Ahmose [Aahmes first ruler of the 18th Dynasty] wrote that when Auaris [Avaris] was taken. The Hyksos retreated to Sharuhen in southern Palestine. But Manetho, many centuries later, wrote that the Hyksos retreated into Palestine and BUILT JERUSALEM; also that at a later date, when a leper colony in Auaris revolted, these rebels summoned the Solymites (the people of Jerusalem) and together conquered Egypt; that these Solymites were extremely cruel to the population, and that one of the lepers, Osarsiph, CHANGED HIS NAME TO MOSES. This confused story reflects the ASSYRIAN CONQUEST OF EGYPT, when Sennacherib and Esarhaddon invaded Palestine and Egypt 'with a great host of Assyrians and ARABS.' The people of Jerusalem NEVER conquered Egypt. Ages in Chaos, pp. 95-96.

106. H1419 גָדוֹל gadowl or shortened gadol gaw-dole') from h1431;

107. The 4th century B.C. Greek historian Hecataeus of Abdera (quoted by Diodorus Siculus) had written that the Egyptians, formerly being troubled by calamities [the Ten Plagues at the time of the Exodus] in order that the divine wrath might be averted, expelled all the [Israelite] aliens gathered together in Egypt. The worship of the gods having been neglected on account of the foreigners in Egypt, the Egyptians were warned by a pestilence to drive away the pollution. Of these,

some, under their leaders Danuss and Cadmus, migrated into Greece; others into other regions, the greater part into Syria [Canaan]. Their leader is said to have been Moses, a man renowned for wisdom and courage, founder and legislator of the state who led them into Judea. Herodotus had said that the Curetes had come to Crete with the Phoenician Prince Cadmus. The Danaoi, or Danaans, which had at onetime possessed colonies in the Black Sea region around the mouths of the rivers Danube, Don, and Dnieper. The chiefskings of the Danaoi, or Danaans, who had claimed descent from the ancient Greco-Egyptian Pharaoh Danaus (Tanaus or Dan I), and also Pharaoh Horemheb (Horemhab or Haremhab — meaning Horus is in Jubilation).

108.   High Priest of Israel

109.   High Priest Breastplate of Cohen Godol Found in Barrow at Stonehenge

110.   Stars Stones and Scholars

111.   Long writes: 'The other, much larger (from Bush *barrow*, half—a—mile south of *Stonehenge*, the richest of all in gold objects), is a solid and substantial ornament, of lozenge form, 7 by 6...89 As we have *discovered*, the *breastplate* identifies its owner as the '*Cohen Gadol*' (*High Priest*) of Ancient Britain, i.e., the High Druid.

112.   2Ch 2:14 The son of a woman of the daughters of Dan, and his father *was* a man of Tyre, skillful to work in gold, and in silver, and with the cunning men of my lord David, thy father.in brass, in iron, in stone, and in timber, in purple, in blue, and in fine linen, and in crimson; also, to grave any manner of graving, and to find out every device which shall be put to him, with thy cunning men,

113.   http:www.johnpratt.comitemsdocsldsmeridian2005 12stones. html

114.   John O'Donovan — 1851 — Ireland pp. 16–20. * *Psalter of Teamhair*, said to have been written by King CORMAC ULFHADA in 227-266AD. See also this link

115. Manethos who was an Egyptian priest who lived in the 3century BC only fragments remain of his work, detailing the history and religion of ancient Egypt p7,41

116. ראֹתֹ tô'ar, to'-ar; from H8388; outline, i.e. figure or appearance:— beautiful, × comely, countenance, fair, × favored, form, × goodly, × resemble, visage. Gen 39.6

117. Newly discovered fortress on Way of Horus in Egypt stood sentinel…

118. http:www.thekeep.org~kunoichikunoichithemestrea msexu ality.html Succubus (Traditional) — The Wiki of the Succubi SuccuWiki

119. Gen 33:17 And Jacob journeyed to SuccothH5523, and built him a house, and made booths H5521 (sukkot) for his cattle: therefore the name of the place is called Succoth.

120. Wadi =dry river bed, El=God Arish

121. http:www.arkdiscovery.comred_sea_crossing.htm

122. 5524 Cukkowth bnowth sook-kohth' ben-ohth'

123. from 5523 and the (irreg.) plural of 1323; booths of (the) daughters; brothels, i.e., idolatrous tents for impure purpose:--Succoth-benoth. See   SH5523 see SH1323– Strong's dictionary.

124. http:www.Bible.caarcheologyBible-archeology-exodus-madaba-map.htm

125. https:en.wikipedia.orgwikiCutting_off_the_nose_to _spite_the_face

126. https:www.ancient.euimage6359https:www.britanni ca. comtopicHyksos-Egyptian-dynasty

127. H3303 yapheh pronounced ya-feh' from 3302; meaning beautiful (literally or figuratively): --+ beautiful, beauty, comely, fair (-est, one), + goodly, pleasant, well. see SH3302; this is where we get the English term 'your fair' from -to'-ar; H8388

128. http:blogs.timesofisrael.comstatue-of-biblical-joseph-found-story-covered-up

129. https:www.studylight.orglexiconshebrew1133.html

130. http:www.dailymail.co.uksciencetecharticle-2022313Up-70-British-men-related-Egyptian-Pharaoh-Tutankhamun.html

131. https:en.wikipedia.orgwikiDanaus

132. https:en.wikipedia.orgwikiHecataeus_of_Abdera

133. Diodorus Siculus on DANAUS & CADMUS IN RHODES

134. Jpost on Elephantine Island - Jewish Temple

135. DANAUS' FLIGHT FROM EGYPT

136. https:books.google.com

137. Prophecies concerning the Two Houses of Israel and Judah. This article is from Volume IX, 1903 (could not find the original only quoted excerpts).

138. https:www.google.comurl?sa=t&rct=j&q=&esrc=s &sourcef

139. http:www.indaweb.comoilapocryphaJasher.pdf many passages are hard to reconcile with the Bible http:logosresourcepages. orgHistoryjasher.htm

140. https:books.google.combooksaboutJuventus_Mundi .htm l?id=L9NLAAAAMAAJ&printsec=frontcover&source =kp_ read_button#v=onepage&q&f=false

141. http:blogs.timesofisrael.comdecoding-the-el-arish-stone-blog-entry-3

142. http:www.ancient-origins.netartifacts-ancient-writingsdoes-ipuwer-papyrus-provide-evidence-events-exodus-006951

143. https:en.wikipedia.orgwikiFamine_Stela

144. http:patternsofevidence.com

145. https:www.youtube.comwatch?v=aBDbDeepyS4

146. https:en.wikipedia.orgwikiBrook_of_Egypt

147. http:www.Bible.caarcheologyBible-archeology-exodus-kadesh-barnea-southern-border-judah-territory-river-of-egypt-wadi-el-arish-tharu-rhinocolu.htm

148. http:www.ancient-origins.netnews-history-archaeologyarcha eological-dig-ancient-fortress-site-egypt-reveals-massive-gate-020325

149. Ex13.17God led them not of the direct(derek H1869) road through the Philistines country (though they were right on the border H7138 – qarow-Look at the use of this word Gen19.20, they were at Succoth-Tharu and Arish all mean the same thing Palm Huts wich was a common sight here.

150.   http:www.palmtalk.orgforumindex.php?topic20825 -what-do-el-arish-and-babinda-have-in-common http:looklex.come. oarish.htm
151.   https:www.awm.gov.aucollectionC176337
152.   https:www.merriam-webster.comdictionarypalm
153.   https:en.wikipedia.orgwikiPalm_branch
154.   https:www.revolvy.commainindex.php?s=El-Arish&item_type=topic
155.   https://news.nationalgeographic.com/news/2008/06/080602-egypt-fort.html
156.   https:en.wikipedia.orgwikiBetween_the_devil_and_the_deep_blue_sea
157.   Exo 34:35 And the children of Israel saw the face of Moses, that the skin of Moses' face shone: and Moses put the vail upon his face again, until he went in to speak with him.
158.   https:dictionary.cambridge.orgdictionaryenglishhold-out
159.   The Bible uses the Hebrew term yad which can be singular or plural H3027 clearly it was two hands as we have a wall on both sides and Moses cause both sides to come together Ex14.26 compare Ex17.12 same Hebrew word for hands.
160.   http:www.ronwyatt.comred_sea_crossing.html
161.   https:en.wikipedia.orgwikiEl_Arish,_Queensland
162.   Definition from-pillar-to-post see cambridge dictionary
163.   https:en.wikipedia.orgwikiHoremheb
164.   https:www.britannica.complaceAl-Arish
165.   https:claudemariottini.com20140701josephs-coat-of-many-colors Golden boy – meaning favorite, turns out that not only was Joseph Jacob's favorite but also God's, richly ornamental robe with Gold sown into it. The Israelites corrupted this and made a Golden (boy) Calf 2Ki 10:29 But Jehu did not turn aside from the sins of Jeroboam the son of Nebat, which he made Israel to sin—that is, the golden-h2091 calves that were in Bethel and in Dan.

166. Palestine into Britain p128 Rev. L. G. A. ROBERTS, Com. R.N.

167. Keating General History of Ireland p64

168. Google books Ogygia Homers says Sacred Island That Ireland should have been known in some vague way to Homer does not seem so improbable when we find Orpheus of Crotona who flourished in the age of Pisistratus 540 BC and therefore not long if at all after Homer alluding to Ireland in his Argonautica. An additional reason for identifying Ogygia with Ireland is supplied by the meaning of the name Ogyges was a very ancient King of Thebes hence Ogygia comes to have the meaning of ancient with necessarily the ideas of sacredness and venerableness superadded Thus it is equivalent to Insula Sacra.

169. The history of Ireland by Geoffrey Keating Parthelon sec vi history of Ireland p.157

170. Partholón son of Sera, son of Sru, son of Esru, son of Fraimint, son of Fathacht, son of Magog, son of Japheth P69Keat-From middle Greece, i.e. 'Migdonia,' Partholón set out. It is the way which he took (was) through the 'Torrian' Sea to Sicily, and with the right hand toward Spain till he reached Ireland. Two months and a half he was on the sea till he took harbor in Innbhear Sceine, [252] in the western part of Munster, the fourteenth day in the month May. It is of it this verse was recited [as the poet says]: --p70Keat General History

171. The fourteenth, on (day of) Mars,

172. They put their noble barks

173. The History of Ireland — Page 159 — Google Books Resulthttps:books.google.combooks?id=Br8-AQAAMAAJ-Geoffrey Keating, David Comyn, Patrick Stephen Dinneen 902 — Ireland…and a half he was on the sea till he took harbor in Innbhear Sceine, 1 in the western part of Munster, the fourteenth day in the month May. It is of it this verse was recited [as the poet says]: — The fourteenth, on (day of) Mars, they put their noble

barks *into the port of fair lands, blue, clear, In Innbhear Scéine of bright shields.*

174.   Geoffrey Keating, David Comyn, Patrick Stephen Dinneen- 1902 - Ireland…and a half he was on the sea till he took harbor in Innbhear Sceine, 1 in the western part of Munster, the fourteenth day in the month May. It is of it this verse was recited [as the poet says]: — The fourteenth, on (day of) Mars, they put their noble barks *into the port of fair lands, blue, clear, In Innbhear Scéine of bright shields.*

175.   Aber and Inver (place name elements) — Wikipedia

176.   https:en.wikipedia.orgwikiAber_and_Inver_(placen ame_elements)

177.   Aber and Inver are common elements in place-names of Celtic origin. Both mean 'confluence of waters' or 'river mouth'. Their distribution reflects the geographical influence of the Brittonic and Goidelic language groups, respectively. Contents. [hide]. 1 Aber; 2 Inver; 3 Syntax; 4 Use in British colonies; 5 List of place-names.

178.   https:en.wikipedia.orgwikiMygdonia

179.   Koch, John T. *Celtic Culture: A Historical Encyclopedia.* ABC-CLIO, 2006. pp.1693-1695 13James MacKillop, *Dictionary of Celtic Mythology*, Oxford University Press, p. 366

180.   Keating history of Ireland place names (Foras Feasa) see Dan, Dun and Don etc.

181.   John O'Donovan — 1851 — Ireland pp. 16–20. * *Psalter of Teamhair*

182.   http:www.heraldmag.orgolBContentsdictionariesSH ebrew.pdf

183.   J   is-only-400-500-years-old-was-there-a-j-sound-that-preceded

184.   John is often referred as *Iohannes, gift of God also Ian https:en. wikipedia.orgwikiIan*

185.   a Guy 5695 `egel ay-ghel from the same as 5696; a (male) calf (as frisking round), especially one nearly grown (i.e. a steer): --bullock, calf. see SH5696

186. http:www.heorot.dkbeowulf-rede-text.html   verses 180 & 190
187. https:www.phrases.org.ukmeaningsdarkest-hour.html
188. Injustice quote John Shelby Spong
189. https:www.deseretnews.comtop8025Cleanliness-is-next-to-Godliness-9-misquoted-Bible-phrases.html
190. https:www.phrases.org.ukmeaningsfingers-and-thumbs.html 'Giijb, Whan he should get ought, eche fynger is a thumbe.'
191. https:www.urbandictionary.comdefine.php?term=Paybacks%20 a%20bitch%21
192. https:www.merriam-webster.comdictionarykeep%20the%20 faith
193. https:www.omniglot.comimageswritingoldenglish_aBC.gif
194. https:en.wikipedia.orgwikiYogh
195. https:www.omniglot.comimageswritingogham.gif
196. https:archive.orgstreamaffinitybetweenh00straaffinitybetween h00stra_djvu.txt
197. https:forum.wordreference.comthreadsis-the-hebrew-welsh-connection-more-than-a-myth.2568833
198. https:www.blueletterBible.orgsearchDictionaryviewTopic. cfm?topic=IT0001524
199. https:www.blueletterBible.orgsearchDictionaryviewTopic. cfm?topic=VT0000295
200. https:www.brainyquote.comquotesrichard_m_nixon_138431? src=t_great_nation
201. https:en.wikipedia.orgwikiRed_coat_(military_uniform) #Early_instances
202. https:en.wikipedia.orgwikiMilitary_colours,_standards_and_ guidons
203. https:www.torahresource.compdf-articlesthe-pitfalls-in-using-Strong's-numbers.pdf
204. https:en.wikipedia.orgwikiElephantine
205. https:en.wikipedia.orgwikiFlag_of_Israel
206. https:en.wikipedia.orgwikiAlbion
207. http:www.sheknows.combaby-namesnamedamian

208.   http:www.ancestraljourneys.orgcelticscotlowlands.s
html
209.   https:idioms.thefreedictionary.comspill+the+beans
210.   https:idioms.thefreedictionary.comwait+for+the+ot
her+shoe+to+drop
211.   https:idioms.thefreedictionary.comcleanliness+is+n
ext+to+god liness
212.   http:www.chabad.orgtheJewishWomanarticle_cdoai
d1541 jewishThe-Mikvah.htm
213.   https:en.wikipedia.orgwikiShooting_the_messenger
214.   https:www.phrases.org.ukmeaningsbells-and-
whistles.html
215.   https:en.wikipedia.orgwikiPurple
216.   https:en.wikipedia.orgwikiPhoenician_language
Phoenician was written with the Phoenician script, an abjad (consonantary) originating from the Proto-Canaanite alphabet that also became the basis for the Greek alphabet and, via an **Etruscan adaptation**, the Latin alphabet. The Punic form of the script gradually developed somewhat different and more cursive letter shapes; in the 3rd century BC, it also began to exhibit a tendency to mark the presence of vowels, especially final vowels, with an aleph or sometimes an ayin. Furthermore, around the time of the Second Punic War, an even more cursive form began to develop[13], and it gave rise to a variety referred to as Neo-Punic, which existed alongside the more conservative form and became predominant sometime after the Battle of Carthage (c. 149 BC).[14]

217.   https:en.wikipedia.orgwikiAbjad
218.   The only name that Patrick uses for himself in his own writings is PATR C Us, which gives Old Irish *Pátraic* and Modern Irish *Pádraig* ([ˈp^ˠaːd̪ ˠɾˠəɪ]), English *Patrick*, Welsh *Padrig* Cornish *Petroc*.
219.   _____ **Eze 1:7** And their feet were straight feet; and the sole of their feet was like the sole of a calf 's H5695 foot: and they sparkled like the color of burnished brass (burnished brass looks like gold).

220. http:serendip.brynmawr.edubiologyb103f03web2tli ben.html#3

221. H250 'Ezrachiy ez-raw-khee' patronymic from 2246; an Ezrachite or descendant of Zerach, Ezrahite. 2244 chaba' khaw-baw' a primitive root to secretly hide (self), do secretly. (see 2245) chabab khaw-bab' a primitive root properly, to hide (as in the bosom), i.e. to cherish (with affection), love. 2246 Chobab kho-bawb' from 2245; cherished; Chobab, father-in-law of Mose. Also2247 chabah khaw-bah' a primitive root (compare 2245); to secrete:-hide (self). see SH2245. So the name Ezrachite or Zarhites is linked to a root meaning to secretly hide, like God did with the Zarhites (Mahol)

222. Mat 10:26, Mar 4:22, 'For there is nothing hidden which will not be revealed, nor has anything been kept secret but that it should come to light. Luk 8:17, Luk 12:2

223. Here we must remark, that the river Iberus, (now the Ebro) from which, some say Ireland was denominated (populated i.e. Milesians-Zarahites came from) — Part II 0' 'Flaherty's Ogygia. 119

224. AN ESSAY TOWARD AN HISTORY OF THE English Tongue 1773 By JOHN FREE DD he speaks of the Sarmatae (Samaritans who originally came from Iran 3BC Babylon. They were Israelites taken by the Assyrians a Germanic people. The Assyrians followed us across Europe but they stayed in Germany.

225. Part II 0' 'Flaherty's Ogygia. 119 Here we must remark that the river Iberus (now the Ebro) from which, fome fay Ireland was denominated (note 5), I think denominated means populated, again Irber and Ebro are derivations of the same origin erber, Herber Hiberians, Hebrews. Num 24:24 H5677

226. Eber – Herber – Hebrews Ebro – HeyBro 5676 `eber ay'-ber from 5674; properly, a region across; but used only adverbially (with or without a preposition) on the opposite side (especially of the Jordan; usually meaning the east)X against, beyond, by, X from, over, passage, quarter, (other, this) side, straight. see SH5674 -

Gesenius' Hebrew-Chaldee Lexicon [?] says region beyond the sea i.e west Jer. 25.44

227. Langer'sbookonworldhistoryp26,27andWikipedia-Assyria

228. Armenian-people-physical-characteristics

229. It is no surprise that the Armenian nation is very good at wrestling, and it is considered the #1 sport in the country. Most of the Olympic medals come to Armenia from wrestling. See web site under ref47

230. https://www.quora.com/Is-it-true-that-original-Armenians-were-blonde-and-blue-eyed

231. https://www.youtube.com/watch?v=FayeNeawzqM

232. There is a Hebrew word for sack's 8242 saq however this is not what is used for this scripture h4969 H572 — 'amtachath stretchable container.

233. Num. 2.5-9,Due33.18-19 ad Gen49.13-15

234. Land of milk and honey idiom means https://dictionary.cambridge.org/us/dictionary/english/land-of-milk-and-honey The Bible list https://www.blueletterBible.org/search/search.cfm?Criteria=land+of+milk+and+honey&t=KJV#s=s_ primary_0_1

235. https://www.quora.com/What-is-the-meaning-of-hay-day-and-where-did-it-originate

236. If I were to translate these word I would say Benach = ben means son of Ach Akan was a Zaraite that committed a great crime in Israel and his family was killed (Josh 7.1 H5912), he also belonged to the tribe of Zerah and would be a prince of Judah the line came to Ireland and the breach was healed or possibly in Hebrew lbenach means 3843 lbenah leb-ay-naw' white house de=God re=king albanne= white kingdom or white house and there are many similar sounding words like Laban, Lebanon.

237. Every professor in his art, of the latter classes, is called Ollamh P 86 O'Flaherty's Ogygia, Part I.

238. p130 O'Flaherty's Ogygia, Part II. Year 3276. Finnacta, the son of king Ollam fodla, reigned monarch

of Ireland twenty years. Year 3236. Ollam fodla of the house of Hir, the son of Fiach, swayed the scepter forty-years.

239. p130 O'Flaherty's Ogygia, Part II — year3433. The annals of Dunnegal(Doneagle)assign him 22 years, from the poem of G. Coeman; and another copy of the fame poem allows 2 1. However the book of Cluamnacnois, which I follow^ asserts he reigned 20 only.

240. Foldhla is a tribal name – O'Flaherty says P29 Ogygia it was the original name of the Ireland — But particularly it has three Irifh names in common, Ere, Fodla, and Banba(Banbha meaning sacred mountain top in both Hebrew and Irish see "names of Ireland" Ch. 14), from three sisters of the royal blood, of the Danans, who were the last queens of that people, as is universally recorded by all our historians. This island has five names, as Fiach the Scholiast wrote above a thousand years ago, Ere, Fodla, Banba, Fail, and Elga.

241. http://www.giveshare.org/israel/locationtribes.html http://www.nordiskisrael.dk/artikler/gad_spain_portug al.html http://stevenmcollins.com/WordPress/which-tribe-do-spain-and-portugal-belong/

242. http://hebrewnations.com/articles/biblical-proof/criteria/ spaintest.html

243. H693 אֲרֻבָּה 'ărubbâh, ar-oob-baw'; feminine participle passive of H693 (as if for lurking); a window; (by implication) a window, dovecot (**because of the pigeon-holes**), chimney, window.

244. English Language History   Old English (c. 500 – c. 1100) Notice the tribes of Angles, Saxon's Jutes and Normans are called Germanic because they came from Scythia via the land route (Hallstatt-Celts) via modern-day German.

245. Polybius, Dionyfius, Ptolemy, and of the Latin writers, Fella, Avienus, Apuleius, and Pliny, b. 4. Nat. Kill. Ancient writers from Ogygia p31

246. The temperature of the climate and fertility of the soil had deservedly conferred on it the name of the Sacred

island, which was given to it many ages before the birth of Christ by the Greeks: for from hieron which means holy, Ierna (P32 Ogygia)

247. H3414 Yirmyah yir-meh-yaw' or Yirmyahuw {yir-meh-yaw'-hoo}; from 7311 and 3050; Jah will rise; Jirmejah,...:--Jeremiah. H7311 ruwm room a primitive root; to be high actively, to rise or raise (in various applications, literally or figuratively):--bring up, exalt (self), extol, give, go up, haughty, heave (up), (be, lift up on, make on, set up on, too) high(-er, one), hold up, levy, lift(-er) up, (be) lofty, (X a-)loud, mount up, offer (up), + presumptuously, (be) promote(-ion), proud, set up, tall(-er), take (away, off, up), breed worms.

248. H3050 Yahh – yaw contraction for 3068, and meaning the same; Jah, the sacred name:--Jah, the Lord, most vehement. Compare names in '-iah,' also names beginning with Je Je(sus h3442) Yeshua or ending with iah, ian, ya, jah (link)

249. Argus, or Cecrops, ruled over the Argives; Gaedheal was said to be sprung from. (P388 Keating HoI)

250. Post captivity names of Israel by Rev Wm Pascoe, Missing Links discovered in Assyrian tablets E. Raymond Capt.

251. ANNALS OF THE KINGDOM OF IRELAND, BY THE FOUR MASTERS, FROM THE EARLIEST PERIOD TO THE YEAR 1616. Introductory remarks page-x

252. Milidh, Milesian, Mile, male etc. = 4390 male' maw-lay' or malae means prophesy fulfilled or fulfilled (Esth. 7:5) {maw-law'}; a primitive root, to fill or (intransitively) be full of, in a wide application (literally and figuratively):--accomplish, confirm, + consecrate, be at an end, be expired, be fenced, fill, fulfill, (be, become, X draw, give in, go) full(-ly, -ly set, tale), (over-)flow, fulness, furnish, gather (selves, together), presume, replenish, satisfy, set, space, take a (hand-)full, + have wholly. 4391 mla' mel-aw' (Aramaic) corresponding to 4390; to fill: fill, be full. See SH4390 4392 male' maw-lay' from 4390; full (literally or

273

figuratively) or filling (literally); also (concretely) fulness; adverbially, fully:--X she that was with child, fill(-ed, -ed with), full(-ly), multitude, as is worth. see SH4390 4393 mlo' mel-o' rarely mlowf {mel-o'}; or mlow (Ezekiel 41:8), {mel-o'}; from 4390; fulness (literally or figuratively):--X all along, X all that is (there-)in, fill, (X that whereof...was) full, fulness, (hand-)full, multitude. See SH4390 4394 millu' mil-loo' from 4390; a fulfilling (only in plural), i.e. (literally) a setting (of gems-or stone), or (technically) consecration (also concretely, a dedicatory sacrifice):-- consecration, be set. see SH4390 4395 mle'ah mel-ay-aw' feminine of 4392; something fulfilled, i.e. abundance (of produce):--(first of ripe fruit, fulness. see SH4392 4396 millu'ah mil-loo-aw' feminine of 4394; a filling, i.e. setting (of gems stone):--inclosing, setting.see SH4394 But perhaps an even more apro pros word -

253. Thus, Tanift, fecund to the prince in rank and authority; and from this the title of Taniflry-law is derived by Davis * and Ware 'f. Each of the other candidates of the family is called Riegb damna, which is royal; that is, a fubjedt qualified to receive the * In cafu Taniftriae. f Antiquities of Ireland, c.8 — Part I, O'Flaherty s Ogygia. p85

254. And a little after, he informs us that Susana, a city of Spain, was built by the Sarmatiar\s, (Samaritans), who all acknowledge being Scythians, in this line: Sarmaticos attolkns Susana Muros. Here we must remark, that the river Iberus, (now the Ebro), from which some say Ireland was denominated, takes its rise in Cantabria, Part II 0''Flaherty's Ogygia.p119

255. Jos 24:2 And Joshua said unto all the people, Thus saith the LORD God of Israel, Your fathers dwelt on the other side H5676 of the flood in old time, even Terah, the father of Abraham, and the father of Nachor: and they served other gods.

256. Part I. 0'Flaherty s Ogygia. p27 "Biscay bay, in Cantabria, (anciently called the Scythian) that being the

next land to it, at an immense distance; the British Sea, the British Armorica." This is the area where the Red hand of Zerah i.e. the Milesians allegedly came from, Keating forsa p117 XXI. "Of the coming of the sons of Milidh to Ireland."

257. Milesian family in Ireland Keating Foras Feasa p118-119,also in Ogygia — Tea, teamhair Tamar Tara etc, and Anuls of the four maters p30.

258. Ethan the Ezrihite (Zarahite) wrote Psalm 89, see v 25.

259. http://www.ringbell.co.uk/info/hdist.htm

260. http://www.libraryireland.com/Pedigrees1/Stem.php

261. The highest peaks in Brittany reach over 1000 meters high

262. History of the European nations. 3d ed. 1841 https://books. google.com/books?id=-NEtAAAAYAAJ James Cowles Prichard 1841 — Anthropology This tale has been alluded to by writers of late times as a probable tradition,…, *Tuatha De-Danann*, and *Milesians*, though said to have come to Ireland from different countries, all *spoke* the Gaoidhealg or Gaelic *language*.

263. Sons on Mil (prophesy) Brigantees tower breoghan - Spain Galicia map of where the tower was said to be located. This would mean the distance would be over 600 miles.

264. Ithel h384-God is with me, short form El-h410-god, Uwl-h193 mighty or strong as in Ith'ul, Ittai or Ithai Ith-h863-with me.

265. Teamor, Teamor, teamor, Tamar, Tea, Tara, Tiaras- princesses crown, all variations of the.

266. May Day traditions: Maypole, May Queen and Morris dancing

267. Don a derivative of Dan, i.e. Dun etc h1835

268. H4354 Makiyriy patronymical from 4353; a Makirite or descend. Of Makir:--of Machir. see SH4353 MACHIR or HA-MACHIRI? Not sure if I want this in? hypelink to a book I haven't read?

269. Names of tamar – p55 Keating GHoI TEE BOUNDARIES OF MEATH, AS TIIEY WERE IMPROVED BY TUATHALL TEACHTMHAR.

270. Arguments for and against Teai Tephi https://www.cai.org/ Bible-studies/tea-tephi-never-existed http://jahtruth.net/tephis um.htm

271. Ollam Fodhla set up Tara and the Red Hand of Ulster p59 Forsh KHoI

272. The title given was Ollamh Fodhla, to the son of Fiacha Finscothach, p53 Annals of the 4 masters, and — P163 K-GH-Also before a crew take to their racing craft, they have some preliminary practice in a wide pair-oared boat, called a tub pair. This practice is called tubbing. The same term is also applied to the coaching given to new oarsmen. (Prison), imprisonment. 'Nantes from the Rents (Fuller's or Tullwood's Rents in Holborn), smugged to rites, pilled, expects a tubbing;' inscription in a prison cell. Tub-man, an appointment given to a barrister -Tub-thumping (common), street preaching. Another, who waxed rather warm, was requested not to do any tub-thumping.— Funny Folhs. To Web site

273. Idioms are one of our ways of communicating; we commonly use phrases or idioms that convey a special meaning. I believe God built them into us so we could remember our past. Caught between a rock and a hard place means you have a tough decision with no seemingly good options

274. This is the difference between an idiom and a phrase: A phrase is 'a small group of words standing together as a conceptual unit', while an idiom is 'a group of words established by usage as having a meaning not deducible from those of the individual words.' Jul 22, 2011

275. FLUSH OUT OR FLESH OUT

276. Page x introduction annals of the four masters, and again Herber (Hebrews) mentioned Ivii, of course the name is commonly associated with Jeremiah in Ireland Emher and anglicized Herber, p27,29, 34, Dumha-Aichir: i. e. Aicher's or Heber's mound p.146 – 'race of

Heber mac Mileadh, p61-Emhear, Ever which means Ollam, or Heber mentioned, many high heaps i.e. signpost listed for them p29.

277. https://en.wikipedia.org/wiki/Red_line_(phrase)
278. https://en.wikipedia.org/wiki/Black_sheep
279. Lbn original spelling of the name without the vowels that only were introduced 600ad.
280. http://www.abarim-publications.com/Meaning/Galeed.html
281. https://en.wikipedia.org/wiki/Hip_(slang) there are differing view on the hip term, I think much of the statement is correct,
282. https://en.wikipedia.org/wiki/David_Rohl
283. https://www.ucg.org/world-news-and-prophecy/a-place-called-megiddo-the-worlds-battleground https://www.pinteres t.com/pin/548242954608967332/ https://www.thattheworld mayknow.com/the-valley-of-jezreel-viewcd-from-megiddo
284. Makhir Gen 50:23 Yosef saw Efrayim's children to the third generation. The children also of Makhir, the son of Menashsheh, were born on Yosef 's knees (H4353 NHB) And again in Joshua 17.1 it talks of Manassehs son 'This was the allotment for the tribe of Manasseh as Joseph's firstborn, that is, for Makir, Manasseh's firstborn. Makir was the ancestor of the Gileadites, who had received Gilead and Bashan because the Makirites were great soldiers. Let me paraphrase in modern terms the A'Makir'ians (Americans) where kick ass soldiers' (truth is all Israel could be kick ass soldiers with the right training and General, Patten and Montgomery WWII).
285. P31 Annals of the 4 masters Troy and Teamhair.
286. H8024 — שׁ֑וֹלָ֥נִי Shê lânîy, shay-law-nee'; from H7956 with the last part being decendant i.e. Laniy
287. https://www.blueletterBible.org/lang/lexicon/lexicon.cfm?Strong's=H5906&t=KJV – read Gesenius' Hebrew-Chaldee Lexicon on this link
288. Number in Scripture — By E. W. Bullinger – page 107

289. Ogygia p 27
290. Page 110 Keating General History
291. Britannia, Brit am Yah means covenant Brit=*H1285 – běriyth, h5971 am*=peoples or tribe h3050 Yahh – yaw contraction for 3068 -Yah, aka Ian or ia = God. Britannia means covenant people of God! The ancient name of these Island and Albans (Laban H3836) White House-500BC it was known by these Hebrew names. The white house and 'Brit am Yah' = 'covenant people of God.'
292. Keating general Hist. p108 poem on Mil or Mile, also known as Milesian, his real name was Galamh. https://miadhachain. weebly.com/milesius-galamh.html
293. Ith, aka Ithe and Ithel=h384-God is with me, short form El-h410-god, Uwl-h193 mighty or strong as in Ith'ul, Ittai or Ithai Ith-h863-with me. Eatan=EthanH386, God has strengthend, Scot=Sukkot H5521, Tea, Teamhear, Temhair, Tara Tiara etc = Tamer *erection-pillar*h8564 and h8558, Er = h6147, Herber, Eber Ebro= h5677 is the father of the term Hebrews Heremon Chermown (silent c, changes pronunciation) Sanctuary (H2768), Amergin, Emhear fin, = yIrm eyah = *Yirměyah*H3414, which means Yah will rise or 'Whom Yehovah has appointed' h3050 (248) h7311 (247). 1288 baw-rak-Baruch Jeremiah's scribe. See ref 252 for Milesian – prophesy fulfilled. Galamh, I this this is Gwilliam= 114 in Welsh-hebrew Joy of the lord or People.
294. 1524 giyl gheel meaning joy, happiness, and am H5971 — `am meaning people or nations Giylam Guillam, also Ian means gift of God., or God favored, from John-Yon and Yonathan 3076 Yhowchanan
295. Phinehas, H6372 mouth of serpent or brass.
296. Egle'ish Hebrew Strong's -h5695 & H376 Ox-man also Egla'ish 5697-376 calf, cow, heifer.& eglah 5882 En-eglaim. Pronounced An Eglaim — Fountain of two calfs will gore them with there horns (Deu33.17)
297. El-Arish /Succot name of staging area for the exodus el=god H410, H3423 = *y'Arash sounds like Irish* a

primitive root to occupy by driving out previous tenants, and possessing in their place, just as God predicted!, Th'Ar(sh)ish H8659 and it speaks of the region of the stone! And the Naphee (Navy). Also we have it written in the stars, that y'Arash will never be taken into captivity — navy (H590*oniy oNi(p)hee)* was named Th'Ar'shish (1Ki 10:22) and when we look in Job 38:32 The Ollam speaks out of the storm to Job(Arcturus) Job 38:32 Arcturus (h5906 ע̇ י ש *`Ayish*) with his sons? wee little ones.

298. Arcturus (h5906 ש ע י ש `Ayish) takes its name Arcturus takes its name from its nearness to the sky Bears, Big and Little Bears, Ursa Major, and Ursa Minor. From Arktouros orArctophilax, 'the Bear Guard' and also called the Bear Watcher' actually bearn watcher as in child. The 'Herdsman' as in shepherd or **'driver of oxen'** i.e. The ancient symbol of Jospeh was the Ox as in Arktouros (ark tarus) "bear-ward" and Bootes, "cow-herd." Arcturus is the brightest star in the constellation of Bootes the Herdsman so it is…with his sons? wee little ones-(ref) also striking is Ark Taurus — Arc Turus – It was used by Th'Arshish oNi(v) y, to navigate at night I am sure they often thought about the prophesies of Yahwey.

299. The original name of London was (Luwndan) Lunw'Dan'Ian (**Londinium**) meaning Dwelling place (or abode) of Dan by Gods grace. 3885 luwn pronounced lun – h1835 Dan. In (Ephraim, the Brits) be willing to serve thee, or abide H3885 by thy crib? (manger to be fed by God).

300. 4376 makar maw-kar' a primitive root; to sell, literally as merchandise, a daughter in marriage, into slavery literally or figuratively.

301. 4425 mliylah, mel-ee-law' from 4449 (in the sense of cropping, compare 4135), a head of grain (as cut off), foreskin it where Brit Milah is from, i.e. covenant of circumcision.

302. Ogygia Letter of the Author. P liii

303. Tuathal Teachtmhar-p164, many many names of Teach in Ireland Tea, da. of Lughaidh, s. of Ioth (Ithe), w. of Eireamhon; one of the seven chief women who came with the Milesians; built a fortress at Teamhair (Tara), which is named from her. P 564 Keating fenias forsa. Fact, the name land is a contraction of LunDan, Egel'lund, Sukkot'Lund, Er'luwnd! Psa 91:1 He that dwelleth in the secret place of the most High shall abide -luwn(d) H3885) under the shadow of the Almighty and again Job 39:9, Will the unicorn

304. O'Flaherty Ogygia p Ixvil also of note is that the Picts got wives from the Milesian

305. God said the Israelites would be oppressed and in a land not of their own for 400 years or 4 generations. After this time, God himself carried us on eagles' wings, but even then, the promised land was not free for the taking; it had to be taken by forces, and this process took hundreds of years,

306. Page 38 BRITISH HISTORY TRACED FROM EGYPT AND PALISTINE — Rev. L. G. A. ROBERTS, Com. R.N

307. Armagh (Armor or arma) according to wikipedia comes from Ard and Mhacha, Hebrew Ard h714 to subdue, meaning tough, strong, hard and Mhacha in Hebrew appears to connect to macha'neh H4264, we can see from the Irish place names that both magan (magen), and machan are in use – as well as Magh and some with Maghain. It appears that the name magh is from macha'neh as identified with Armagh, but is it possible that some of the magh's or magh variants come from maghen, meaning shield as in that of Abraham (h4043מָגֵן magen), we must remember that the spelling varied a lot and would often get misspelled so its phonetics that's important –.Ard means to subdue (H714) — ʼArdַאְרָךַד ʼArdîy, ar-dee; patronymic from H714; Ard H716 Ardites = "I shall subdue" the descendants of Ard Ard'magh shield that subdue's. Also, we have the Brit slang term "he's hard" meaning

tough, someone who can kick a donkey's ass's or subdue, disarm.

308. Tuatha De Dan (ites) came to Ireland 1200-700BC Forensic evidence P497 Foras Feasa Keating the stone of scone aka **Lia Fail**, a stone brought to Ireland by the Tuatha De Danann, said to 'roar' under the foot of the rightful king. of Ireland; silent since the time of Conchubhar.

309. The Welsh name does not have land or ish afterward and speaks of a different clan of Israel, they still spoke Celtic/Hebrew).

310. Celtic Culture: A Historical Encyclopedia edited by John Thomas Koch page 152 Bagpipes

311. http://www.doyle.com.au/great_irish_warpipe.htm

312. https://archive.org/stream/cu31924022329977#page /n31/ mode/2up/search/story+of+the+organ herbew origin p1 &2

313. https://www.vocabulary.com/dictionary/windbag

314. http://www.hebrew4christians.com/Grammar/Unit_ Two/ Introduction/introduction.html

315. https://archive.org/stream/cu31924022329977#page /n29/ mode/2up/search/psandherin symphony meant bagpipe M-A

316. http://www.britam.org/HebrewBagpipes.html, http://www.bag pipes.co.uk/irishbagpipes.html, celtic culture Irish bagpipes, https://www.google.com/search?q=irish+bagpiples+ula id&ie= utf-8&oe=utf-8&client=firefox-b-1, http://www.Bible-history. com/sketches/ancient/dulcimer-goatskin.html

317. Cymry 1583 Gamliy'el gam-lee-ale' Gamlee means reward Gamlee'el reward from God from 1580 and 410; the reward of God; Gamliel, an Israelite:--Gamaliel. see SH1580 see SH410

318. David Ben-Gurion declared the establishment of the Jewish state on May 14, 1948. This was followed by public Shabbat services.

319. There have been kings to the number of 181 (Monarchs), who have governed Ireland from the first

king Heremon & Tamar of this line to Roderic the last king O'Flaherty p. 57 Ogygia part 1

320. https://wahiduddin.net/words/name_god.htm

321. 1434 gdil(Gord) this Hebrew word means cord and is linked with Godel h1433 and h1431, h1432.

322. 1508 gizrah ghiz-raw' 'his raw' person who has been cut and their skin is raw see1506, **1625**

323. Yogh used for /x/: *God spede þe plouȝ: & sende us kọrne inolk. link*

324. Q-*Celtic has no* F, J or P. Neither *is* there a P http://www.faculty. ucr.edu/~legneref/bronze/ogamScri.htm

325. Phonogram, or alphabetic, where each cuneiform sign represented one letter of an alphabet. http://www.ancient-hebrew.org/m/ Bible_ugarit.html

326. 7939 sakar saw-kawr' *saw cash* reward of payment 3485 Yissaskar yis-saw-kawr' *he saw cash* he will bring a reward; 814 'eshkar esh-cawr' *its cash* for 7939; a gratuity:--gift, present.

327. 3966 m`od meh-ode' *method* force, might (a force something that caused it to happen we could also call method?)181 'uwd ood from an unused root meaning to rake together; a poker (for turning or gathering embers) what God is saying here Gen15.1 He is Abram's shield *magen* and *method* (the force or means) of obtaining great reward *saw cash.*

328. Zerah, H2226, Zerach meaning a ray of light or hope, also Zera & Zara =seed 2233 zera` zeh'-rah planting seed, H2234 zra` zer-ah' seed.

329. H6558 Partsiy par-tsee' patronymically from 6557; a Partsite (collectively) or descendants of Perets:--Pharzites. Parez i.e. Zerah's twin brother! 6556 perets peh'-rets from 6555; a break (literally or figuratively):--breach, breaking forth (in), X forth, gap. 6557 Perets peh'-rets the same as 6556; Perets, the name of two Israelites:--Perez, Pharez. 6555 parats paw-rats' a primitive root; to break out (in many applications, direct and indirect, literal and figurative):--X abroad, make a abroad, scatter!

330. 5912 `Akan from an unused root meaning to trouble; troublesome; Akan, an Israelite: Achan. Compare 5917. 5917 `Akar aw-kawr' from 5916; troublesome; Akar, an Israelite: Achar. See 5916 `akar aw-kar' a primitive root; properly, to roil water; figuratively, to disturb or afflict: --trouble, stir. see SH5912, Akan, an Israelite:--Achan. Compare 5917. I also see similarity in this 253 'ach awkh a variation for 162; Oh! (expressive of grief or surprise):--ah, alas. 162 'ahahh a-haw,' apparently a primitive word expressing pain exclamatorily.

331. 3115 Yowkebed yo-keh'-bed from 3068 contracted and 3513; Jehovah-gloried; Jokebed, the mother of Moses-Jochebed. see SH3068 see SH3513 3513 kabad kaw-bad' or kabed {kaw-bade'}; a primitive root; to be heavy, i.e., in a bad sense (burdensome, severe, dull) or in a good sense (numerous, rich, honorable; causatively, to make weighty (in the same two senses):--abounding with, more grievously afflict, boast, be chargeable, X be dim, glorify, be (make) glorious (things), glory, (very) great, be grievous, harden, be (make) heavy, be heavier, lay heavily, (bring to, come to, do, get, be had in) honor (self), (be) honorable (man), lade, X more be laid, make self many, nobles, prevail, promote (to honor), be rich, be (go) sore, stop

332. Mystery of ancient egypts red haired mummies

333. Why-do-we-bless-our-sons-to-be-like-Ephraim-and-Manasseh

334. https://en.wikipedia.org/wiki/Mullah the term refers to all the other so-called religious leaders, but clearly has an implication for us today!

335. https://www.Bible-history.com/map_fall_of_judah/fallofjudah_fall_of_jerusalem.html

336. 4583 ma`own a place you own, a habitation also Gods habitation Jer 25:30, your dwelling also Samaria h8111 שׁ מרון Shomĕ r own or a place of your own or dwelling place. 6619 Pithom pee-thome' of Egyptian derivation; Pithom, a place in Egypt:-Pithom a pee home in Egypt.

337. British History traced for Egypt and Patestine. Rev. L.G.A. Roberts, com R.N 1927, Petavius cir. 1659 A.D Sir Walter Raleigh cir. 1586 A.D. pub. 1786. Bk. II., p. 240 — the references above also corroborate 3 of these migrations.

338. Connection between Israel, Phoenicians and Greeks — Hiram (Solomon Hired him h2438 חִירָם ○Chiyram to assist in the work of the temple, , also worthy of note is that the free masons trace their origin back to Hiram Abif): Josephus Ant V8 Chapter 5.3 '**Menander also, one who translated the** Tyrian archives out of the dialect of the Phoenicians into the Greek language, makes mention of these two kings, where he says this: 'When Abibalus was dead, his son Hiram received the kingdom from him, who, when he had lived fifty-three years, reigned thirty-four.'…he both built the temple of Hercules and that of Astarte.

339. Now Solomon sent for an artificer out of Tyre, whose name was Hiram; he was by birth of the tribe of Naphtali, on the mother's side, (for she was of that tribe,) but his father was Ur, of the stock of the Israelites. Josephus Ant Vol L8 Chap 4.3. See also 1Ki 7:14 2Ch 2:14.

340. Gen 25:25 And the first came out red, all over like a hairy garment; and they called his name Esau. H6215 Interesting that this doesn't mean read but his son Edom does, (h6215 עֵשָׂו ○'Esav he saw red-(father of Edom= h123 ○אֱדֹם 'Edom= Red)

341. Keatings General History of Ireland p 75 All the original inhabitants of the island were the descendants of Magog – this may be close to the truth, however often they say the subsequent waves of migrations Tuatha de Danann and Milesians also came from Magog, this is not their origin some Scythians did come through Magog before eventually reaching Ireland.

342. Keatings History of Ireland, throughout his book he writes it as Tuatha de Danann's p. 75, O'Flaherty Ogygia, calls them Tuatha de Danonn p17, and Danan and O'Flaherty says the name Danann's comes from the

Danes part 1, p19, the name Danes comes from "native of Denmark," from Danish Daner (replacing Old English Dene (plural)); used in Old English of Northmen generally. Perhaps ultimately from a source related to Old High German tanar "sand bank," in reference to their homeland (*or their father family line*); or from Proto-Germanic *den- "low ground," for the same reason. Applied 1774 to a breed of large dogs. Danegeld not known by that name in Old English (really what about Donegal), or until 1086, long after the end of the Viking depredations. Supposedly originally a tax to pay for protection from the Northmen (either to outfit defensive armies or to buy peace). Danelaw (c.1050) was the Danish law in force over that large part of England under Viking rule after c.878; the application to the land itself is modern (1837).

343. Yahweh, is a transliteration form the Tetragrammaton יהוה (YHWH or YHVH h3068 יְהֹוָה Yĕhovah, Jehovah), which is said to actually exists only of vowels, personally all these letters could sound a vowel but they could also sound a consonant, (see EIH alphabet section) Yod=Y,J,I and E, Hey =H, he, hi, ha,, ae, ea, Waw/Vav=W,V, O, & U, oo, uu.. There is evidence to show that the original 6th letter of Hebrew sounded a W, but changed over time to also include a V, while today's Hebrew they only have the V. The Paleo Hebrew is considered a consonantal script, i.e, no vowels, or missing vowels and the Jews consider God's name so sacred that when they reading would pronounce Adoni instead. Due to this and other reasons, most scholars are unsure how to pronounce it, but two main contenders YeHoVaH and YaHWaY. Remember the 6th letter of Paelo Hebrew was originally a Waw and it is now a Vav. Historically folks have had problems pronouncing W's and sometimes replace them with V to make it easier like vhere (where) have you been. But the opposite can also be true for instance the Russians pronounce Vodka as Wadka.

344. https://en.wikipedia.org/wiki/Milesians_(Irish) This theme is general back up by Keating Gen His of Ireland p. Foras Feasa XXI. Of the coming of the sons of Milidh to Ireland as follows: p177. The Danites and Milesian's ancient map

345. Ogygia, O'Flaherty — The Translators Address, vii places the arrival of the Gaels 489BC. O'Flaherty at the time says he computes the arrival of the Gaels to the time when Solomon was on the throne of Israel 950BC ibib page 103.

346. The "Hyksos" as Amalekites

347. What does an Eagle mean, God said he brought Israel out of Egypt on eagles wings, symbolic of God doing the work accomplishing his goal. Also we know that the Eagle is a symbol of Dan and Dan is a merchant! Powerful wings, and long feathers means it comes from a distance, varied colors, we know that Joseph had a coat of many colors and varied colors is a symbol of Joseph/Israel, (Dan, Judah, Levi, Joseph others) also later color became a symbol of authority, the higher the rank the more the colors. Top of the cedar, we can see that the king of Babylon was symbolized by a tree top and Daniel interpreted the dream, it means high, the kingly line taken to a city of traders, Jews, & Dan's with Ephraim & Manasseh, Th'Arshish. Lebanon is a symbol of a white mountain, i.e. an allegory of Israel (the white house).

348. http://www.heraldry.ws/info/article12.html High kings of Ireland.

349. ANNALS OF THE KINGDOM OF IRELAND. P 43

350. Hercules and Samson are the same people link

351. Although Dai was formerly used as a name in its own right prior to the late 15th century, possibly derived from a Welsh word meaning "shining." The name was very popular in Wales, leading to the situation whereby in England, "Taffy" or "Taff" (imitating the Welsh pronunciation of "Dafydd") became used as a pejorative nickname for Welshmen regardless of their actual name link. Also we have the following: The term "Taffy" may

be a merging of the common Welsh name "Dafydd" (Welsh pronunciation: [ˈdavið]) and the Welsh river"Taff" on which Cardiff is built, and seems to have been in use by the mid-eighteenth century.[3] The rhyme may be related to one published in Tommy Thumb's Pretty Song Book, printed in London around 1744, which had the lyrics:. Taffy was born On a Moon Shiny Night, His head in the Pipkin, His Heels upright.[2] etc. etc.

352. David Louis flute of Moses listen it sounds like the Irish flute, and don't forget the Harp.

353. https://www.adath-shalom.ca/history_of_hebrew.htm#varieties

354. https://www.myjewishlearning.com/article/the-conventi ons-of-biblical-poetry/

355. H5521 cukkah sook-kaw' fem of 5520; a hut or lair: -- booth, cottage, covert, pavilion, tabernacle, tent. 5522 cikkuwth sik-kooth' feminine of 5519; an (idolatrous) booth: -tabernacle. 5523 Cukkowth sook-kohth' or Cukkoth {sook-kohth'}; plural of 5521; booths; Succoth, the name of a place in Egypt and of three in Palestine: Succoth. 5524 Cukkowth bnowth sook-kohth' ben-ohth' from 5523 and the (irreg.) plural of 1323; booths of (the) daughters; brothels, i.e., idolatrous tents for impure purpose: -Succoth-benoth. 5525 Cukkiy sook-kee' partial from an unknown name (perhaps 5520); a Sukkite, or inhabitant of someplace near Egypt (i.e., hut-dwellers): Sukkiims. 5526 cakak saw-kak' or sakak (Exod. 33:22) {saw-kak'}; a primitive root; properly, to entwine as a screen; by implication, to fence in, cover over, (figuratively) protect: -cover, defense, defend, hedge in, join together, set, shut up.

356. Canadian Researcher, Dr. Doug Petrovitch is the first person in history to translate these 16 inscriptions and it all started when he realized they were in ancient Hebrew. This refutes the previous notion that Phoenician was the first alphabet and proves beyond doubt that Phoenician was derived directly from

Hebrew which is in fact the true Proto-Canaanite alphabet, Dr Petrovitch says Samuel developed the first Paleo Hebrew, see fig A.

357. A 15th century treatise on Ogham, *The Book of Ballymote*, confirms that ogham was a secret, ritualistic language.

358. Isaac's name as it was originally pronounced sounds like 'Its Jack' (h3327 יִצְחָק, *Yitschaq, Yits'chaq* Its Jack).

359. Baton and the name bat appear to come from the Hebrew word bad(t) H905 these were the staves that carried the Ark Exo 25:13, according to the edenics.net website a similar term was the scepter spoken of in Genesis 49.10 H7626 – shebet-scepter. Briton (celtic *Brython)* and baton sound similar and are clearly used together in scripture. In addition, the ark of Noah was known as תֵּבָה têbâh which appears to be a derivative of bad, according to the Edenics web site. And we have the Ark of the covenant, which was called (Num 10:33) Arown Brit, (ar own Brit, **Briyth)**, and soon to be revealed will be the Brit'ish. It does appear that bad-on bat-on is a Hebrew word see #361.

360. *Ararat* (sometimes *Ararad*) is the Greek version of the Hebrew spelling (H780: אֲרָרָט, 'A*RaRaT*) of the name Urartu Urfa, Ur, Armenia, Shem land, land where Laban lived - rarat = "the curse reversed: precipitation of curse" a mountainous region of eastern Armenia, between the river Araxes and the lakes Van and Oroomiah, the site where Noah's ark came to rest.

361. *Brit'on* The most common name on i.e. own from 202 'own (one) probably from the same as 205 (in the sense of effort, but successful); ability, power, (figuratively) wealth, force, goods, might, strength, substance. 203 'Own one the same as 202, On, an Israelite, On. see **H204** 'Own one or (shortened); On (one) of Egyptian derivation(?) On, a city of Egypt:-- On. 37 times in the bible. Briton, means strength or power or might of the covenant and is normally associated with the first-born, Reuben but remember God made Ephraim the first-born Genesis 49:3 Reuben,

you are my first-born, my might, and the first fruits of my strength, pre-eminent in pride and pre-eminent in power. And in Deuteronomy 21:17 but he shall acknowledge the first-born, the son of the disliked, by giving him a double portion of all that he has, for he is the first issue of his strength; the right of the first-born is his.

362.	Does the word יְהֹ֗ וֹ סוּמְפֹ *cuwmpownĕyah* means a composition of music to Yah (Exo. 15:2), see H7892 שִׁיר. shiyr=song, 6440 פָּנִים.p.paniym= face of, or presence of, anadh=YGod? H3050 יָּהּ Yâhh, contraction for H3068, and meaning the same; Jah,the sacred name:—Jah, the Lord, most vehement. Compare names in '-iah,' '-jah.' The Hebrew words are very similar Shiyr paniym yah or shir 6831 Tsphowniy tsef-o-nee' or tsefonee yah Exo 15:2 — this requires more work sorry!

363.	According to 'Oxford History of Music the first know mention of the bagpipe was in the area of Cannan (Israel) 1000 BC.

364.	http://www.johnpratt.com/items/docs/lds/meridian/2 005/12sons.html 12 tibes are said to have been associated with the 12 zodiac signs.

365.	Here is the google link to *"etymology of Irish"*.

366.	The awesome prophesies made by God to David (D'vid) 2 Samuel 7, God had given David rest from all his enemies and then he tells David that he will plant Israel in a place of safety (v.10) and that he will establish a house and throne forever! This is the prophecy the Jews of *Jurin* (Ireland) were alluding to! And remember to dwel (luwn) in the secret hiding place of God, underneath his wings: Job 39:28 She dwelleth and abideth H3885 on the rock, upon the crag of the rock, and the strong place .Psa 25:13 His soul shall dwell H3885 at ease; and his seed shall inherit the earth. Psa 91:1 He that dwelleth in the secret place of the most High shall abide H3885 under the shadow of the Almighty. Please read Ps25 and Ps 91 they tell of Yah way's promise to the Brit's also see section on Jeremiah' commission for Ezekiels prophesies.

367. C.S. Lewis was God a mad man, liar or really God? Lord or Lunatic argument.

368. Dannus and Belius, his mother? Was this one of the sons of Jacob and from the tribe of Dan Who were the Ancient Danites part II The Mysterious Tribe of Dan

369. https://en.wikipedia.org/wiki/Mining_in_Roman_Britain

370. Holy covenant listed in Daniel **H6944 – qodesh** baqqōḏeš as a transliteration listed in https://biblehub.com/str/hebrew/6944. htm similar to the English name bequeath a holy alliance

371. Latham's Ethnology of Europe p. 157, suggests the traveling about of Danai is the tribe of Dan, Argive Danai, also called *Heraclidae* – Lacedaemonians are Argives and Heraclidae and are Hebrew.

372. Gladstone tells us the Tuatha de Danaans of Ireland came from the Danai of Greece. (1Maccabees 22).

373. http://www.Bible-history.com/maps/2-table-of-nations.html

374. https://www.ancient.eu/image/6154/eratosthenes-map-of-the-world/ A reconstructed map of the known world according to Eratosthenes (276-195 BCE), the Greek Alexandrian scholar from Cyrene. Also you can see the three oldest maps of the know world here: https://periklisdeligiannis.wordpress.com/2018/04/16/world-maps-of-ancient-geographers-part-ii/ And we have the world's oldest map reconstruction being — The World According to Homer (B.C. 900). The World According to Hecataeus (about B.C. 500). The World According to Herodotus (about B.C. 440). The World According to Democritus about B.C. 300. The World According to Eratosthenes and Strabo (from about B.C. 200 to A. D. 20). Western Europe According to Strabo. The World According to Ptolemy (about A.D. 160). India According to Ptolemy. Great Britain According to Ptolemy.

375. Ogygia p130 speaks of Olam Fodah.

376. Primarily due to the potato famine and other hardships the Irish migrated in mass to the USA. It is

estimated that as many as 4.5 million Irish arrived in America between 1820 and 1930. Between 1820 and 1860, the Irish constituted over one third of all immigrants to the United States. In the 1840s, they comprised nearly half of all immigrants to this nation (Link).

377.   Hebrew is whirlwind galgal h1534, ok its not gale or blowing a gael however it does mean a rolling, wheel or stone and whirlwind and is a strong contender for the origin of our Egelish term gale, notice the terms from an old Norse term used in seafaring! Also, bible hub says the wind leading to a gale https://biblehub.com/str/hebrew/1534.htm.

378.   Fight between Danites and Milesians on Sliabh Mis mountain side Annals of the four-master page 25.

379.   Annals of the four masters *This was the year in which Eremhon and Emher ruled Ireland"* https://celt.ucc.ie/published/ T100005A/text005.html

380.   H8081 Shemen thick fatty oil, olive or fat or animal fat its what we call an emission from a penis, I am sure this was not what Jacob put on the Tamarrun, because God is very clear about a nocturnal emission or discharge of semen making a person unclean — Lev 15:15 read all Leviticus 15 for clarity, it must have happened later that we started using the term. The website Edenics.net say that the English word semen is from the Hebrew word shemen meaning grease or fat. http://www. edenics.net/english=SEMEN.

381.   *Murtagh*   *MacEirc* https://en.wikipedia.org/wiki/List_of_kings_ of_D%C3%A1l_Riata This lists the kings of Northern Ireland and Scotland from about 500AD-1603AD, Fergus the great-king James VI that united the thrones of Scotland to England. Then rules Great Britain 1603-today! https://en.wikipedia.org/ wiki/James_VI_and_I

382.   Tea Tephi is listed in their account, I mention this in passing Bible Ts^{e}phîy; H6825 from H6822, meaning watch tower or strong hold, perhaps this this is exactly

what Tara was Tae Tephi, watch town of the new Britons?

383.   Laban's father, Bethuel, was the son of Nachor (Snore), Abraham's older brother. In addition, Laban was thrice related by marriage to Abraham's family: his sister Rebecca married Isaac, and his two daughters, Leah and Rachel, both married Jacob. Thus, Laban was Abraham's great-nephew, Isaac's cousin and brother-in-law, and Jacob's uncle and father-in-law

384.   Family Tree DNA Genealogy by Genetics, Ltd. World Headquarters. R1b1b2 represents the largest haplogroup for Armenians in general and project members in particular. It has been estimated to be 8,000 years old, according to Vince Vizachero, who runs the haplogroup R-ht35 Project.

385.   http://www.polgeonow.com/2012/06/feature-queen-elizabeths-16-countries.html

386.   The original Hebrew was written in Paleo or, as some say

387.   The devil comes in many name sin the Bible, Baalzebub, בַּעַל זְבוּב (h1176 Ba`al Zĕbuwb), Lucifer (1966 heylel hay- lale'), Demons are called shed or shade (שֵׁד shêd, shade; from H7736), but what about the English word Devil or evil this comes from 4 possible Hebrew words h5760 Aivyl-ungoldly h5765 ăval -unrighteous, 66 evel-evil and 67 avval-wicked, we also have Satan — h7854 Satan-arch-enemy of good.

388.   http://www.nordiskisrael.dk/artikler/jory_brooks_hebrew_and_english.html

389.   https://idioms.thefreedictionary.com/once+bitten%2c+twice+shy

390.   Hebrew for a male donkey is H2543 חֲמוֹר chamowr its from the root h2560, same as the word root that Samson (h2560) uses but does anyone know what it really means in the NIV they collected 100 biblical Hebrew scholars and this is what they say — Then Samson said, "With a donkey's jawbone I have made donkeys[asses] of them. With a donkey's jawbone I have killed a thousand men." NIV.

391.   We can see that Isaac instructed Jacob to go to his family line and get a daughter. Specifically, to the House of Bethuel, and get a wife from his son Laban, i.e., the white house. Essentially, all the females came from the white house, i.e., Laban. The family line of the tribes of Israel now begins. Jacob worked at the "white house" for over 14 years, perhaps 20 in total. Names used in Britain that correspond to the term white house are:- Alban, Albion, Albanion, and Albiōnōn the name Judging from Avienus's Ora Maritima to which it is considered to have served as a source, the Massaliote Periplus (originally written in the 6th century BC, translated by Avienus at the end of the 4th century), does not use the name Britannia; instead, it speaks of nēsos Iernōn kai Albiōnōn "the islands of the Iernians and the Albiones." [10] Likewise, Pytheas (ca. 320 BC), as directly or indirectly quoted in the surviving excerpts of his works in later writers, speaks of Albiōn and Iernē (Britain and Ireland). Pytheas's grasp of the νῆσος Πρεττανική (nēsos Prettanikē, "Prettanic island") is somewhat blurry and appears to include anything he considers a western island, including Thule.

392.   **P-Celtic (Brythonic) Period**: P-Celtic languages, also known as Brythonic languages, began to diverge from other Celtic languages around the 1st millennium BCE. The P-Celtic languages were spoken in Britain and parts of mainland Europe (e.g., Gaul). The primary Brythonic languages include Welsh, Cornish, and Breton (in Brittany, France

393.   BRITON, BRITISH, BRITANNIA - Briton - **Earliest References**: The term "Briton" is first known from the writings of Pytheas, a Greek geographer who explored the British Isles around 330-320 BC. Although his original works are lost, subsequent writers frequently referenced his descriptions of the inhabitants of Britain. The Greeks called the people of Britain the Pretanoí or Bretanoí. Pliny's "Natural History" mentions the older name for the island, Albion, while Avienius refers to it as "insula Albionum," meaning "island of the

293

Albions." The Latin term for the Britons was Britanni. The P-Celtic ethnonym *Pritanī* is reconstructed from Common Celtic *kʷritu*, related to Old Irish *cruth* and Old Welsh *pryd*. This term likely means "people of the forms" and is associated with the Latin *Picti*, meaning "painted people." The Old Welsh term for the Picts was *Prydyn*.   British The medieval Welsh form of Latin *Britanni* was *Brython* (both singular and plural). The term *Brython* was introduced into English by John Rhys in 1884 to refer specifically to P-Celtic speakers of Great Britain, differentiating them from Goidelic speakers.   The adjective *Brythonic* relates to this group of languages, and the term "Brittonic languages" emerged in the early 20th century.   Britannia is the Latin name for the island of Britain and has been used since Roman times to refer to the British Isles.
Britannia has also been personified as a female figure representing Britain, often depicted in art and coinage.
     The connection between *Pritani* and the terms *cruth* (Old Irish) and *pryd* (Old Welsh) involves the concept of form and appearance, but for me, they are not linked, it is a hypothetical constructed root.   Said   to   be from **Common Celtic *kʷritu*   Old   Welsh   The Welsh *prydydd*,** "maker of forms", was also a term for the highest grade of <u>a bard</u>. ⁽daBar), spoken word Hebrew. Pryd'ydd   I believe they have gotten this totally wrong Britain, British Britania, do not relate to *Pritanī* as a painted man, but relate to Old Irish *Briathar,* word, speech, saying covenant, solemn declaration, and *Bráth (noun):* Judgement on a solemn, declaration broken, these come from the Hebrew Brith (Brit), in fact, Brit'ish (H1285, H376) means covenant man in Hebrew, a blood oath in Celtic and Hebrew, would use the same term Briathar, or Brath, and (Brith or Brit in Hebrew).   Old   Irish   Words Related   to   Solemn   Declarations   and   Covenants: **Bríathar (noun):Meaning**: Word, speech, saying.
     Context: Often used in legal or formal contexts, indicating a solemn declaration or statement.

Example Usage: "bríathar" in legal texts could refer to an oath or a formal promise, reflecting the seriousness and binding nature of the words spoken. **Bráth (noun)**: **Meaning**: Judgment, doom. **Context**: Often used in a legal or apocalyptic sense, indicating a final decision or end of times. **Example Usage**: "bráth" could refer to a final judgment or decision, often with a sense of irrevocability and solemnity.

Significance in Legal and Formal Contexts:

Bríathar: The use of "bríathar" in legal contexts underscores the importance of spoken words as binding agreements or covenants. In many ancient cultures, including Celtic societies, spoken oaths and promises held great weight and were considered sacred. **Bráth**: The term "bráth" conveys a sense of ultimate judgment or fate. In legal terms, it could be used to describe a final verdict, while in a more apocalyptic or eschatological context, it might refer to the end times or final reckoning. Connection to the Concept of Covenant: **Solemn Declaration**: Both terms align with the idea of a covenant as a solemn declaration. "Bríathar" emphasizes the spoken aspect, while "bráth" highlights the finality and seriousness of the declaration.

Binding Agreement: In legal and formal contexts, these words reflect the binding nature of covenants. Just as a "bríathar" is a spoken promise that one is bound to keep, a "bráth" is a final decision that one must adhere to. These Old Irish terms demonstrate the cultural significance of speech and judgment in solemn declarations and covenants, illustrating the deep respect for words and promises in ancient legal and formal practices, similar to the Hebrew word Brith meaning covenant, that if broken would be a judgement impending disaster - 1285 בְּרִית bĕriyth Brits, the Hebrew word בְּרִית (bĕriyth), which is often transliterated as "berith" or "brit." This word indeed means "covenant" in Hebrew and is used extensively in the Hebrew Bible to refer to agreements or promises, especially those made by God with the Israelites.

Analysis of the Word בְּרִית (bĕriyth) **Meaning**: Covenant, agreement, pledge. **Usage**: It is used to describe solemn agreements, often between God and humans, such as the covenants made with Noah, Abraham, Moses, and David.**Implications**: The breaking of a covenant (בְּרִית) often implied severe consequences or divine judgment, reflecting the serious and binding nature of these agreements. Connection to "Brits" and "Brith"   **Brits**: The term "Brits" in the image likely refers to the people of Britain. The connection to בְּרִית (bĕriyth) could be explored through historical and linguistic studies, as some theories suggest links between ancient Hebrew and Celtic languages.   **Brith**: As you mentioned, "Brith" is closely related to "bĕriyth," and it can be associated with covenants or agreements that, if broken, could lead to judgment or disaster.   Etymology and Usage in Historical Context -   **Etymology**: The word "bĕriyth" is derived from a root that means "to cut," referencing the ancient practice of cutting animals in half as part of making a covenant (a practice symbolizing the seriousness of the agreement).

Historical Context: Covenants were foundational in ancient societies, establishing relationships between tribes, nations, and deities. The concept of a covenant was central to the identity and religious practices of the Israelites. Conclusion   The word בְּרִית (**bĕriyth**) encapsulates **the concept of a binding and solemn agreement, with significant religious and cultural implications. The connection to the term "Brits" might be a point of interest in exploring historical and linguistic links between ancient Hebrew and the languages or peoples of the British Isles.**

394.   Zaragossa, (said by some to mean stronghold of Zarah, where or Zarah Garda, ZARA the first to pop out from Tamar's womb, but Perez breached for, even though Zerah got the scarlet cord tied around his hand (see the flag of Northern Ireland) the Iberian town that preceded Roman colonization was said to be called

Sal'duie[7] or *Sal'duba*.[8] (unknown meaning perhaps Sal=salt or water, suffix **"-duie"** possibly "city" or "settlement," but not uncommon around Spain).

The Romans and Greeks called the ancient city *Caesar Augusta* (in Greek Καισαραυγοῦστα),[9][10] from which derive the Arabic name سرقسطة*Sar aqsṭa* (used during the Al-Andalus period), the medieval *Çaragoça*, and the modern *Zaragoza*. on the Ebro River. For some reason, I still think that Sal and SAR could be related to ZARA, which means seed or rising Zar, (H2226 זֶרַח Zerach Leader of the Jews in Ireland, STAR of David and scarlet cord-(H2225 dawning, shining זֶרַח zerach, from H2224; a rising of light-STAR) Gen 38:30 KJV 30 And afterward came out his brother, that had the scarlet thread upon his hand: and his name was called Zarah. as the sun and was the name of the proposed inhabitance of Spain prior to going to Ireland. CEASAR, CZAR and is the name of the Roman supreme leader (highest leader Ceasor (uncertain origin; Pliny derives it from caesaries "head of hair," because the future dictator was born with a full one; Century Dictionary suggests Latin caesius "bluish-gray" (of the eyes), also used as a proper name, caesarian. Maybe a king a crown, Tiara (Tara?) from Hebrew consider (2918   טִירָה tiyrah castle, palace, row, habitation 5850 עֲטָרָה ʻăṭârâh, TIARA ʻăṭârâh, from H5849; a crown h5849 עָטַר ʻâṭar, a primitive root; to encircle (for attack or protection); especially to crown (literally or figuratively). Also Tzar sound like Zar(a) who was a prince of the Jews, as rising ZAR -STAR 2094 זָהַר zâhar, zaw-har'; a primitive root; to gleam; figuratively, to enlighten (by caution), admonish, shine, teach, (give) warn(-ing) (see Ishtar, Ashtoreth-astor'eth, Easter-matrix).

395. Place of safety, a place where Israel will not be disturbed, this is alluded to in Gen 49.22 where Jacob says that Ephraim will be a fruitful vine that will climb over the **wall**. A wall is defensive and provides security, a place where people feel safe like Jericho, it was

thought that their walls were impossible to overcome. 2 Sam 7..10 God tells David after he had given him rest from his enemies that he will (future tense וְשַׂמְתִּי the inclusion of the prefix ו Waw/Vav indicates future tense), plant Israel where they will be secure, again suggest a natural border. As Gen 49.22 suggested (see also 1Ch 17.9, Ps 80.8, Jer 18.9, Amo 9.15, Ps 89.22, Isa 60.18, Hose 2.18, Rev 21.4). We know that God will bring the ultimate peace and safety, and restore a symbolic number of Israel to the promised land of Israel, but he also looked at the world and designed that Israel would inhabit the Islands of the sea (Britain, , Australia, New Zealand, even America, Canada are places of the western coastlands, with a natural sea wall and rivers as protection)

Notes

1. Notice that they nearly always use contemporary names; Moses and the prophets often did this also in the Bible, unless God directed them to use a special name of hidden meaning **Owlam** H5769
2. I have copies and accounts of O'Flaherty from 1760, where the spelling was a little different than it is now, and F was used instead of the S in much of his book.
3. https://josephandisraelinegypt.wordpress.com/tag/david-down/
4. http://Biblehub.com/timeline/ 1898 BC Tamar deceives Judah, Genesis 38, 9 months later twin boys.
5. This was cut straight from his book with his wording, and his misspelling f 's were used in place of s's throughout most of his writing a common practice back then.
6. Names of Ireland from Ogygia by O'Flaherty 1793 p27-33 Banbah or Banna, banbh this is by some believed to be sacred promontory i.e. hill of sacrifice (p30) this is bamah h1116 in Hebrew a sacred high place of worship also could mean hog or back of an animal or person.
7. The Dead Sea Scrolls, uncovered in 1946–1948 near Qumran revealed ancient Jewish texts overwhelmingly in Hebrew, not Aramaic... Alongside Aramaic, Hebrew co-existed within Israel as a spoken language. Most scholars now date the demise of Hebrew as a spoken language to the end of the Roman Period, or about 200 CE.
8. Punctuation/inflection emphasis is mine. e.g., tharshish would be th'ar'shish
9. Naos   obelisk
   https:www.google.comsearch?q=Tharu+in+Egyptian%2C+Naos+&ie=utf-8&oe=utf-8&client=firefox-b-1
10. In Exodus 14.2-3, it speaks of the Arabian side of the true red sea crossing is Baal Zephon, historians say the crossing of the red sea was through a shallow sea of reeds, how wrong they are, as we have already see, even our idiom history tells the truth!

11. This section of the book is paraphrased; examples are Gen 17, Gen48.17-20, 49.22-26 and Deu 33.13-17

12. The book of Jasher is non-conical, as such its not considered part of the Bible however the Bible does quote form this book (2Sa 1:18, Jos 10:13).

13. This appears to be an error, I cannot find additional supporting Hebrew, it might be correct as a Judge needs to run a straight, honest course, Dan is also a sea fairing race.

14. I am not saying its wrong to use the name Jesus, God knows our hearts and so long as we respect him and us a name appropriately, its fine, also the name Je is even in Hebrew considered to be a name of God. See #248, Jesus had a sign written in Latin, Hebrew and Greek Luk 23:38, the original language of the Apostles, who were predominantly from Galilee is generally considered to be ancient Aramaic, they would pronounce his name as Eashoa but others say his name in Hebrew Yeshu, also we have Yeshua (Jesus h3442)

15. Stronghold of Zarah, referenced in E. Raymond Capt book Missing Links Discovered in Assyrian Tablets p65; while it is possible that the Zarahite branch of Judah, came from this region, the etymology of Saragoza, does not bear this out.

16. https://cafeastrology.com/zodiactaurus.html This is also a constellation Taurus the bull, which we will not take the time to discuss here. https://en.wikipedia.org/wiki/Bo%C3%B6tes (bootes link).

17. As in Egel'ish, Hebrew has many silent letters; in the Hebrew language, almost all cases of silent letters are silent aleph – 6].א] Many words that have a silent aleph in Hebrew have an equivalent word in Arabic. Often, the 'S' is silent, as is the Aleph https://en.wikipedia.org/wiki/Silent_letter

18. Urfa reminds me of my aunt's name, Bertha, which I believe comes from the Hebrew Bertha daughter of Jehovah, Bertha, my second mother's name (Aunt Bertha — H1332 – Bithyah Bithiah = 'daughter of Jehovah'a

daughter of a Pharaoh and wife of Mered of Judah, from Bath H1323 =Daughter and Jah H3050 God. Most likely, where did we get the term birth from, i.e., birth of a new daughter? We also have Itha, Ith, aka Ithe and Ithel=h384. God is with me, short form El-h410-God, Uwl-h193 mighty or strong as in Ith'ul, Ittai or Ithai Ith-h863-with me. Not as close a sound but perhaps a connection?

19. Strong's 1116 bamah bam-maw' from an unused root (meaning to be high); an elevation, height, high place, wave, singular of 1120 Bamowth baw-moth' plural of 1116; heights; or (fully) Bamowth Bahal {baw-moth' bah'-al}; from the same and 1168; heights of Baal; Bamoth or Bamoth-Baal, a place East of the Jordan, Bamoth, Bamoth-baal. see SH1116 see SH1168. 1168 Ba`al bah'-al the same as 1167; Baal, a Phoenician deity, Baal,(plural) Baalim (see SH1167). At one point, I found a connsc-tion with Height elevation and back, especially hog back with its prominent arch, but no cants seem to find it.

List Of Figures

Figure A

Biblical "Hebrew to English" Alphabet
Hebrew is the first and oldest alphabet: 1859 BC

Pictograms Egyptian Hieroglyphics 1859 BC (Gardiner's Sign List #)	Sounds Like	Phonograms Mosaic Hieroglypic Hebrew Alphabet 1859 - 550 BC (First Hebrew Phonogram Alphabet 1859 - 1100 BC)	Paleo-Hebrew 1100-550BC	Echograms English Modern	Aramaic Hebrew Square Hebrew 550 BC - 70 AD (First Century)	Masoretic Hebrew Vowelled Hebrew 600 AD - present (Vowels, dots, dashes were invented by Masoretes 600 AD) did not exist before.
(F1)	K	Aleph Cattle	∢	A	א	Silent stop, like the "-" in "A-ha".
(O1) (O4)	Pr /H	Bayit House	◿	B,V	ב	B as in Bet (With dot) / V as in Vet
(S38)	Kobt	Gahar Bend	⅄	G	ג	G as in Gift
(O31)	.	Delet Door	△	D	ד	D as in Door
(A28)	Hi	Halal Praise	⅄	H,E	ה	H as in Hay
(O30)	Shut	Vaw Pillar Support	Y	V,O,U	ו	V as in Vine, Vowel "u" as in "Flute", Vowel "o" as in "Hole"
(D13)	inh	Zeah Sweat (Brow)	Z	Z	ז	Z as in Zechariah
(O6) / (V28)	Hwt /H	Haser/Hut Enclosure/Thread	目	H,Ch	ח	Ch as in Bach
(F35)	D	Tov Good	⊗	Th	ט	Th as in Thin
(D36) (D47)	A	Yad Hand	𐤉	I,Y,J	י	Y as in Yes, Vowel "i" as in machine, Vowel "ey" as in "they".
(D28)	K	Kap Palms	✓	K,Ch	ך,כ	K as in King (With dot), Ch as in Bach
(S39)	Wt	Lamad Teach	L	L	ל	L as in Learn
(N35)	N	Mayim Water	ⱳ	M	ם,מ	M as in Memory
(I9) (D19)	F	Nahas Snake	∤	N	ן,נ	N as in Now
(O6) (F13)	- / Bz	Sear/Sarah Hair/Stink	ⱦ	S,X	ס	S as in Support
D	IR	Ayin Eye	O	O	ע	Silent guttural in the back of the throat
(D21)	R	Peh Mouth	⌐	P,Ph	ף,פ	P as in Power (with dot), Ph as in Phone
V33	Sar	Seror Sack	⌐	Ts	ץ,צ	Ts as in Sits
V28	Wd	Qur Spun fiber	⌐	Q	ק	C as in Cry (more guttural than Kaph)
D1	Tp	Resh Head	⌐	R	ר	R as in Rush
D27	Mnd	Sadayim Breasts	W	S,Sh	ש	Sh as in Shine (right dot), S as in Sun (left dot)
M42	Wn	Tayis Male goat	x †	T,Th	ת	T as in Time (dot), Th as in Theme

Egyptian epigraphical data in this chart, in part from "The World's Oldest Alphabet", Douglas Petrovich, 2016 AD

www.bible.ca/manuscripts

Figure B

Euboean Greek	Model Etruscan	Archaic Etruscan	Late Etruscan	Latin	Phonetic Value
A A	A	A	A	A	[a]
B	𐌁			B	[b]
< C	𐌂	)	Ɔ	C G	[k]
▷	𐌃			D	[d]
�digamma E	𐌄	∃	∃	E	[e]
F	𐌅	𐌅	𐌅	F	[w]
I	I	I	⌶Ⱶ	(Z)	[z]
⊟ H	𐌇	𐌇	⊟⊘	H	[h]
⊕ ⊗ ⊙	⊗	⊗ O	⊙ O		[tʰ]
I	I	I	I	I	[i]
K	K	K		K	[k]
L	𐌋	𐌋	𐌋	L	[l]
ᛖ M	𐌌	𐌌	𐌌	M	[m]
ᛄ N	𐌍	𐌍	𐌍	N	[n]
Ξ	⊞				[s]
O	O			O	[o]
Γ	𐌐	𐌐	𐌐	P	[p]
M	M	M	M		[ʃ]
φ	𐌒	𐌒		Q	[q]
P	𐌓	𐌓	𐌃	R	[r]
﹥	﹦	﹦	﹦	S	[s]
T	T	T	⊤Ⱶ	T	[t]
Ⱶ V Y	Y	Y	V	V	[u]
X	X	X			[ks]
Φ Ⓟ	Φ	Φ	Φ		[pʰ]
Ψ ⱴ	Ψ	Ψ	Ψ		[kʰ]
		(𐌚 8)	8		[f]

Figure C

Ancient Semitic/Hebrew							Modern Hebrew			Greek		Latin
Early	Middle	Late	Name	Picture	Meaning	Sound	Letter	Name	Sound	Ancient	Modern	
𐤀	𐤀	א	El	Ox head	Strong, Power, Leader	ah, eh	א	Aleph	silent	A	A	A
𐤁	𐤁	ב	Bet	Tent floorplan	Family, House, In	b, bb(v)	ב	Beyt	b, bb(v)	B	B	B
𐤂	𐤂	ג	Gam	Foot	Gather, Walk	g	ג	Gimel	g	Γ	Γ	C G
𐤃	𐤃	ד	Dal	Door	Move, Hang, Entrance	d	ד	Dalet	d	Δ	Δ	D
𐤄	𐤄	ה	Hey	Man with arms raised	Look, Reveal, Breath	h, eh	ה	Hey	h	E	E	E
𐤅	𐤅	ו	Waw	Tent peg	Add, Secure, Hook	w, o, u	ו	Vav	v	F		F
𐤆	𐤆	ז	Zan	Mattock	Food, Cut, Nourish	z	ז	Zayin	z	Z	Z	Z
𐤇	𐤇	ח	Hhet	Tent wall	Outside, Divide, Half	hh	ח	Chet	hh	H	H	H
𐤈	𐤈	ט	Tet	Basket	Surround, Contain, Mud	t	ט	Tet	t	Θ	Θ	
𐤉	𐤉	י	Yad	Arm and closed hand	Work, Throw, Worship	y, ee	י	Yud	y	I	I	I J
𐤊	𐤊	כ	Kaph	Open palm	Bend, Open, Allow, Tame	k, kh	כ	Kaph	k, kh	K	K	K
𐤋	𐤋	ל	Lam	Shepherd Staff	Teach, Yoke, To, Bind	l	ל	Lamed	l	Λ	Λ	L
𐤌	𐤌	מ	Mam	Water	Chaos, Mighty, Blood	m	מ	Mem	m	M	M	M
𐤍	𐤍	נ	Nun	Seed	Continue, Heir, Son	n	נ	Nun	n	N	N	N
𐤎	𐤎	ס	Sin	Thorn	Grab, Hate, Protect	s	ס	Samech	s	Ξ	Ξ	X
𐤏	𐤏	ע	Ghah	Eye	Watch, Know, Shade	gh(ng)	ע	Ayin	silent	O	O	O
𐤐	𐤐	פ	Pey	Mouth	Blow, Scatter, Edge	p, ph(f)	פ	Pey	p, ph(f)	Π	Π	P
𐤑	𐤑	צ	Tsad	Trail	Journey, chase, hunt	ts	צ	Tsade	ts	M		
𐤒	𐤒	ק	Quph	Sun on the horizon	Condense, Circle, Time	q	ק	Quph	q	Q		Q
𐤓	𐤓	ר	Rosh	Head of a man	First, Top, Beginning	r	ר	Resh	r	Ρ	Ρ	R
𐤔	𐤔	ש	Shin	Two front teeth	Sharp, Press, Eat, Two	sh	ש	Shin / Sin	sh, s	Σ	Σ	S
𐤕	𐤕	ת	Taw	Crossed sticks	Mark, Sign, Signal, Monument	t	ת	Tav	t	T	T	T
𐤘			Ghah	Rope	Twist, Dark, Wicked	gh		For additional information on this letter see. www.ancient-hebrew.org/alphabet_changes.html					

Ancient Hebrew Research Center   www.ancient-hebrew.org

Figure D

Figure E

Below, I list many names from both the Tuatha de Danann and Milesians kings list, as taken from Keating General History of Ireland, Section 21 XXI.

As to the sons of Milidh (Mil, Male), they got together an army to come to Ireland and avenge Ioth on the Tuatha De Danann and on the children of Cearmad and to wrest Ireland from them; and the full number of leaders they had to rule the warriors was Milidh Eibhle (the Hebrew, i.e., Erber), Fuad, Breagha, excellent Bladh, Lughaidh, Muirtheimhne from the lake, Buas, Breas, Buaidhne of great vigor, Donn, Ir, Eibhear, Eireamhon, Aimhirgin, Colpa Eibhear, Airioch, Arannan, Cuala, Cuailgne, and generous Nay, Muimhne, Luighne, and Laighne, Fulman, Manntan, gentle Bile, Er, Orba, Fearon, Feirghein, En, Un, Eatan Goistean bright, Seadgha, Sobhairce, Suirghe, Palap, son of noble Eireamhon, Ioth Caicher, son of Manntan.

There are a handful of sources slightly predating the *Lebor Gabála Érenn* covering significant portions of essentially the same list of Milesian High Kings (though following a discrepant chronology), starting with the *Laud Synchronisms* estimated to have been compiled c. 1021 (part of Laud 610). The oldest section of the *Lebor Gabála Érenn* "Roll of Kings" is taken from the poems of Gilla Cómáin mac Gilla Samthainde, written c. 1072.[4]

Early Modern works like the *Annals of the Four Masters*[5] and Geoffrey Keating's *Foras Feasa ar Éirinn*[6] continued this tradition based on later Irish annals. Keating's chronology, based on reign lengths, is longer than the synchronised chronology of the *Lebor Gabála*, and the *Four Masters'* chronology is even longer.

- **LGE**: synchronized dates from *Lebor Gabála Érenn*

- **FFE**: chronology based on reign lengths given in Geoffrey Keating's *Forus Feasa ar Erinn*.

- **AFM**: chronology from the *Annals of the Four Masters*

Milesian Kings	LGE	FFE	AFM
Eber Finn and Érimón		1287–1286 BC	1700 BC
Érimón		1286–1272 BC	1700–1684 BC
Muimne, Luigne and Laigne		1272–1269 BC	1684–1681 BC
Ér, Orba, Ferón and Fergna		1269 BC	1681 BC
Íriel Fáid		1269–1259 BC	1681–1671 BC
Ethriel		1259–1239 BC	1671–1651 BC
Conmáel		1239–1209 BC	1651–1621 BC
Tigernmas		1209–1159 BC	1621–1544 BC
			Interregnum 1544–1537 BC
Eochaid Étgudach		1159–1155 BC	1537–1533 BC
Cermna Finn and Sobairce		1155–1115 BC	1533–1493 BC

Eochaid Faebar Glas		1115–1095 BC	1493–1473 BC
Fíachu Labrainne		1095–1071 BC	1473–1449 BC
Eochu Mumu		1071–1050 BC	1449–1428 BC
Óengus Olmucaid		1050–1032 BC	1428–1410 BC
Énna Airgdech		1032–1005 BC	1410–1383 BC
Rothechtaid mac Main		1005–980 BC	1383–1358 BC
Sétna Airt		980–975 BC	1358–1353 BC
Fíachu Fínscothach		975–955 BC	1353–1333 BC
Muinemón		955–950 BC	1333–1328 BC
Faildergdóit		950–943 BC	1328–1318 BC
Ollom Fotla		943–913 BC	1318–1278 BC

Fínnachta		913–895 BC	1278–1258 BC
Slánoll		895–880 BC	1257–1241 BC
Géde Ollgothach		880–863 BC	1241–1231 BC
Fíachu Findoilches		863–833 BC	1231–1209 BC
Berngal	7th century BC	833–831 BC	1209–1197 BC
Ailill mac Slánuill	7th century BC	831–815 BC	1197–1181 BC
Sírna Sáeglach	7th century BC	814–794 BC	1181–1031 BC
Rothechtaid Rotha	7th century BC	794–787 BC	1031–1024 BC
Elim Olfínechta	7th century BC	787–786 BC	1024–1023 BC
Gíallchad	7th century BC	786–777 BC	1023–1014 BC

Art Imlech	7th–6th century BC	777–755 BC	1014–1002 BC
Nuadu Finn Fáil	7th–6th century BC	755–735 BC	1002–962 BC
Bres Rí	7th–6th century BC	735–726 BC	962–953 BC
Eochu Apthach	6th–5th century BC	726–725 BC	953–952 BC
Finn mac Blatha	6th–5th century BC	725–705 BC	952–930 BC
Sétna Innarraid	5th century BC	705–685 BC	930–910 BC
Siomón Brecc	5th century BC	685–679 BC	910–904 BC
Dui Finn	5th century BC	679–674 BC	904–894 BC
Muiredach Bolgrach	5th century BC	674–670 BC	894–893 BC
Énna Derg	5th century BC	670–658 BC	893–881 BC
Lugaid Íardonn	5th century BC	658–649 BC	881–872 BC
Sírlám	5th century BC	649–633 BC	872–856 BC
Eochu Uairches	5th century BC	633–621 BC	856–844 BC

Eochu Fíadmuine and Conaing Bececlach	5th century BC	621–616 BC	844–839 BC
Lugaid Lámderg and Conaing Bececlach	5th century BC	616–609 BC	839–832 BC
Conaing Bececlach (alone)	5th century BC	609–599 BC	832–812 BC

Name	Century		
Art mac Lugdach	5th century BC	599–593 BC	812–806 BC
Fíachu Tolgrach		593–586 BC	806–796 BC
Ailill Finn	5th–4th century BC	586–577 BC	796–785 BC
Eochu mac Ailella	5th–4th century BC	577–570 BC	785–778 BC
Airgetmar	4th century BC	570–547 BC	778–748 BC
Dui Ladrach	4th century BC	547–537 BC	748–738 BC
Lugaid Laigdech	4th century BC	537–530 BC	738–731 BC
Áed Rúad	4th century BC	530–509 BC	731–724 BC
Díthorba	4th century BC	509–488 BC	724–717 BC
Cimbáeth	4th century BC	488–468 BC	717–710 BC
Áed Rúad (2nd time)			710–703 BC
Díthorba (2nd time)			703–696 BC
Cimbáeth (2nd time)			696–689 BC
Áed Rúad (3rd time)			689–682 BC
Díthorba (3rd time)			682–675 BC
Cimbáeth (3rd time)			675–668 BC
Cimbáeth and Queen Macha			668–661 BC

Name	Century		
Macha Mong Ruad (alone)	4th–3cc BC	468–461 BC	661–654 BC
Rechtaid Rígderg	4th–3rd century BC	461–441 BC	654–634 BC

311

Úgaine Mor	3rd century BC	441–411 BC	634–594 BC
Raighan		551 BC	594 BC
Cineth		524 BC	551 BC
Flann Da Cuileagain		480 BC	524 BC
Heremon		435 BC	480 BC
Bodbchad		411 BC	435 BC
Lóegaire Lorc	3rd century BC	411–409 BC	594–592 BC
Cobthach Cóel Breg	3rd century BC	409–379 BC	592–542 BC
Labraid Loingsech	3rd century BC	379–369 BC	542–523 BC
Meilge Molbthach	3rd century BC	369–362 BC	523–506 BC
Mug Corb	3rd century BC	362–355 BC	506–499 BC
Óengus Ollom	3rd century BC	355–337 BC	499–481 BC
Irereo	3rd century BC	337–330 BC	481–474 BC
Fer Corb	3rd century BC	330–319 BC	474–463 BC
Connla Cáem	3rd century BC	319–315 BC	463–443 BC
Ailill Caisfiaclach	3rd–2nd century BC	315–290 BC	443–418 BC
Adamair	3rd–2nd century BC	290–285 BC	418–414 BC
Eochaid Ailtlethan	3rd–2nd century BC	285–274 BC	414–396 BC
Fergus Fortamail	2nd century BC	274–262 BC	396–385 BC

Óengus Tuirmech Temrach	2nd century BC	262–232 BC	385–326 BC
Conall Collamrach	2nd century BC	232–226 BC	326–320 BC

Nia Segamain	2nd century BC	226–219 BC	320–313 BC
Énna Aignech	2nd century BC	219–191 BC	313–293 BC
Crimthann Coscrach	2nd century BC	191–184 BC	293–289 BC
Rudraige mac Sithrigi	2nd–1st century BC	184–154 BC	289–219 BC
Finnat Már	2nd–1st century BC	154–151 BC	219–210 BC
Bresal Bó-Díbad	2nd–1st century BC	151–140 BC	210–199 BC
Lugaid Luaigne	2nd–1st century BC	140–135 BC	199–184 BC
Congal Cláiringnech	1st century BC	135–120 BC	184–169 BC
Dui Dallta Dedad	1st century BC	120–110 BC	169–159 BC
Fachtna Fáthach	1st century BC	110–94 BC	159–143 BC
Eochu Feidlech	1st century BC	94–82 BC	143–131 BC
Eochu Airem	1st century BC	82–70 BC	131–116 BC
Eterscél	1BC–1 AD	70–64 BC	116–111 BC
Nuadu Necht	1st century	64–63 BC	111–110 BC
Conaire Mór	1st century	63–33 BC	110–40 BC
Lugaid Riab nDerg	1st century	33–13 BC	33–9 BC
Conchobar Abradruad	1st century	13–12 BC	9–8 BC
	Cairbre Cinnchait 1st century	Crimthann Nia Náir 12 BC – AD 5	Crimthann Nia Náir 8 BC – AD 9

313

	Feradach Finnfechtnach 1st century	Feradach Finnfechtnach AD 5–25	Cairbre Cinnchait AD 9–14
	Fíatach Finn 1st century	Fiatach Finn 25–28	Feradach Finnfechtnach 14–36
	Fíachu Finnolach 1st century	Fiacha Finnfolaidh 28–55	Fiatach Finn 36–39
	Elim mac Conrach 2nd century	Cairbre Cinnchait 55–60	Fiacha Finnfolaidh 39–56
		Elim mac Conrach 60–80	Elim mac Conrach 56–76

Goidelic Kings	LGE	FFE	AFM	Dynasty – Sept
Tuathal Techtmar		80–100	76–106	Connachta (ancestor)
Mal mac Rochride		100–104	106–110	Ulaid
Fedlimid Rechtmar		104–113	110–119	Connachta (ancestor)
Cathair Mór	2c	113–116	119–122	Laigin
Conn Cétchathach		116–136	122–157	Connachta (ancestor)
Conaire Cóem		136–143	157–165	Clanna Dedad – Síl Conairi (ancestor)
Art mac Cuinn		143–173	165–195	Connachta
Lugaid mac Con		173–203	195–225	Dáirine – Corcu Loígde
Fergus Dubdétach		203–204	225–226	Ulaid
Cormac mac Airt		204–244	226–266	Connachta
Eochaid Gonnat		244–245	266–267	Ulaid?
Cairbre Lifechair		245–272	267–284	Connachta
Fothad Cairpthech and Fothad Airgthech		272–273	284–285	Dáirine – Corcu Loígde
Fíacha Sroiptine		273–306	285–322	
Colla Uais		306–310	322–326	Connachta
Muiredach Tirech		310–343	326–356	
Cáelbad		343–344	356–357	Ulaid?
Eochaid Mugmedon		344–351	357–365	Connachta
Crimthann mac Fidaig		351–368	365–376	Érainn?

Niall Noígíallach (generally thought historical)		368–395	376–405	Connachta – Uí Néill (ancestor)
Nath Í (probably did not reign at Tara)		395–418	405–428	Connachta – Uí Fiachrach
Lóegaire mac Néill (historical)		418–448	428–458	Connachta – Uí Néill

Kings of Ireland t	459–831	Dynasty – Sept
Ailill Molt	59–478	Connachta – Uí Fiachrach
Lugaid mac Lóegairi	479–503	Uí Néill – Cenél Lóegairi
Muirchertach mac Ercae	504–527	Uí Néill – Cenél nEógain
Túathal Máelgarb	528–538	Uí Néill – Cenél Coirpri
Diarmait mac Cerbaill	539–558	Uí Néill – Cenél Conaill
Domhnall and Fearghus	559–561	Uí Néill – Cenél nEógain
Eochaidh and Baedan	562–563	Uí Néill – Cenél nEógain
Ainmuire mac Sétnai	564–566	Uí Néill – Cenél Conaill
Báetán mac Ninnedo	567	Uí Néill – Cenél Conaill
Áed mac Ainmuirech	568–594	Uí Néill – Cenél Conaill
Áed Sláine and Colmán Rímid	595–600	Uí Néill – Cenél Conaill and Cenél nEógain
Áed Uaridnach	601–607	Uí Néill – Cenél nEógain
Máel Coba mac Áedo	608–610	Uí Néill – Cenél Conaill
Suibne Menn	611–623	Uí Néill – Cenél nEógain
Domnall mac Áedo	624–639	Uí Néill – Cenél Conaill
Cellach and Conall	640–656	Uí Néill – Cenél Conaill

Diarmait and Blathmac	657–664	Uí Néill – Síl nÁedo Sláine
Sechnassach	665–669	Uí Néill – Síl nÁedo Sláine
Cenn Fáelad	670–673	Uí Néill – Síl nÁedo Sláine
Fínsnechta Fledach	674–693	Uí Néill – Síl nÁedo Sláine
Loingsech mac Óengusso	694–701	Uí Néill – Cenél Conaill
Congal Cennmagair	702–708	Uí Néill – Cenél Conaill
Fergal mac Máele Dúin	709–718	Uí Néill – Cenél nEógain
Fogartach mac Néill	719	Uí Néill – Síl nÁedo Sláine
Cináed mac Írgalaig	720–722	Uí Néill – Síl nÁedo Sláine
Flaithbertach mac Loingsig	723–729	Uí Néill – Cenél Conaill
Áed Allán	730–738	Uí Néill – Cenél nEógain
Domnall Midi	739–758	Uí Néill – ClannCholmáin
Niall Frossach	759–765	Uí Néill – Cenél nEógain
Donnchad Midi	766–792	Uí Néill – Clann Cholmáin
Áed Oirdnide	793–819	Uí Néill – Cenél n Eógain
Conchobar mac Donnchada	819–833	Uí Néill – Clann Cholmáin
Niall Caille 833–846 (according to ThePeerage.com)	832–846	Uí Néill – Cenél n Eógain
or Feidlimid mac Crimthainn)	836–841	or Eóganachta – Eóganacht Chaisil
Kings of Ireland	**832–1318**	**Dynasty – Sept**
Máel Sechnaill mac Máele Ruanaid	846–860	Uí Néill – ClannCholmáin
Áed Findliath	861–876	Uí Néill – Cenél nEógain

Flann Sinna	877–914	Uí Néill – ClannCholmáin
Niall Glúndub	915–917	Uí Néill – Cenél nEógain
Donnchad Donn	918–942	Uí Néill – ClannCholmáin
Congalach Cnogba	943–954	Uí Néill – Síl nÁedo Sláine
Domnall ua Néill	955–978	Uí Néill – Cenél nEógain
Máel Sechnaill mac Domnaill	979–1002	Uí Néill – ClannCholmáin
Brian Bóruma	1002–1014	Dál gCais
Máel Sechnaill mac Domnaill (restored)	1014–1022	Uí Néill – ClannCholmáin
Donnchad mac Briain	died 1064 (with opposition)	Dál gCais
Diarmait mac Maíl na mBó	died 1072 (with opposition)	Uí Cheinnselaig
Toirdelbach Ua Briain	died 1086 (with opposition)	Dál gCais – Ua Briain
Domnall Ua Lochlainn	died 1121 (with opposition)	Uí Néill – Cenél nEógain
Muirchertach Ua Briain	died 1119 (with opposition)	Dál gCais – Ua Briain
Toirdelbach Ua Conchobair	1119–1156	Uí Briúin – Ua Conchobair
Muirchertach Mac Lochlainn	1156–1166	Uí Néill – Cenél nEógain
Ruaidrí Ua Conchobair	1166–1198	Uí Briúin – Ua Conchobair

Index

Note that the Index English-Hebrew links, are a combination of phonetic, etymological, thematic and idiomatic, and while I concede that not all, connections have been thoroughly investigated from an etymological standpoint, they do tie in via other methods. The process of cognates (whether real or false), and more detailed root source corroboration is discussed more fully in "English is Hebrew".

In addition, please bear in mind that PIE roots are made up they are proposed, based on guesses and assumptions that do not understand the origins of the Celts, Gauls, and Germanic people, which I have traced back to the Bible and the Lost Ten tribes of Israel. These do include the Red Hand of Zerah (Jews) that was joined by Jeremiah to the Parez lineage via Hezekiah (the last kings of Judah), daughters

An example of the Etymology/thematic/phonetic connection is Aaron, whose Biblical etymology is unknown or obscure. However Aaron was the first high priest, he was God's representative on earth as a judge, prophet, and administrator. His lineage became the Aaronic line, Aaron (Aaronic)therefore could mean leader or master, he was God's representative on earth, ie. God's holy one, strong leader, like (a)Iron. It was only from the Aaronic lineage that the high priest was chosen.

Aaron – H175 אַהֲרֹן (Aharon), meaning "light-bringer" or "ark" as in the sacred chest. (Num 10:33)

Aaron IRON was the first high priest, he was holy, strong powerful, IRON Aaronic Ironic,

IRON, Aaron thought to be from Old Irish iarn, Welsh haiarn others thin PIE *is-(e)ro- "powerful, holy" it's from Aaron first high priest

Aarony IRONY, IRONIC, condition opposite to what might be expected, Aaron's sons, made Illegal fire, and got fired, burned alive hence Aarony

Abraham, Abram – H85 אַבְרָהָם ('Avraham), H87 אַבְרָם ('Avram)

Abro, (Thematic-HeBro Hebrow, brother), and a bro short form of brother from BaSaR H1320, or h1197 בָּעַר bâ'ar, baw-ar (*bhrater),

ABRO, is a fellow -Hebrew, see H5676, h5677

Abro-E'BeR(o) – H5680 עִבְרִי ('Ibrîy) - from H5676, meaning "region beyond" or "over," referring to crossing over, as in across the Jordan.

Academy, Grove of Akademos HaKaR h1970, DaMaH h1819

Achar, Ache'n (h5912 &H253 'ach)

Ache, Achken H9512 Sore as in Ache, form Achar.

Ahab-H256, brother father

Alban, Albany, Albania, LBN, (see Laban and Lebanon)

Aleph, Eleph, Ps119, margin, Aleph. Ps119, margin, Aleph 504 ox, H502: אָלַף ('âlaph) – Verb "to learn" or "to teach." H503: אָלַף ('âlaph) – Verb meaning "to produce thousands" "H504: אֶלֶף ('eleph) – Noun "ox" or "cattle. Training, teach, "H505: אֶלֶף ('eleph) – Noun "thousand."H506: אֲלַף ('ălaph) – Aramaic form of "thousand."H507: אֶלֶף ('eleph) – Proper noun a city in Benjamin.

AMERICA, 5971 עַמְּךָ 'am·me·kā Your people, People of Jehovah

America, Am H5971 & Makir Ma-kirite(s) H4353

America, the people of Makir, also God's people

Anarkim, (Anarchy), něphiyl h5303, H6062 Ankiy-Lanky-tall Deu 2:10

Arcturus, H5906 `Ayish, Ark Taurus

Arish, El Irish, God of the Irish

Ark of the Covenant-0727 אֲרוֹן 'arown aw-rone or אָרֹן 'ârôn; from H717 (in the sense of gathering); a box, ark, chest, coffin.ark, chest, coffin 0712 אַרְגָּז 'argâz, ar-gawz'; perhaps from H7264 (in the sense of being suspended), a box (as a pannier), coffer.Ar own Brit-sounds English to me

Ark, Noah, no akh-at rest (120y to build-Gen6.3)

Armenia Unknow etymology? H780, אֲרָרַט 'Ărâraṭ, ar-aw-rat'; of foreign origin, Armina (in Old Persian), Harminuya (in Elamite), and Urashtu (in Babylonian)

Armour, H0579 אַרְמוֹן 'armôwn, ar-mone'; armown/armour from an unused root (meaning to be elevated and protected); a citadel (from its height),castle, palace etc.

Arown Brit, (ar own Brit, Briyth)

Aryan —IRAN, Arman Assyrian, Germany   5867 עֵילָם 'Êylâm, ay-lawm'; oor עוֹלָם 'Ôwlâm; (Ezra 10:2; Jeremiah 49:36), probably from H5956; hidden, i.e. distant; Elam, a son of Shem and his descendants, with their country; Persia, Elam.

0758 אֲרָם Aram, arawm from the same as H759; the highland; Aram or Syria, and its inhabitants; also the name of the son of Shem, a grandson of Nahor, and of an Israelite:—Aram, Mesopotamia, Syria, Syrians.

0759 אַרְמוֹן 'armôwn, ar-mone'; from an unused root (meaning to be elevated); a citadel (from its height), castle, palace. Compare H2038

Baal (H1167): בעל (Ba'al) - Lord or master.

Baal Zephon (Red Sea Crossing H1189)

Baalzebub, devil, el of Ekron H1176

Babble, to mumble h894

Babylon, Babylonians, Babble – H894, H895, H896 בָּבֶל (Babel) – meaning Babylon

Bag-gab (reverse letters) H5689 and heavy breathing metaphor- sex

Bagpipes -gab (reverse uw bag-neh'-bel-H5035)

Barley, bar Beer, seʻôwrâh-see hair from hairy ears h8184

Bat – H905 בַּד (bad) - meaning alone.

Bath (daughter) – H1323 בַּת (bat) - meaning daughter.

Bath (measure) – H1324 בַּת (bath) - measure for liquid.

Bathsheba – H1339 בַּת־שֶׁבַע (Bathsheba) - meaning daughter of an oath.

Baton – H905 (bad) - meaning alone, H202 אוֹן (on) - strength.

Bellows – H5035 נֵבֶל (nebel) - meaning musical or skin container.

Bertha – Related to H1332 בִּתְיָה (Bithyah), meaning "daughter of Yah."

Bethel – H1008 בֵּית אֵל (Bethel) - meaning house of God.

Beyth hash-Shittah – H1029 בֵּית הַשִּׁטָּה (Beth Hashittah), meaning house of the acacia tree.

Boustrophedon – Term for writing style that alternates direction with each line, often used in ancient scripts.

Bow and British longbow – Traditional English weapon. Chap.6 Joseph ,Ephraim, Manasseh

Breastplate – H2833 חֹשֶׁן (choshen) - breastplate worn by the High Priest.

Brigante –ancient British tribe see Chap. 13 Milesians..

Brit (Lead Covenant Tribe) – Ephraim & Manasseh, associated with H1285 בְּרִית (berit) - meaning covenant.

Brit Milah – H4139 מִילָה (milah) - meaning circumcision.

Brit'am – H1285 (berit), H5971 (am - people).

Brit'on – H1285 (berit), H202 (on)

Britain – Derived from Brit, meaning covenant.

Britannia – H1285 (berit), H5971 (am - people), H3050 (Yah - God).

British Brit'ish – H1285 בְּרִית (berit) - meaning covenant, H3129 (yashar suffix) as "ish."

Bull – H7214 רְאֵם (reem).

Bull and Bush prophesy, Chap.6 Joseph Ephraim Manasseh

Bulldog British Chap 16

Bullshxx – Related to H5695 עֵגֶל (egel - young bull or calf) and H7214 רְאֵם (reem - wild ox), Chapt 6

Chaldeans – H3778 כַּשְׂדִּים (Kasdim) - meaning Chaldean or astrologers.

Chittim, Kittim, Kitty – H3794 כִּתִּים (Kittim) - reference to Cyprus and regions.

Choshen – H2833 חֹשֶׁן (choshen) - breastplate.

Coach – H3581 כֹּחַ (koach) - meaning, train, strength or power.

Cumri, Kimri – OMRI H6018 עָמְרִי ʻāmrî Refers to Welsh, linked to Cymry.

Cyprus – G2953 Κύπρος (Kupros) in Greek.

Damian, Damah – H1819 דָּמָה (damah) - meaning to meditate or compare; linked to ian-G2491.

Dan – H1835 דָּן (Dan) - meaning judge.

Daniel – H1840 דָּנִיֵּאל (Daniel) - meaning God is my judge.

Danite's – H1839 דָּנִי (Daniy) - meaning of the tribe of Dan.

David – H1732 דָּוִד (David) - meaning beloved.

Don (teacher) – H136 אֲדֹנָי (Adonay) - meaning Lord or master.

Dravidians – Chapt. 13 Ethnographic division

Eber – H5676 עֵבֶר (Eber) - meaning across or beyond.

Eber, OVER, a'ver h5676, across river, not from here, across the pond, not from here OVER (עֵבֶר AVR).

Ebro (related to Hebrew) – H5677 עֵבֶר (Eber) - meaning beyond.

Ebro river in Spain Iberian Peninsula and the Hibērī or Ibērī "Ibēr" or "Hibēr"

Ebro–Hebrew, HeyBro, family, tribe friend h5677, Gen10.21

Edenics — English has over50,000 root words from Hebrew.

Egel (young bull) – H5695 עֵגֶל (egel) - meaning calf.

Egel Egel'ish Bull tribe, see Aleph, young bull, h5695

Egel, ish – H5695, H376 אִישׁ (ish) - meaning man, linked to young bull.

Egel, ish young bull, h5695, h376

Egypt – H4714 מִצְרַיִם (Mitsrayim) - referring to Egypt.

Egypt, h4714, Mitsrayim, -slave-misery

Eleph – H505 אֶלֶף (eleph) - meaning 1,000 or a group/tribe.

Elephant, Elephantine (Aleph-ant) – Eleph H504 אֶלֶף Ok Kline family

Elihanah bat Gael-h5941, h2583 or, h1323, h7069

Elkanah, H511 Samuel son of, means God has created, EL=God, QaNa=Cain, KIN, KINFOLK, GENE, GENESIS.

Elo Hello short form Elohim long form HELLO (Elo) we invoke God name everytime we greet someone.

Elohim, H430 אֱלֹהִים no niquid 'LHYM' or a LHYmy a follower of God

Enoch – H2585 חֲנוֹךְ (Chanok) - meaning dedicated.

Ephraim – H669 אֶפְרַיִם (Ephrayim) - meaning fruitful.

Er – H6147 עֵר (Er) - meaning watchful.

Er'land, Er'ish – Derived from Er, linked to H6147 עֵר (Er).

Er'land, Er'ish h376

Er'line, Er-heir to the throne Judas son who died h6147 "heir, heiress" PIE root *ghe- "to be empty, left behind.

Ethan – H387 אֵיתָן (Ethan) - meaning strong or enduring.

Evil – H5766 עָוֶל (avel) - meaning injustice or unrighteousness.

Ezekiel – H3168 יְחֶזְקֵאל (Yechezqe'l) - meaning God strengthens.

Fair – H3303 יָפֶה (yafeh) - meaning beautiful.

Gael – H1350 גָּאַל (ga'al) - meaning to redeem.

323

Gaelic – Gaels redeemed of God, or a witness, see Gael or Galed

Galed – H1567 גַּלְעֵד (Galed) - meaning heap of witness.

Glottochronology The study of languages to determine when they diverged from being the same language

God Heal, Gaedheal – H1419 גָּדוֹל (gadol) - meaning great.

Guttenberg Bible – Refers to the first major book printed using movable type by Johann Gutenberg.

Gwilliam – H1534 גִּילָם (Gilam) - joy of the people, did the Celts inherit it becase of Galam, h1534 giyl'am, Proto-Germanic *helmaz "protective covering" (from PIE root *kel- (1) "to cover, conceal, save;" compare helm

Ha, Hi and Hey praise, H see HI YAH, Origin of YHWH, See English is Hebrew for full text and Alphabet

Hallstatt Celtic – Term referencing Celtic origins and early Iron Age culture.

Hebrides, unknown origin but Celts and Hebrew call crossing, Eber's -consider Avon: Derived from the Brythonic/Celtic word abona, meaning "river." Aber: A Celtic prefix meaning "confluence" or "mouth of a river" (e.g., Aberdeen, Aberystwyth). Avon, **Eber Chap. 13** Eber H5677 region beyond, see **Hibernia**.

Hell Yeah (Elijah) – H452 אֵלִיָּה 'Êlîyâh - meaning my God is Yah.

Hello (Elohim) – H430 אֱלֹהִים (Elohim), H433 אֱלוֹהַּ (Eloah) invoking Gods name.

Hermon and Hemon – H2768 חֶרְמוֹן (Hermon), H2763 חָרַם (charam) - meaning banned or dedicated.

HeyBro, Eber – Herber – Hebrews Ebro, see Eber

Heyday – Related to the fifth letter Hey (ה) in Hebrew, Jospeh and Abraham.

Hi Yah – H1961 הָיָה (hayah) - meaning to be or exist, invoking the name of, h430, h433.

Hibernia, Ibear, Iberus, Iberia, Spain, **Hibernia** evolved from **Iveriu**, the similarity to **Eber/Ivri**, Iberian Peninsular and Ebro river, all etymologically connect Celts to Eber, Eber H5677 region beyond.

High Priest – H1433 גָּדוֹל (gadol) - meaning great or high, for high priest H3548 כֹּהֵן (kohen).

Hosanna – H1954 אוֹשֵׁעַ (hoshia) - meaning save now , Oshea = "salvation"

Israel — see His Royal Highness H3478 יִשְׂרָאֵל Yisrâ'êl, "He will rule as God"

Ithel or Ith – No specific Strong's reference.

Jack – H3290 יַעֲקֹב (Yaakov) - meaning heel holder.

Jacobites, ideology originated with James VI and I, who in 1603 became the first monarch to rule all three kingdoms King James Bible-From JACOB H3290 יַעֲקֹב

Jehovah – H3068 יְהֹוָה (Yehovah), H3050 יָהּ (Yah), Ye over-lord, h3068 Yahh, yes, yours, h3050

Jeremiah – H3414 יִרְמְיָהוּ (Yirmeyahu) - meaning Yahweh will raise, Eemhear in Ireland.

Jeremiah's commission Chap.. 8 Kingly line moved to Ireland

Jeroboam – H3379 יָרָבְעָם (Ya'rob'am) - meaning the people will contend.

Jerusalem – H3390 יְרוּשָׁלַם (Yerushalayim) - meaning city of peace.

Jews spoke Gaelic Chapt. 10, also see EIH large section on this topic

Jezebel – H348 אִיזֶבֶל (Izevel) - meaning unchaste.

Joshua – H1954 יְהוֹשׁוּעַ (Yehoshua) - meaning Yahweh saves.

Jubilee – H8643 תְּרוּעָה (teruah) - meaning shout or sound of trumpet.

Kitty, Kittee also see Kittee Chittim H3794, cHit am = "bruisers" Chap. 13 Milesian Jer 2:10

Lᵉbânôwn – Related to Lebanon H3844 לְבָנוֹן (Lebanon) - meaning whiteness.

Lyson (Samuel)

Megan – H4043 מָגֵן (magen) - meaning shield, said to come from Peal -Middle Persian marvarit "pearl." a shell a shield, h4043 The plural feminine form, mᵉginnâh (מְגִנָּה), aligns with Celtic traditions where female warriors and goddesses, like Medb and Macha, hold protective and sovereign roles.

Men (ish) – H376 אִישׁ (ish) - meaning man.

Milidh, Mil, Milesian – H4390-92 מָלֵא (male) - meaning to fill or fulfill.

Money – H4489 מָעוֹת (maoth) - meaning coins or wages, pay.

Navy – H590 אֳנִיָּה (aniyah) - meaning ship.

On – H202 or (on) - meaning strength, or strength of the firstborn.

Organ-uwgab-h5748, from h5689

Ox turning-Boustrophedon see ref 20

Ox, Calf, Bullock, h5695, egel

Palm, tree: As in erect, Tamra H8558 תָּמָר (Tamar)

Party: To be jubilant, Jewbilant H6558 פָּרַץ (Parats)

Passover: Pause-awkward-hop, pe-hs-akh H6452 פֶּסַח (Pesach)

Perez: Breach, also see Party, Jubilee, and Zerah H6556 פֶּרֶץ (Perets)

Phineas: A priestly figure H6372 פִּינְחָס (Pinchas)

Priest (High): Kohen Gadol (High Priest) H3548 כֹּהֵן (Kohen)

Rachel: Female biblical name H7354 רָחֵל (Rachel)

Raw: Naked, see in the raw H7200 רָאָה (Ra'ah)

Royalty, Israel: Yis'rael; "He will rule as God," His Royal Highness H3478 יִשְׂרָאֵל (Yisrael)

Sabbath: Rest H7676 שַׁבָּת (Shabbat)

Safe: Threshold, money store; see Yosaf H5592 סַף (Saf)

Salvation: Yeshua, Yesh sure H3442, H3444 יֵשׁוּעַ (Yeshua), יְשׁוּעָה (Yeshuah)

Samaritans: Home r own H8118 שֹׁמְרוֹן (Shomron)

Sarah: Jacob's wife, the queen mother H8283 שָׂרָה (Sarah)

Soke: With water or oil H5480 סוּךְ (Sukh)

Sukkot: Booths, shelters, etc. H5519 סֻכּוֹת (Sukkot)

Taurus: Tor-Sor-Torus, The Bull; from Aramaic TOR H8450, H7794, H7788 תּוֹר (Tor), שׁוֹר (Shor)

Unicorn: Often interpreted as a wild ox H7214 רְאֵם (Re'em)

Union Jack: Related to Jacob (see Jack) H3290 יַעֲקֹב (Yaakov)

Yank (heel holder) – H6117 עָקֵב (aqev) - meaning to grab or hold.

Zaragoza on Ebro river Spain Zerah (2226 זֶרַח) Gossa (1588 גַּן gan, hedge in Ganan Garden, protect) strong hold of Zera although current etymology says not

About This book

This book has been thirty years in the making. In the spring of 1987, Damian started a night-and-day study into a book and a belief system that, amazingly enough, neither he nor many people had heard of before.

The book was titled The United States and Britain in Prophecy, and the belief system was that God had preordained the world's greatest nation and the world's greatest company of nations as a promise made to the patriarchs!

Was this true, Damian's quest to uncover the hidden past, an odyssey over 30 years in the making. Not only was it true, but the staggering evidence and earth-shattering knowledge that God poured into his soul became the catalyst for this book.

I cannot wait to see the look on Abraham, Jacob, Joseph, and Daniels faces

Indeed, it was so much so that on his amazing journey, he discovered many more compelling details about the true nature of these two great peoples, and this book is the culmination of his efforts over this period of time.

GODS SIGNAL to Damian. He had been carrying an old unfinished watercolor. He first started in 1982 while working for the Royal Saudi Air Force as an expat. This painting has been carried across four continents. He rediscovered it in late 2017 and finished it shortly afterward. This (he felt) was a sign that it was time to write his book.

How will the journey end? Please read the book and discover the earth-shattering information that God poured into his soul and, indeed, into his book!

We Are Israel is the culmination of over three decades of relentless research and discovery, uncovering the astonishing connections between the ancient Hebrews and the modern English-speaking world. Damian Myler embarks on a profound journey that traces the roots of language, culture, and even genetics back to biblical origins, revealing truths that have been hidden in plain sight for millennia.

This book delves into the profound influence of the early patriarchs on our daily lives—from the idioms we use to the very names of our cities and countries. Did you know that expressions like "you're fired" or "your 86'ed" are rooted in ancient texts? Or that the very DNA within us carries a divine signature, connecting us to the promises made to Abraham, Jacob, and Joseph?

We Are Israel takes you on a riveting exploration through time, following the Hebrews from Egypt to the Promised Land and beyond—to Greece, Tuscany, Spain, and the British Isles. It traces the evolution of language from Paleo-Hebrew to modern English, uncovering the hidden meanings behind names and words that shape our understanding of the world today.

But this book goes beyond etymology. It explores the biblical prophecies fulfilled in the journeys of Jeremiah and the king's daughters, the sacred lineage preserved through the ages and the remarkable story of how these ancient promises have manifested in the nations of today.

With meticulous research and undeniable proof, We Are Israel reveals the extraordinary connection between the Bible, Israel, and the English-speaking peoples. This is not just a book; it's a revelation—an invitation to discover the divine heritage that has been woven into the fabric of our history and our future.

www.ingramcontent.com/pod-product-compliance
Lightning Source LLC
Chambersburg PA
CBHW060759120626
46557CB00001B/27